CONTENTS

Cover Picture: The Lamb Inn, Burford, Oxfordshire (see page 25).

Key to symbols 2

How to use this guide 3

Introduction from The Lamb Inn,
Winner of the Johansens 1995 Inns Award for Excellence 4

Johansens 1995 Awards for Excellence 5

Johansens Recommended Inns with Restaurants in England 7

Johansens Recommended Inns with Restaurants in Wales 157

Johansens Recommended Inns with Restaurants in Scotland 165

'Mini Listings' of Johansens Country Houses and Small Hotels (published in full in the Johansens Recommended Country Houses and Small Hotels Guide 1996) 173

Maps of the British Isles showing all Johansens Recommendations 180

Indexes 187

Johansens Guides Order Forms and Guest Survey Reports 193

INTRODUCTION BY THE EDITOR

Johansens guides, now in their 15th year, have developed from one single hotel guide into what this year is a set of five – Recommended Hotels, Recommended Inns with Restaurants, Recommended Country Houses and Small Hotels, Recommended Business Meetings Venues and now, for the first time, Johansens Recommended Hotels in Europe. The market place has grown and we have grown with it. Our principles, nevertheless, have remained constant. The annual inspection of candidates for inclusion in our guides reinforced by the thousands of reports from Johansens guide-users sustains our criterion of excellence.

We are publishers and as such we form the link between two groups of clients: hoteliers who, if accepted for membership, pay an annual fee and their guests, who are in many cases purchasers of our guides. We value both these relationships hoping that our contribution to excellence in hospitality, now not only in Britain but in all Europe, will be of great benefit to the diverse clientele which we so proudly serve.

Rodney Exton, Editor.

KEY TO SYMBOLS

13 rms Total number of rooms

MasterCard accepted

Visa accepted

American Express accepted

Diners Club accepted

Quiet location

Access for wheelchairs to at least one bedroom and public rooms

Chef-patron

M 20 Meeting/conference facilities with maximum number of delegates

8 Children welcome, with minimum age where applicable

Dogs accommodated in rooms or kennels

At least one room has a four-poster bed

Cable/satellite TV in all bedrooms

Direct-dial telephone in all bedrooms

No-smoking rooms (at least one no-smoking bedroom)

Lift available for guests' use

Indoor swimming pool

Outdoor swimming pool

Tennis court at hotel

Croquet lawn at hotel

Fishing can be arranged

Golf course on site or nearby, which has an arrangement with hotel allowing guests to play

Shooting can be arranged

Riding can be arranged

Hotel has a helicopter landing pad

Licensed for wedding ceremonies

13 rms Nombre de chambres

MasterCard accepté

Visa accepté

American Express accepté

Diners Club accepté

Un lieu tranquille

Accès handicapé

Chef-patron

M 20 Salle de conférences – capacité maximale

8 Enfants bienvenus

Chiens autorisés

Lit à colonnes

TV câblée/satellite dans les chambres

Téléphone dans les chambres

Chambres non-fumeurs

Ascensrur

Piscine couverte

Piscine de plein air

Tennis à l'hôtel

Croquet à l'hôtel

Pêche

Golf

Chasse

Chevaux de selle

Hélipad

Cérémonies de noces

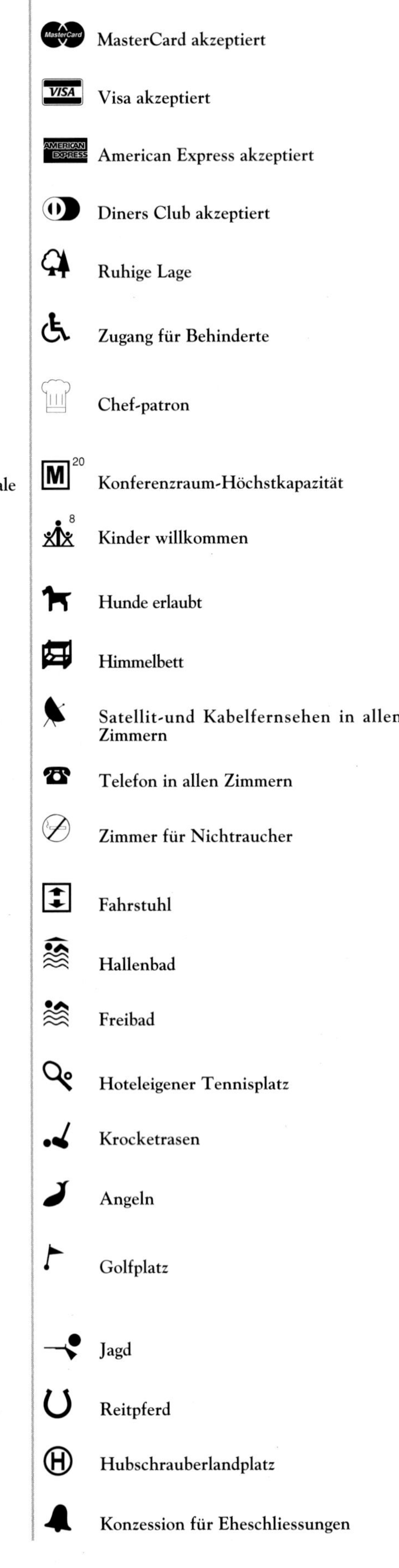

13 rms Anzahl der Zimmer

MasterCard akzeptiert

Visa akzeptiert

American Express akzeptiert

Diners Club akzeptiert

Ruhige Lage

Zugang für Behinderte

Chef-patron

M 20 Konferenzraum-Höchstkapazität

8 Kinder willkommen

Hunde erlaubt

Himmelbett

Satellit-und Kabelfernsehen in allen Zimmern

Telefon in allen Zimmern

Zimmer für Nichtraucher

Fahrstuhl

Hallenbad

Freibad

Hoteleigener Tennisplatz

Krocketrasen

Angeln

Golfplatz

Jagd

Reitpferd

Hubschrauberlandplatz

Konzession für Eheschliessungen

Published by
Johansens, 175-179 St John Street, London EC1V 4RP
Tel: 0171-490 3090 Fax: 0171-490 2538
Find Johansens on the Internet at: http://www.johansen.com

Hobsons Publishing plc,
a subsidiary of the Daily Mail and General Trust plc
ISBN 1 86017 130 3
Printed in England by St Ives plc
Colour origination by East Anglian Engraving
Distributed in the UK and Europe by Biblios PDS Ltd, Partridge Green, West Sussex, RH13 8LD. In North America by general sales agent: SunWelcome, INC., Clearwater, Florida (direct sales) and The Cimino Publishing Group, INC. New York (bookstores). In Australia and New Zealand by Bookwise International, Findon, South Australia.

HOW TO USE THIS GUIDE

If you want to identify an Inn or Restaurant whose name you already know, look for it in the national indexes on pages 187–190.

If you want to find an Inn or Restaurant in a particular area you can

- Turn to the Maps on pages 180–186
- Search the Indexes by County on pages 187–190
- Look for the Town where you wish to stay in the main body of the Guide. This is divided into Countries. Place names in each Country are in alphabetical order.

The Indexes list the Inns and Restaurants by Counties, they also show those with facilities such as conference centres, swimming, etc.

The Maps cover five different regions. Each Inn or Restaurant symbol (a red triangle) relates to a Inn or Restaurant in this guide in or near the location shown.

Mini Listings pages 173–179: The Country Houses and Small Hotels (a green square) on the Maps are listed in order of place names and divided nationally so that, if you cannot find a Inn or Restaurant locally, you may be able to find a Country House or a Small Hotel nearby at which to stay.

The Prices, in most cases, refer to the cost of one night's accommodation, with breakfast, for two people. Prices are also shown for single occupancy. These rates are correct at the time of going to press but they should always be checked.

INTRODUCTION

By Caroline and Richard de Wolf of the Lamb Inn at Burford, Oxfordshire, Winner of the 1995 Johansens Inns with Restaurants Award

---

We are delighted to have won the Johansens 1995 Inn of the Year Award.

When we came to The Lamb in 1982, we felt we were very lucky to have acquired this historic inn in the beautiful Cotswold town of Burford.

Although part of the Lamb's charm was that it had not been over modernised in the past and had retained much of its original character, we also knew that we had many years of hard work and investment ahead of us to upgrade the building and facilities to bring them up to present day standards. The kitchens were like a set from Upstairs & Downstairs, while en suite bathrooms and central heating were almost non-existent. Step by step over the last thirteen years we have transformed every part of the building – kitchens, lounges, bedrooms have been rebuilt, refurbished or re-equipped. All sixteen bedrooms now have their own en suite bathrooms and many have been enlarged. All are within the main building as we wanted to avoid having annexe bedrooms.

Throughout this programme of improvements we were constantly aware (and frequently reminded by our guests) that we must not spoil the unique character of the inn which makes it so special.

Our overall aim has been to create a comfortable and informal, yet civilised place to stay. We genuinely enjoy providing a warm welcome, good food and real sense of hospitality, and we are supported in this by an enthusiastic and experienced staff, many of whom have been with us from the start. It is very rewarding to have our efforts endorsed by the number of guests who return to us again and again.

We have always found the Johansens Guide to Recommended Inns with Restaurants a most attractive and well presented book. Johansens' policy of selective entry into the guide as a result of regular visits from their inspectors ensures the quality of the establishments it features.

It gives a great sense of achievement for everyone at The Lamb to know we have won the 1995 Johansens Inn of the Year Award and we would like to thank all involved at Johansens for their support and also the many guests who sent in their survey reports.

EVERY LANGUAGE SPEAKS MASTERCARD

JOHANSENS AWARDS FOR EXCELLENCE

The names of the winners of the 1996 Awards will be published in the 1997 editions of Johansens guides.

The winners of the 1995 Awards are listed below. They were presented with their certificates at the Johansens Annual Awards dinner, held at The Savoy on 31st October 1994, by Giles Shepard CBE.

WINNERS OF THE 1995 JOHANSENS AWARDS

Johansens Country Hotel Award for Excellence
Amberley Castle, Arundel, West Sussex

Johansens City Hotel Award for Excellence
The Chester Grosvenor, Chester, Cheshire

Johansens Country House Award for Excellence
Coopershill House, Riverstown, Co Sligo

Johansens Inn Award for Excellence
The Lamb, Burford, Oxford

Johansens Most Excellent Value for Money Award
Lower Bache, Leominster, Herefordshire

Johansens Most Excellent Service Award
Hotel Maes-Y-Neuadd, Harlech, Gwynedd

Candidates for awards derive from two main sources: from the thousands of Johansens guide users who send us guest survey reports commending hotels, inn and country houses in which they have stayed and from our team of twelve regional inspectors who regularly visit all properties in our guides. Guest survey report forms can be found on pages 487–496. They are a vital part of our continuous process of assessment and they are the decisive factor in choosing the value for money and the most excellent service awards.

The judges each year are invited from among the winners of previous years awards.

The Judges for the 1995 Awards were:-

David Shentall, Kinloch House, Winner of the 1994 Johansens Country Hotel Award
Malcolm Reed, The Swallow, Birmingham, Winner of the 1994 Johansens City Hotel Award
Hugo Jeune, The Rising Sun, Lynmouth, Winner of the 1991 Johansens Inn Award
Anne McClure, 4 South Parade, York, Winner of the 1994 Johansens Value for Money Award

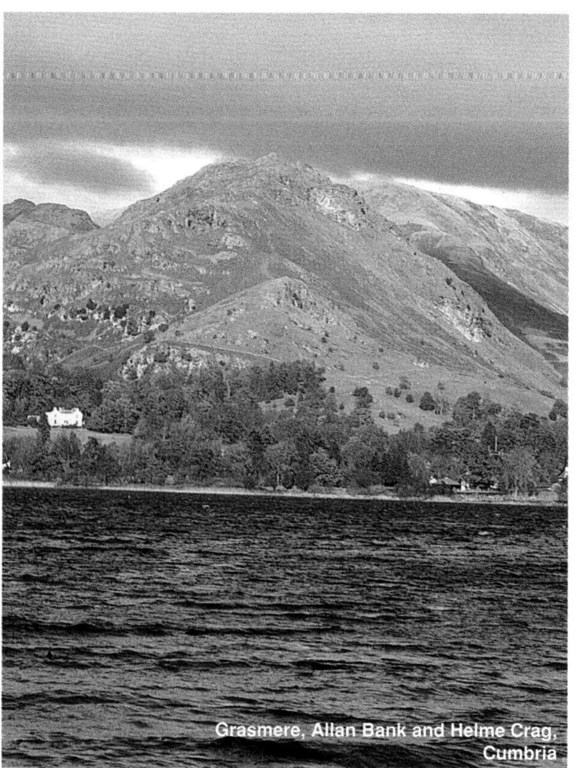

Johansens Recommended Inns with Restaurants in England

Castles, cathedrals, museums, great country houses and the opportunity to stay in areas of historical importance, England has much to offer. Whatever your leisure interests, there's a network of more than 550 Tourist Information Centres throughout England offering friendly, free advice on places to visit, entertainment, local facilities and travel information.

British Travel Centre
12 Regent Street
Piccadilly Circus
London SW1Y 4PQ
(Personal callers only)

English Heritage
Keysign House
429 Oxford Street
London W1R 2HD
Tel: 0171-973 3396
Offers an unrivalled choice of properties to visit.

Historic Houses Association
2 Chester Street
London SW1X 7BB
Tel: 0171-259 5688
Ensures the survival of historic houses and gardens in private ownership in Great Britain.

The National Trust
36 Queen Anne's Gate
London SW1H 9AS
Tel: 0171-222 9251
Cares for more than 590,000 acres of countryside and over 400 historic buildings.

THE HEART OF ENGLAND
Here you have the essence of England, the country's very heart. From the thatched villages of Shakespeare Country, to some of the world's finest potteries in Stoke on Trent.

The Heart of England Tourist Board
PO Box 15
Worcester
Worcestershire WR5 1BR
Tel: 01905 763436

CUMBRIA
England's most beautiful lakes and tallest mountains reach out from the Lake District National Park to a landscape of spectacular coasts, hills and dales.

Cumbria Tourist Board
Ashleigh
Holly Road
Windermere
Cumbria LA23 2AQ
Tel: 015394 44444

NORTHUMBRIA
The north east region of England is steeped in folklore and history and is celebrated as one of the most important centres of early English Christianity.

Northumbria Tourist Board
Aykley Heads
Durham
Co Durham DH1 5UX
Tel: 0191-384 6905

THE NORTH WEST
This region offers the very best in history and heritage, stunning countryside and vibrant towns and cities including Chester, Lancaster, Liverpool and Manchester.

The North West Tourist Board
Swan House
Swan Meadow Road
Wigan Pier
Wigan WN3 5BB
Tel: 01942 821222

YORKSHIRE & HUMBERSIDE
Scenic coastline with lively resorts, and spectacular seascapes. Unspoilt natural grandeur in dales and moors. Historic cities, picturesque villages, impressive castles and stately homes.

Yorkshire & Humberside Tourist Board
312 Tadcaster Road
York
North Yorkshire YO2 2HF
Tel: 01904 707961

EAST MIDLANDS
This region includes the coastal resorts of Lincolnshire, waterways such as the Grand Union Canal, the Trent & Mersey Canal and the Rivers Trent, Soar and Witham. Most of the Peak District National Park lies in Derbyshire.

East Midlands Tourist Board
Exchequergate
Lincoln
Lincolnshire LN2 1PZ
01522 531521

EAST ANGLIA
A place of farms and pine forests, quiet villages and thatched cottages, medieval towns and charming cities, lively seaside resorts and quaint villages.

East Anglia Tourist Board
Toppesfield Hall
Hadleigh
Suffolk IP7 5DN
Tel: 01473 822922

WEST COUNTRY
England's favourite holiday destination with a mild climate all year round and over 600 miles of contrasting coastline. Discover another world of legend, mystery and romance.

West Country Tourist Board
60 St Davids Hill
Exeter
Devon EX4 4SY
Tel: 01392 76351

SOUTHERN ENGLAND
This area has connections with great literary figures. In the 19th century, Oxford was a centre for the pre-Raphaelite painters and many of their works can still be viewed in the city.

Southern Tourist Board
40 Chamberlayne Road
Eastleigh
Hampshire SO50 5JH
Tel: 01703 620006

SOUTH EAST
The region has 257 miles of coastline stretching from Gravesend, Kent, to the Witterings, West Sussex. The Channel Tunnel links this corner of England to mainland Europe.

South East England Tourist Board
The Old Brew House
Warwick Park
Royal Tunbridge Wells
Kent TN2 5TU
Tel: 01892 540766

THE RED LION INN

THE GREEN, ADDERBURY, NR BANBURY, OXFORDSHIRE OX17 3LU
TEL: 01295 810269 FAX: 01295 811906

OWNERS: Michael and Andrea Mortimer

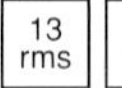  

  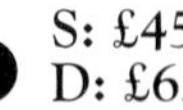

S: £45
D: £65

Inn: Situated in the historic village of Adderbury and overlooking the picturesque village green. The Red Lion is a magnificent example of a traditional coaching inn. This ancient royalist hostelry pre-dates the Civil War and local folklore pinpoints it as a Royalist bolt hole and the secret tunnel which was used to flee from the Parliamentarians is now part of the wine vaults. Devotees of English heritage will delight in the wealth of old oak and stone chimney pieces which have been carefully preserved and visitors cannot fail to be impressed by the tasteful interior decoration which is consistent throughout. Each of the bedrooms is individually appointed to the highest standard, drawing inspiration from a bygone era yet still offering all the modern amenities. Individual rooms are available for private functions, also separate meeting rooms and a board room suitable for business meetings or conferences in a propitious environment for special occasions. The Red Lion is recommended for the quality in addition to its general ambience. **Restaurant:** Formal and informal meals are available in the bars or the restaurant. Traditional inn food is presented generously and without fuss in a friendly, stylish atmosphere. **Nearby:** Oxford, Blenheim Palace, Stratford-upon-Avon and the Cotswolds. **Directions: The Red Lion is three miles south of Banbury on the A4260 Oxford road (formerly the A423), six miles from the M40 junction 10 or four miles from junction 11.**

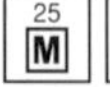   

For hotel location, see maps on pages 180–186

ARROW MILL HOTEL AND RESTAURANT

ARROW, NEAR ALCESTER, WARWICKSHIRE B49 5NL
TEL: 01789 762419 FAX: 01789 765170

OWNERS: The Woodhams Family

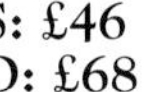

S: £46
D: £68

Inn: Once a working flour mill, Arrow Mill is proud of its listing in the Domesday Book, when it was valued at three shillings and sixpence. Today it remains a historic and charming building, although it offers its guests the most modern and comfortable accommodation. Its rustic charm, enhanced by log fires and exposed beams, is complemented by a spectacular yet secluded riverside setting. Creature comforts are plentiful in the individually furnished bedrooms and panoramic views take in the mill pond, River Arrow and surrounding countryside. **Restaurant:** A highly trained team of chefs uses only market-fresh ingredients in maintaining their uncompromising standards. The Millstream Restaurant incorporates the original working floor of the mill, with its wheel still driven by the flowing stream. It offers an à la carte menu and carefully selected wine list to satisfy the most discriminating palate. Similarly high standards are assured by the luncheons from the Miller's Table. Residential conferences, business meetings, hospitality days and product launches can all be accommodated. **Nearby:** Stratford-upon-Avon, Warwick Castle and the Cotswolds are all nearby. Arrow Mill is closed from 26 December for two weeks. **Directions: Set back from the A435 1 mile south of Alcester.**

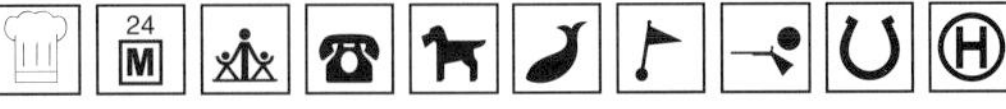

For hotel location, see maps on pages 180–186

The Boathouse Brasserie

HOUGHTON BRIDGE, AMBERLEY, NR ARUNDEL, WEST SUSSEX BN18 9LR
TEL: 01798 831059 FAX: 01798 831063

OWNERS: Howard and Susie Macnamara
CHEFS: Keith Baker and Derrick Clarke

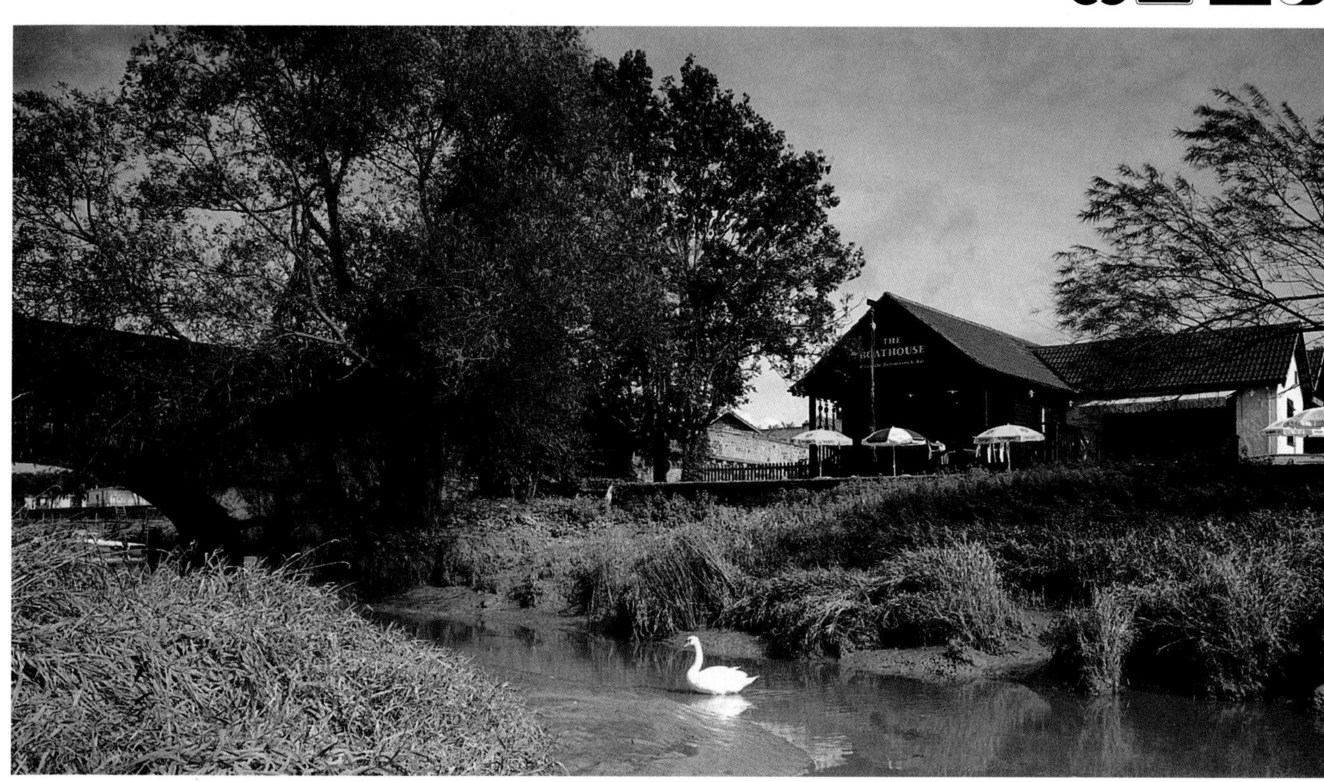

Restaurant: This delightful restaurant is on the River Arun at the site of the ancient Houghton Wharf. It is under the same private ownership as the White Horse Inn at Sutton. The inn is full of character, strewn with charts and maritime bric-a-brac, and is Edwardian in style. Weather permitting, you may prefer to enjoy your meal out on the open wooden deck or under the verandah. The attractive staff are friendly and attentive. The Carvery, is without doubt, the speciality here – succulent roast meats are on display, carved for you by the chefs. There is a small but impressive à la carte menu and the fresh fish is a worthy alternative. Extra seasonal dishes are shown on the blackboard in the bar. There is a fine selection of sweets, a good cheeseboard and probably the best cup of coffee you'll find anywhere. The set price lunch (two-courses and coffee) is good value and very popular. On Sunday it is advisable to book well ahead. The wine list is well chosen and reasonably priced. **Nearby:** Arundel Castle, Petworth House, Parham House, Chichester (Festival Theatre), and Goodwood Racecourse. Being on the Southdowns Way there are some good walks to be had. The Amberley Chalkpits Industrial Museum is nearby. **Directions: The Boathouse is on the B2139 (Arundel to Storrington Road) where it crosses the River Arun.**

For hotel location, see maps on pages 180–186

The New Dungeon Ghyll Hotel

GREAT LANGDALE, AMBLESIDE, CUMBRIA LA22 9JY
TEL: 015394 37213 FAX: 015394 37666

OWNER: John Winter Smith
MANAGERS: Ian and Rebecca Manley

  S: £40–£45
D: £60–£70

Inn: The splendour of Lakeland's most majestic fells is the setting for The New Dungeon Ghyll Hotel. It is built on the site of an ancient Norse settlement, but was rebuilt as a Victorian Hotel in the 1830s. Bought by John Smith in 1991 and completely refurbished, the hotel sits in its own lawned gardens in a spectacular position beneath the Langdale Pikes and Pavey Ark. The comfortable bedrooms are all en suite and offer colour TV, tea and coffee making facilities and direct dial telephones. There are two bars with open fires and the Residents' Bar has an original slate floor. **Restaurant:** The dining room enjoys panoramic views of the Valley and the Fells beyond. A table d'hôte menu is offered and includes a varied choice of both English and continental dishes. Generous portions are served to satisfy the hearty appetite of a keen walker. A good selection of wines is available to complement the cuisine. **Nearby:** The Langdale Valley offers wonderful walking and climbing opportunities in England's most beautiful corner, with abundant wildlife and many places of historical and literary importance. From the hotel guests can walk up Stickle Ghyll to Stickle Tarn and onwards to Paveyarc Harrison Stickle and numerous other pikes. **Directions: M6 junction 36 A591. Through Windermere to Ambleside. Follow A593 towards Coniston, turn right onto B5343 to Langdale. The hotel is two miles past Chapelstyle on the right.**

For hotel location, see maps on pages 180–186

THE ROYAL OAK INN

BONGATE, APPLEBY-IN-WESTMORLAND, CUMBRIA CA16 6UN
TEL: 017683 51463 FAX: 017683 52300

OWNERS: Colin and Hilary Cheyne
CHEF: Hilary Cheyne

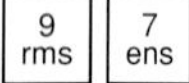

S: £38–£48
D: £60–£72

Inn: The Royal Oak has been a coaching inn since the 1600s and parts of the building are 750 years old. It is a well cared for, traditional hostelry, situated in the oldest part of the north Pennine town of Appleby-in-Westmorland. The oak panelling, beams, stone walls and open fires combine to give the inn its warm, inviting atmosphere. The bedrooms are all individually furnished and all have a private bathroom. Facilities for ironing and clothes-drying are available. Guests will find the owners hospitable and their staff attentive, providing an efficient service. **Restaurant:** An extensive selection of fresh fish, local meat and vegetarian dishes, together with some unusual specialities, are offered to suit all tastes. There are two dining rooms, one of which is non-smoking, and an extensive wine list of over 70 bins. A full Westmorland breakfast is served to set visitors up for a day of sightseeing. Hand-pumped ales plus malt whiskies are offered in the Snug and Taproom bars and The Royal Oak was awarded Cumbria Pub of the Year 1992 by CAMRA. **Nearby:** The inn is well placed for visitors wishing to explore the celebrated scenery of the high moorlands, as well as the numerous castles and historic houses in the area. Running through Appleby is the Settle to Carlisle railway which traverses spectacular, remote countryside. **Directions: The inn can easily be located on the south-east approach to Appleby from the A66 Penrith–Scotch Corner road.**

For hotel location, see maps on pages 180–186

OLD BEAMS RESTAURANT WITH ROOMS

WATERHOUSES, STAFFORDSHIRE ST10 3HW
TEL: 01538 308254 FAX: 01538 308157

OWNERS: Nigel and Ann Wallis
CHEF: Nigel Wallis

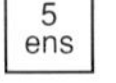

S: £55–£72
D: £70–£89.95

Inn: Dating back to 1746, this attractive house has been lovingly refurbished by owners Nigel and Ann Wallis, who bought it 1980 with the aim of creating a top-class provincial restaurant. For guests who wish to extend their visit, The Old Beams provides accommodation of a very high standard. The beautifully decorated bedrooms are individually styled; they have the luxury of hand-made beds and provide all the little extras to make your stay memorable. There is an oak-beamed reception and bar area, where pre-dinner drinks can be enjoyed by an open fire. An enchanting garden provides many of the fresh vegetables and herbs used in Nigel's creative cooking. **Restaurant:** Chef-patron Nigel Wallis has earned a well deserved reputation for his superb cuisine. The menus offer a choice of exceptional dishes, served with inspired sauces and garnishes. Meals can be enjoyed in the main restaurant or in the conservatory with its lush foliage. An award-winning wine list, which offers over 130 bins, is augmented by a fine selection of whiskies and brandies. During the summer drinks and coffee are often served in the garden. **Nearby:** The Old Beams Restaurant is ideally situated for visiting the Peak National Park, Alton Towers theme park, Chatsworth and other famous houses, and the Staffordshire potteries' visitor centres. **Directions: The Old Beams Restaurant is on the A523 Ashbourne–Leek road, about 35 minutes' drive from the M6 or M1.**

THE KINGS ARMS HOTEL AND RESTAURANT

MARKET PLACE, ASKRIGG-IN-WENSLEYDALE, NORTH YORKSHIRE DL8 3HQ
TEL: 01969 650258 FAX: 01969 650635

OWNERS: Ray and Liz Hopwood
CHEF: John Barber

10 rms | 10 ens

S: £50–£75
D: £75–£110

Inn: Ray and Liz Hopwood welcome you to their country Georgian manor house in the tiny village of Askrigg. It is set amid some of Britain's most emotive scenery, as captured on canvas by Turner during his stay in the early 1800s. Originally built in 1760 to house the racing stables, the building became an inn in 1810 and it established a tradition of warm hospitality and good food. There are three distinctive bars: one – the back parlour – is better known ass The Drover's Arms from the BBC TV series *All Creatures Great and Small*. In each of the distinctive and comfortable bars guests can enjoy an award-winning bar meal with ales from the cask. Beautifully styled bedrooms include richly draped four-poster, half-tester and brass beds; all thoughtfully appointed to ensure the utmost comfort. **Restaurant:** The panelled Clubroom Restaurant epitomises the era of elegance and sophistication. Only the finest fresh produce, fish and game in season are used for the dishes that comprise the fixed price à la carte menu. Special dinners are held regularly to celebrate significant events in the calendar. An award-winning wine list complements the menu. The Silks Grill offers steaks, games and fresh fish. It is also available for private functions. **Nearby:** The Yorkshire Dales, Settle–Carlisle Railway, Aysgarth Falls and Brontë country. **Directions: In the centre of Askrigg, ½ mile from the A684 near Bainbridge. This road links the A1 at Leeming Bar with the M6 at Sedbergh (junction 37).**

For hotel location, see maps on pages 180–186

THE WINDMILL AT BADBY

MAIN STREET, BADBY, NR DAVENTRY, NORTHAMPTONSHIRE NN11 6AN
TEL: 01327 702363 FAX: 01327 311521

OWNERS: John Freestone and Carol Sutton
CHEF: Gavin Baxter

S: £35–£42.50
D: £49–£59

Inn: The Windmill Inn Hotel was first established as an inn in the 17th century and is situated in the heart of the pretty village of Badby. A traditional thatched country pub, complete with log fires, The Windmill offers good food and a range of cask-conditioned ales. The owners, with their extensive experience of hotel and pub management, have plenty of ideas for regular activities. Winter Sportsmans Dinners and theme nights with entertainment are popular events. The en suite bedrooms provide comfortable accommodation and the whole hotel is ideally suitable for house party weekends from 12-14 guests. **Restaurant:** Under the skilled eye of Gavin Baxter the kitchen prepares a varied range of freshly cooked dishes. Many specialities are made and these include Stilton mushrooms, char-grilled Cajun chicken, steak and kidney pie, fresh moussaka and poached salmon with new potatoes. Weddings, functions and business conferences are catered for with ease. **Nearby:** The surrounding woods and meadows provide excellent walking (Badby is the start of both the Knightley and Nene Ways). Cycles may be hired. Places to visit include Althorpe, Canons Ashby, Sulgrave Manor (home of the Washingtons), Blenheim Palace, Silverstone Circuit, Warwick and Stratford-upon-Avon. **Directions: The Windmill is in the centre of Badby, a village located off the A361, three miles south of Daventry on the Banbury road.**

For hotel location, see maps on pages 180–186

THE MORRITT ARMS HOTEL

GRETA BRIDGE, NR BARNARD CASTLE, COUNTY DURHAM DL12 9SE
TEL: 01833 627232 FAX: 01833 627392

OWNERS: Peter J. Phillips and Barbara Anne Johnson

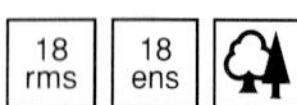

S: £55
D: £70–£95

Inn: Close to the famous beauty spot and subject of one of Turner's paintings, The Meeting of the Waters, The Morritt Arms Hotel is itself a famous meeting place. Built where a Roman fort used to stand, the traditional coaching inn dates back to the 17th century. Staying at 'The Morritt' you will capture the essence of a by-gone era. Scott and Dickens both found inspiration for their writings in the area, and are remembered in the names of two of the hotel's bars. Memories of Dickensian times are evoked through John Gilroy's original mural, celebrating their 50th anniversary in 1996 and welcoming you to the Dickens Bar. **Restaurant:** The oak-panelled Copperfield Restaurant provides the finest of local, British fayre, which is complemented by 150 bins of traditional and New World Wines from our national award-winning wine list. Hearty breakfasts, home-made afternoon teas and discerning bar food with real ales complete the menu. **Nearby:** The area is rich in history and natural beauty on the border between North Yorkshire and the Land of the Prince Bishops. Barnard Castle and Richmond are within easy reach. Other local amenities include racecourses, theatres, golf links, museums and historic ruins. **Directions: The hotel is conveniently located just off the A66 linking A1 (Scotch Corner) with M6 (Penrith). The hotel signs on the A66 direct you to the hotel. Darlington main-line railway station and Teeside airport are both approximately 30 minutes away by car.**

For hotel location, see maps on pages 180–186

The George Hotel

HIGH STREET, ODIHAM, HOOK, HAMPSHIRE RG29 1LP
TEL: 01256 702081 FAX: 01256 704213

OWNERS: Moira and Peter Kelsey
CHEF: Peter Kelsey

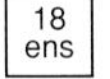
18 rms 18 ens

S: £65
D: £75–£90

Inn: This handsome inn, with 1½ acres of garden orchard, was first granted a licence in 1540. Among its authentic features are wattle and daub walls, timber framing, an antique fireplace and Elizabethan wall paintings. The oak-panelled restaurant was once the area Assize Court and, with a whipping post in the room above, it was only a short trip from sentence to punishment for the unlucky offender! The bedrooms are located both in the main building and newer annexe. The George is a family-run hotel, whose owners offer friendly hospitality and good service. **Restaurant:** The dining room is elegantly furnished, with attractively set tables. Here, the best of good seafood such as sea bass, baked monkfish or fillet of sea bream on saffron noodles is served and always well presented. An extensive choice of lighter meals is also available in the bar. **Nearby:** Local attractions include the Watercress Line Steam Railway at Alton, Birdworld at Farnham, the Old Kiln Agricultural Museum at Tilford, and Basing House near Basingstoke. **Directions: Odiham is one mile from junction 5 of the M3. Take A287 towards Farnham; the hotel is in the centre of the village.**

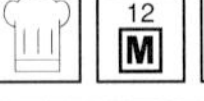   

For hotel location, see maps on pages 180–186

THE WOOLPACK INN

BECKINGTON, NR BATH BA3 6SP
TEL: 01373 831244 FAX: 01373 831223

OWNER: West Country Village Inns Ltd
DIRECTORS: Martin Tarr and Paul Toogood
CHEF: David Woolfall

12 rms | 12 ens

S: £49.50–£59.50
D: £64.50–£94.50

Inn: Situated in the centre of the village of Beckington, on the borders of Somerset, Avon and Wiltshire, The Woolpack is a small coaching inn dating from the 16th century. Legend has it that condemned criminals were allowed a final drink here before being led away to the gallows. The inn has been thoughtfully decorated and furnished to recapture the original character of the building. On the ground floor is the bar area, with its stone floor and open log fire, where fine traditional ale is served. There is also a small lounge. Each of the 12 bedrooms has been individually renovated, each having an en suite bathroom and all modern comforts. **Restaurant:** Guests may enjoy either a quick snack or a more substantial meal in either the Oak Room, Dining or Garden Rooms, where the menus offer freshly prepared dishes, including locally caught game and fish, skillfully cooked by the kitchen team. **Nearby:** There are places to visit nearby in abundance: the Georgian city of Bath, the cathedral cities of Salisbury and Wells, Longleat House and Safari Park, Lacock, Glastonbury, Stourhead, Cheddar Gorge and Wookey Hole, the stone circles at Stonehenge and Avebury, and the tropical bird gardens at Rode. **Directions: Beckington, recently by-passed, is on the A36 Bath–Southampton road on the borders of Somerset, Avon and Wiltshire.**

For hotel location, see maps on pages 180–186

FRESHMANS RESTAURANT

CHURCH HILL, BELBROUGHTON, WORCESTERSHIRE DY9 0DT
TEL: 01562 730467

PROPRIETOR: Annette Wheatley
CHEFS: Annette Wheatley and Rebecca Wheatley-Bodsworth

Restaurant: Freshmans, which has enjoyed previous incarnations as the village workhouse and a coaching inn, now enjoys a widespread reputation for the flair of its chef-patronnes, Annette Wheatley and her daughter, Rebecca. The vibrant past of the building is perpetuated in fine oak beams, gleaming crystal hardware and abundant flowers which decorate the intimate split-level dining room. The main attraction is the food, however. The delightful style of cooking is based on the use of the freshest market ingredients combined with imaginative and, often, unusual flavours. From the simplest of fresh lobster salads to dishes of culinary extravagance, exciting sauces and interesting vegetables, the emphasis is on attention to detail. Fresh shell fish from Orkney, local game, seasonal vegetables and puddings to make the mouth water usually appear on the regularly changing menus. There are often daily specialities, particularly fresh fish, on offer as well. A balanced wine list and very reasonable prices add to the attractions. **Wine:** Good, honest French house wines from £10. Other wines reasonably priced. **Price:** À la carte; lunches from around £10 – dinner from £25 per head. Open for lunch Tuesday to Friday; dinner Tuesday to Saturday. Booking essential. **Directions: Freshmans is adjacent to Belbroughtion Church – M5/junction 4 to Stourbridge, A491 then B4188, turning left at the T-junction in the village.**

CHEFS' SPECIALITIES

●●●●●●●

fresh supreme oysters
simply flash fried in a subtle garlic butter, placed inside its shell with a topping of Mozzarella cheese and herb breadcrumbs and grilled

sirloin of English veal
pan fried in a mildly spicy ginger wine and cream sauce, complemented with flavoursome fresh parsnip chips

Freshman's bread and butter pudding
with Grand Marnier

THE BLUE BELL HOTEL

MARKET PLACE, BELFORD, NORTHUMBERLAND NE70 7NE
TEL: 01668 213543 FAX: 01668 213787

OWNER: Jean Shirley
CHEF: Stephen Owens

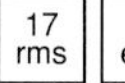

S: £42–£60
D: £80–£98

Inn: This beautifully restored old coaching inn stands in the centre of the village of Belford, near the old Market Cross. The sophisticated Georgian-style interiors are decorated to complement the original features. Luxurious bedrooms provide every modern comfort and are all unique. There is an elegant residents' lounge and two bars, well stocked with fine malts, rare brandies and vintage ports. The hotel also has three acres of walled terraced grounds, with a putting lawn and organic vegetable and herb garden. Dogs by arrangement. **Restaurant:** The emphasis here is on freshness. Fruit and vegetables from the hotel gardens are combined with an excellent supply of fresh local produce such as Cheviot lamb, Tweed salmon and Craster kippers, to create a range of delicious seasonal dishes. Frequently changing à la carte and table d'hôte menus are served in the garden restaurant, which is furnished with locally crafted tables. For a more simple but substantial menu, try the Buttery. **Nearby:** There is much to discover along Northumberland's scenic coastline – the Farne Islands, Lindsifarne and Berwick-upon-Tweed are among the many interesting attractions. Sporting activities which can be enjoyed locally include shooting, fishing, riding and golf. **Directions: Midway between Berwick and Alnwick, about 14 miles south of Berwick and two minutes from the A1. From A1 turn off at Belford/Wooler junction to join the B6349. The hotel is situated in the centre of the village centre.**

For hotel location, see maps on pages 180–186

The Old Manse

VICTORIA STREET, BOURTON-ON-THE-WATER, GLOUCESTERSHIRE GL54 2BX
TEL: 01451 820082 FAX: 01451 810381

OWNERS: Oswald and Audrey Dockery

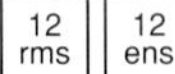

12 rms 12 ens

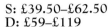

S: £39.50–£62.50
D: £59–£119

Inn: The Old Manse was built in 1748 during a period of wealth for all the settlements of the Cotswold hills. Its first owner was Reverend Benjamin Beddome, the village baptist pastor. In recent years, traditional Cotswold stone has been used to add a modern wing to the inn, whilst just a few feet from the porch the wide and shallow River Windrush flows on its way to the Thames. Fully centrally heated, this lovely inn has 12 en suite bedrooms, all with remote control colour TV, radio alarm and tea and coffee making facilities. For added luxury, the Beddome Room boasts a King-size four-poster bed with matching furniture and a double whirlpool spa. **Restaurant:** An elegantly decorated and furnished restaurant offers excellent table d'hôte, à la carte and vegetarian menus and the chef will gladly prepare any special dish on request. Fresh local produce is used wherever possible and there is an extensive wine list to complement the cuisine. **Nearby:** Bourton-on-the-Water has its own motor museum (with one of the country's largest collections of vintage advertising signs), model village (a one-ninth replica of the original), a model railway exhibition and Birdland (with the largest collection of penguins outside America). Also within easy reach is the well-marked footpath route across the wolds of the Oxfordshire Way. **Directions: Bourton-on-the-Water is off the A429 running between Stow-on-the-Wold and Cirencester.**

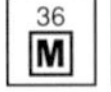

For hotel location, see maps on pages 180–186

THE MANOR HOTEL

WEST BEXINGTON, DORCHESTER, DORSET DT2 9DF
TEL: 01308 897616 FAX: 01308 897035

OWNERS: Richard and Jayne Childs
CHEF: Clive Jobson

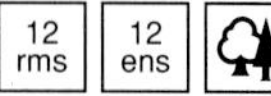

S: from £43
D: from £76

Inn: The Manor Hotel, mentioned in the *The Doomsday Book*, is in a wonderful setting, overlooking the beautiful Dorset countryside and spectacular Lyme Bay. The friendly atmosphere is apparent immediately on entering the inn, while the oak-panelling, stone walls and original fireplaces remind guests they are in the midst of history. **Restaurant:** The restaurant is brilliant, with two or three course menus that include wonderful fish choices – monkfish and scallop kebabs, lobster, oysters and crab & haddock quiche – and game, venison escalopes or pigeon salad with forest mushrooms. Vegetarian dishes also feature, and there is a children's menu. The wine list is exciting. Buffet meals, also including seafood, are served in the cosy cellar bar. There is an attractive conservatory for relaxing while outside children have their own play area. There are twelve charming en suite bedrooms and those at the top of the house have splendid views over the sea. **Nearby:** This is Thomas Hardy (Bridport is *Port Bredy*) country and there are also an abundance of famous gardens and historic houses to visit. Chesil Beach and the Abbotsbury Swannery are nearby and many water sports and country pursuits can be enjoyed. **Directions: West Bexington is on the B3157, five miles east of Bridport, 11 miles from Dorchester and Weymouth.**

For hotel location, see maps on pages 180–186

Poppies at the Roebuck

BRIMFIELD, LUDLOW, SHROPSHIRE SY8 4NE
TEL: 01584 711230 FAX: 01584 711654

OWNER: Carole Evans

S: £45
D: £60

Inn: This highly commended traditional inn is situated in the charming village of Brimfield. In 1992 it won the coveted 'Ronay Pub of the Year' award. The inn's three comfortable bedrooms are pleasantly decorated and furnished and all have en suite bathrooms. **Restaurant:** An extensive variety of dishes is available on the interesting menu. The tempting cuisine includes main courses such as roast herb crusted rack of lamb on a spinach roundel served with a redcurrant and mint sauce; pan fried sea bass on a tomato and saffron sauce, garnished with crispy fried vegetables; and roast fillet of Herefordshire beef served on a purée of horse radish and mange–tout with a red wine sauce and glazed shallots. À la carte main course prices range from around £17 to £23. For sweet sample the delights of rhubarb and orange terrine with crème fraîche or iced lime souffle captured in a chocolate tear drop. Most of the puddings cost from around £5.00 to £6.50. Egon Ronay 1995 Cheeseboard of the Year. There is also a good bar menu available. A comprehensive and reasonably priced wine list is provided to complement the cuisine. **Nearby:** National Trust properties include Berrington Hall with a park and lake by Capability Brown. Also closeby are the Welsh Marshes and the town of Leominster with its summer festivals. **Directions: Poppies at the Roebuck is situated off the A49 midway between Ludlow and Leominster.**

Cotswold Gateway Hotel

CHELTENHAM ROAD, BURFORD, OXON OX18 4HX
TEL: 01993 822695 FAX: 01993 823600

RESIDENT DIRECTORS: Dennis and Ann Evans

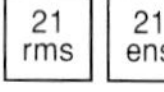

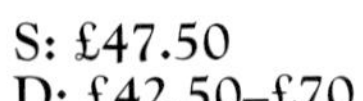

S: £47.50
D: £42.50–£70

Inn: In the days of horse drawn coaches Cotswold Gateway Hotel was a welcome stop over for travellers visiting Burford. Today, this 18th century inn which has been recently lavishly renovated offers its guests every modern comfort and amenity. A friendly and intimate service is offered by the highly trained staff, equal to any found in a family run hotel. All of the bedrooms have been individually designed and furnished and provide a trouser press, alarm clock, television, telephone and tea and coffee making facilities. **Restaurant:** A daily changing menu of traditional English dishes is offered in the spacious and tastefully furnished restaurant, complemented by a good wine list. The comfortable bar is a pleasant place to relax and enjoy a drink, while the coffee shop serves informal meals, tea and refreshments. **Nearby:** Adjacent to the hotel is a mews of specialist antique shops offering an array of fine antique pieces. Burford itself has changed little since the end of the 17th century and its streets are lined with exquisite buildings in the honeyed, locally quarried limestone. There are many other pretty villages to explore. **Directions: Burford is on the A361.**

For hotel location, see maps on pages 180–186

THE LAMB INN

SHEEP STREET, BURFORD, OXFORDSHIRE OX18 4LR
TEL: 01993 823155 FAX: 01993 822228

OWNERS: Richard and Caroline De Wolf
MANAGER: Paul Swain
CHEF: Pascal Clavaud

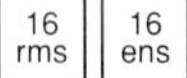

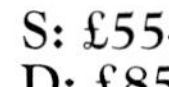

S: £55–£75
D: £85–£95

Inn: The Lamb Inn, in the small Cotswold town of Burford, is everyone's idea of the archetypal English inn, where it is easy to imagine that time has slipped back to some gentler age. The inn is set in a quiet location with a pretty walled garden. To step inside is to recapture something of the spirit of the 14th century: flagged floors, gleaming copper, brass and silver reflect the flicker of log fires and the well-chosen antiques all enhance the sense of history here. The bedrooms, which have recently been refurbished, offer comfortable accommodation, with oak beams, chintz curtains and soft furnishings. **Restaurant:** Guests can enjoy the best of British cooking. Dinner, chosen from a three-course table d'hôte or à la carte menu, is taken in the candlelit pillared dining room and might include such dishes as fresh grilled sardines with lime butter sauce, followed by roast tenderloin of pork wrapped in smoked bacon with a blue cheese cream sauce. Light lunches are served in the bar or in the garden. On Sundays, a traditional three-course lunch is served. Packed lunches and hampers can be provided. **Nearby:** The inn is near the heart of the town, where guests can browse through antiques shops or laze by the waters of the River Windrush. Burford is within easy reach of Oxford, Cheltenham, Stow-on-the-Wold and the many attractive Cotswold villages. **Directions: Sheep Street is off the main street in Burford. Burford is 20 miles west of Oxford.**

THE HOSTE ARMS HOTEL

THE GREEN, BURNHAM MARKET, NORFOLK PE31 8HD
TEL: 01328 738777 FAX: 01328 730103

OWNER: Paul Whittome
MANAGER: Fiona Lyne & Paul Bennett
HEAD CHEF: Leigh Diggins

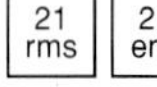

S: £48–£56
D: £66–£92

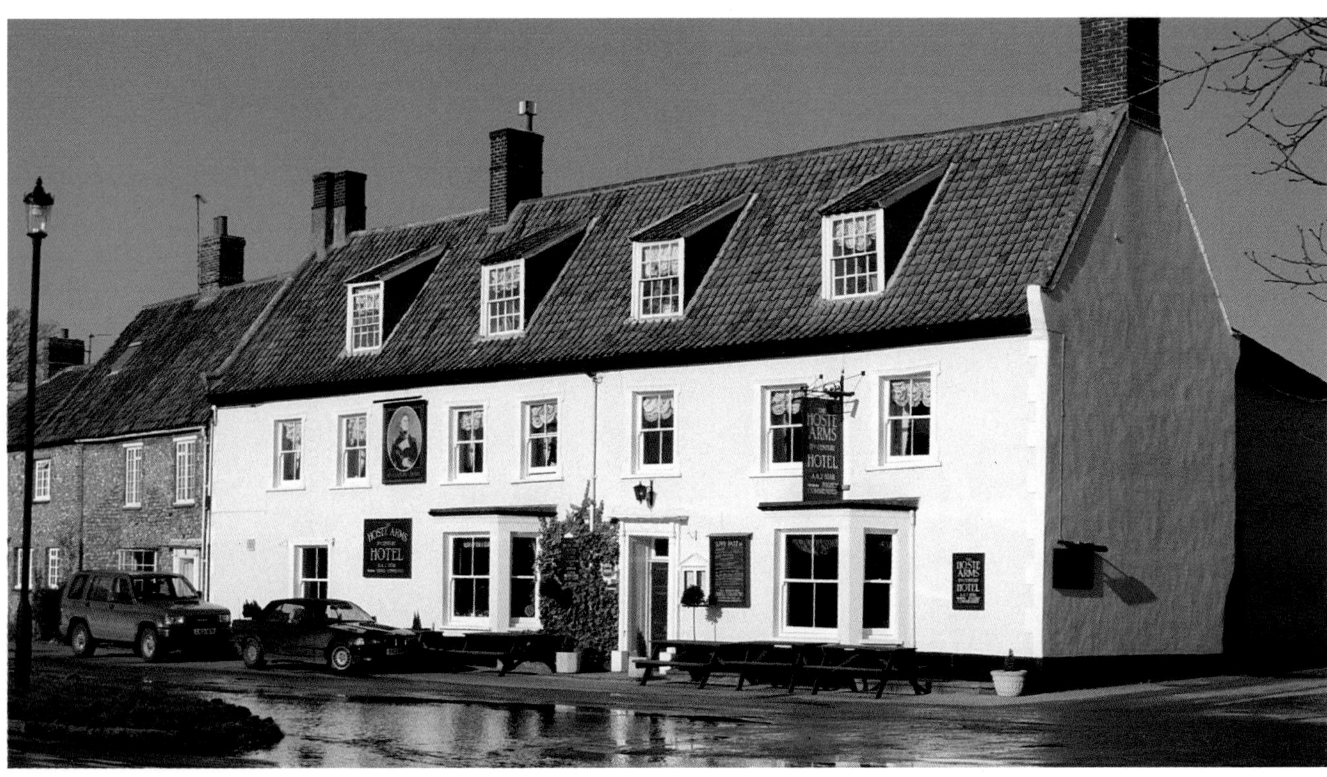

Inn: The Hoste Arms dates back to the 17th century, when it was known as The Pitt Arms, after William Pitt's cousin, a local landowner. Overlooking the green in the picturesque village of Burnham Market, the hotel has recently undergone extensive refurbishments, including the addition of more bedrooms, all en suite. Four rooms have four-poster beds and great care has been taken to preserve any original features. There is a music room with a grand piano, where on Mondays and Fridays Jazz and Rhythm and Blues evenings are held. A panelled function room is available for private parties and conferences. **Restaurant:** The menus are created by head chef Leigh Diggins who applies his extensive skills and experience to create fine cuisine within the à la carte restaurant and modern European menu's in the Brasserie. All wines are personally selected by Paul Bennett. All wines are personally selected by Paul Bennet, with bottles to suit every palate and pocket. **Nearby:** The Hoste Arms is well situated to cater for most interests. There are several stately homes in the area, including Holkham Hall and Sandringham. For nature lovers there are four bird sanctuaries in the area and boat trips can be arranged to Scolt Head Island. Golf enthusiasts are also well catered for. **Directions: Burnham Market is about two miles from the A149 between Brancaster and Wells-next-the-Sea.**

For hotel location, see maps on pages 180–186

BOAR'S HEAD HOTEL

LICHFIELD ROAD, SUDBURY, DERBYSHIRE DE6 5GX
TEL: 01283 820344 FAX: 01283 820075

OWNERS: John and Gail Crooks
CHEF: Jonathon Ridley

22 rms 22 ens

S: from £32
D: from £42

Inn: This 17th century house left the famous Vernon estate through a game of cards! It is now a well known local hostelry, having been run by the Crooks family for many years. Guests arriving should not be deterred by the cold exterior. There is a warm bar, with natural brick walls, horse brasses and a hunting horn. The residents' lounge looks onto a pretty patio where drinks are served in summer months. Much thought has been given to furnishing the delightful bedrooms which have every possible facility, including teletext and Sky television. Visitors enjoy a choice of real ales and excellent home-cooked dishes with the chef's specials listed on a blackboard. **Restaurant:** There are two restaurants, the elegant Royal Boar with an imaginative à la carte menu and the less formal Hunter's Table Carvery and Bistro offering fresh fish, pasta dishes and splendid roasts, both at lunchtime and in the evening. The Royal Boar is closed on Sunday evenings, but is famous for its Sunday lunch. A fascinating wine list covers vineyards worldwide, with 70 entries that include 6 house wines and a selection of 10 half-bottles! **Nearby:** Alton Towers and Uttoxeter Racecourse are lively attractions nearby. Other guests will enjoy Chatsworth House, Tutbury Castle and the Bass Museum. **Directions: The hotel is on the A515, adjacent to the railway crossing, just short of the A50 from Stoke on Trent to Derby.**

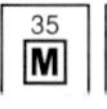   

For hotel location, see maps on pages 180–186

THE OLD VICARAGE

MAIN STREET, BRANSTON, BURTON–UPON–TRENT, STAFFORDSHIRE DE14 3EX
TEL: 01283 533222 FAX: 01283 540258

OWNERS: David and Eileen Boodie
CHEFS: David Boodie and Matthew Bowern

Restaurant: Run by the chef-patron and his wife this excellent restaurant offers an extensive variety of superb dishes to cater for every taste. Speciality dishes include a warm salad of peppered chickens livers with a sherry and shallot sauce, topped with a soft poached egg; char-grilled fillet of beef, roasted peanuts and mange tout with soy and ginger dressing; and monk fish and scallops with vermicelli sauce. There are numerous delicious sweets to chose from, including mango flamed in Armagnac with coconut parfait and fresh raspberries; hot, sticky toffee pudding served with crème anglaise; brandy-snap layered with bananas laced with hot fudge sauce; and warm pancakes filled with a compote of summer fruit and vanilla ice cream. The price of the three course lunch menu is £11.95, while the dinner menu is priced at £22.95. Prices are inclusive of VAT. **Wine:** There are over 150 wines available to complement the cuisine, priced between £7 and £150 with some reasonably priced half bottles. The Restaurant is closed for the first two weeks of August and on every Sunday evening and Monday. **Nearby:** Bass Museum of Brewing, Tutbury Castle and glassworks, Calke Abbey and Sudbury Hall. Visits, which must be pre-booked, can be arranged to the Bass, Marstons and Ind Coope breweries. **Directions: The Old Vicarage restaurant is 400 yards from the A38 Burton South junction in the centre of Branston village and next to the church.**

CHEFS' SPECIALITIES

tartare of dill pickled salmon
with cucumber salad and creme fraîche

pan-fried venison steak
on a bed of braised red cabbage served on a port and juniper sauce

layered chocolate bavarois
served with a light coffee cream

For hotel location, see maps on pages 180–186

THE CHEQUERS INN

FROGGATT EDGE, NR CALVER, DERBYSHIRE S30 1ZB
TEL: 01433 630231

OWNER: Bob Graham
MANAGERS: Isabelle and Euan Bell
CHEF: Brian Holloway

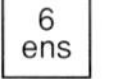

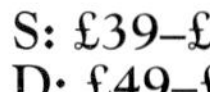

S: £39–£46
D: £49–£59

Inn: A Grade II listed building. The Chequers Inn originally comprised four 16th century houses, rebuilt in the 18th century and now extensively refurbished. It is situated on an old pack horse road in the heart of the Peak National Park. Visitors will see plenty of reminders of the inn's history; a horse-mounting block still stands outside the main building and the old stables house the logs that fuel crackling open fires. Behind the inn, acres of unspoiled woodland lead up to Froggatt Edge, with its panoramic views. Each of the six cottage-style bedrooms has its own identity, and for an extra touch of romance one room has a four poster bed. On most weekends guests can stay free on Sunday night when enjoying a 3 night break including dinner. **Restaurant:** Local chef Brian Holloway creates a wide variety of European and British meals, with several fish dishes and local game in season. The menus are original, exciting and reasonably priced. As an alternative to the restaurant, a choice of hearty bar meals is served every day. Bakewell pudding, the local speciality, is a favourite dessert here – delicious served hot with cream. **Nearby:** This is wonderful walking country: you can leave your car and follow the Derwent River or the Peak trails. Chatsworth House, Haddon Hall, the caverns of Castleton and the market town of Bakewell are all closeby. **Directions: The inn is situated on the old pack horse road, now the B6054 which links Bakewell and Sheffield, 6 miles from Bakewell on Froggatt Edge.**

For hotel location, see maps on pages 180–186

Tyacks Hotel

27 COMMERCIAL STREET, CAMBORNE, CORNWALL TR14 8LD
TEL: 01209 612424 FAX: 01209 612435

OWNERS: St Austell Brewery & Co Ltd
MANAGERS: Terence and Elizabeth Davison
CHEF: Norman Clarke

15 rms | 15 ens

S: £40–£42
D: £75
Suites: £90–£100

Inn: This charming 18th century coaching inn set in the heart of Camborne is just three minutes drive from the main A30 road or less than five minutes from the bus or railway stations. The Tyacks is used by business men and women as well as tourists as a base for travelling in the west of Cornwall. Re-opened in 1992, having been totally refurbished to AA and RAC 3 Star standard the inn has become popular with visitors from all over the world as is reflected in the restaurant's imaginative menus. Adjacent to the restaurant is an attractive lounge bar, ideal for a quiet drink or bar snack. For those people who enjoy a lively pub atmosphere there is the Coach Bar. Beside the hotel entrance, opposite the old stables is a patio and beer garden where drinks and snacks can be enjoyed on a sunny day. **Restaurant:** The à la carte, table d'hôte and vegetarian menus offer a splendid choice of English and Continental using fresh Cornish fish, vegetables and meats. **Nearby:** Camborne School of Mines and Geology Museum, Tehidy Country Park and Golf Club, St Ives Tate Gallery, Penzance and Lands End. The Engines Museum at Poole, the house of William Murdoch, founder of gaslighting, in Redruth. **Directions: From the A30 turn off at the sign for Camborne West the follow signs for town centre. Tyacks Hotel is on the left-hand side.**

For hotel location, see maps on pages 180–186

PANOS HOTEL AND RESTAURANT

154-156 HILLS ROAD, CAMBRIDGE, CAMBRIDGESHIRE CB2 2PB
TEL: 01223 212958 FAX: 01223 210980

OWNER: Genevieve Kretz

6 rms 6 ens

   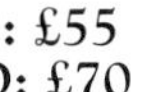

S: £55
D: £70

Inn: This small unpretentious and friendly hotel is managed by Genevieve Kretz. It is close to the centre of town and to the railway station, and has a regular clientèle who return again and again, and regard it as Cambridge's best kept secret. Guests enter the hotel through the attractive conservatory bar, which like the other reception rooms, is filled with fresh flowers arranged by Genevieve. **Restaurant:** The restaurant is recognised to be one of the best in Cambridge, with menus supervised by the owner. The famous Panos charcoal-grilled steaks and flambé dishes are listed beside mezze and sword-fish kebabs. An excellent wine list is available too. Full breakfast is included in the price. The six bedrooms are comfortable and spacious, all with en suite shower facilities, colour television, a radio alarm, writing desk and mini-bar. **Nearby:** The River Cam for those guests who wish to try their hand at punting, and for those preferring dry land the famous Cambridge Botanical Gardens. There are the historic colleges to admire also. Ely Cathedral is not far away and for those who like more activity, there is the racing at Newmarket. **Directions: From city centre follow signs to station and hospital as far as Hills Road. Once on Hills Road carry straight on to traffic lights and railway bridge avoiding fork to station. Panos is immediately on your right. Car park at rear.**

Quy Mill Hotel

NEWMARKET ROAD, STOW-CUM-QUY, CAMBRIDGE CB5 9AG
TEL: 01223 293383 FAX: 01223 293770

OWNER: Mr A.G. Jarvis
MANAGER: Darren Gandley
CHEF: Michael Parr

S: £53.50
D: £66.50

Inn: Quy Mill Hotel, built where there has been a mill since 1066, stands in 11 acres of private parkland. Hotel guests have fishing rights along Quy Water. The nearby Cambridge Science Park makes it ideal for businessmen as well as country-lovers. The new proprietors have improved the forecourt of the hotel and the oak-beamed bar has been transformed into a comfortable lounge. Twenty-three charming en suite bedrooms, recently renovated, overlook the river or farm. A suite, with a four-poster bed, faces the garden. **Restaurant:** The owners have created a traditional ambience, complemented by immaculate service, in The Granary Restaurant where the Mill Wheel is located. The table d'hôte menu offers home made dishes. There is a sophisticated à la carte selection available. The chef will willingly cater for vegetarians and guests with special dietary requirements. The owners enjoy discussing the excellent wine list. **Nearby:** Stow-cum-Quy is three miles from Cambridge with its Botanical Gardens and University. There is racing at Newmarket and Huntingdon. Anglesey Abbey (N.T.) is very near. The locality is ideal for walkers and wildlife lovers. **Directions: Leave M11 at Junction 14, taking the A14 East to the B1102/A1301. Quy Mill is on the left shortly after leaving the A14.**

For hotel location, see maps on pages 180–186

The Falcon Hotel

CASTLE ASHBY, NORTHAMPTON, NORTHAMPTONSHIRE NN7 1LF
TEL: 01604 696200 FAX: 01604 696673

OWNERS: Neville and Jo Watson
CHEF: Neil Helks

S: £50–£62.50
D: £75

Inn: Six miles south of Northampton, in the heart of the Marquess of Northampton's estate, The Falcon is a delightful country hotel, secluded and tranquil, minutes away from the rambling acres of Castle Ashby House. Proprietors Neville and Jo Watson, both committed professionals, have invested energy and enthusiasm into transforming this once modest place into a haven of comfort, excellent food and attentive service. Bedrooms are well furnished, all offering up-to-date appliances and the bathrooms have been recently upgraded. There are fresh flowers, French, Spanish and German are spoken, and dogs are welcome. **Restaurant:** Lunch and dinner which are created where possible from seasonal, home-grown produce, are served in the intimate restaurant which overlooks a lawn with willow trees. The excellent value-for-money cuisine, modern English in flavour, is prepared by chef Neil Helks. A fixed-price menu costs £19.50, including coffee and *petits fours*. There is also an interesting à la carte selection. The extensive wine list, can be studied by guests at their leisure over pre-prandial drinks by a glowing log fire. **Nearby:** Walk in the grounds of Castle Ashby estate. Further afield, visit Woburn, Althorp, Silverstone, Bedford and Stratford. **Directions: Exit M1 junction 14 northbound or 15 southbound. Follow the signs to A428 where Castle Ashby and The Falcon are clearly signposted, six miles south-east of Northampton.**

For hotel location, see maps on pages 180–186

THE GEORGE HOTEL

MARKET PLACE, CASTLE CARY, SOMERSET BA7 7AH
TEL: 01963 350761 FAX: 01963 350035

OWNER: Eltel Ltd
DIRECTORS: Greg and Sue Sparkes
MANAGER: Kim Mitchell CHEF: Martin J. Barrett

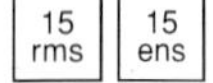

S: £37–£45
D: £65–£75

Inn: The George has played an important part in the history of this unspoilt Somerset town, having been a coaching inn since the 15th century. The charming bedrooms combine modern needs with individual furnishings: – special breaks throughout the year are included in the tariff. Guests will enjoy meeting the local residents in the snug bar (no smoking) and the George Bar which has an elm beam dating back to the 10th century in its inglenook fireplace. Traditional ales are served together with an excellent selection of bar meals. **Restaurant:** This fine panelled restaurant offers an à la carte menu using the finest of local produce, prepared by chef Martin J. Barrett, which is complemented by a well selected wine list. **Nearby:** There are many fine buildings to visit in the town mainly built of 'Cary gingerbread' stone including an 18th century town lock-up known as the 'Roundhouse'. Many National Trust properties and gardens, Wells, Glastonbury, Sherbourne and Longleat are nearby. For sport, Wincanton races, various golf courses, horse riding and ballooning are nearby. **Directions: Castle Cary is signposted off the A303 at Wincanton, reached via the M3 from London. Or via Bath from the M4. There is also a direct train from London Paddington taking 90 minutes.**

For hotel location, see maps on pages 180–186

THE CASTLE INN

CASTLE COMBE, NR CHIPPENHAM, WILTSHIRE SN14 7HN
TEL: 01249 783030 FAX: 01249 782315

OWNERS: Hatton Hotels Group
MANAGER: Craig Bicknell
CHEF: Simon Walker

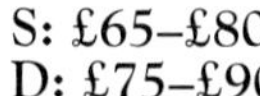

S: £65–£80
D: £75–£90

Inn: This famous inn can trace its origins back to the 12th century, and the restoration completed in 1994 reflects the owners' determination to combine history with discreet modernisation, creating an elegant small hostelry by the market place of this pretty village. The bedrooms are delightful, filled with all modern amenities and luxurious accessories that include towelling robes, fresh fruit, mineral water and homemade cookies. Attention to detail is also reflected in the en suite bathrooms with their antique gold fittings, two having a whirlpool bath and one a Victorian slipper bath. **Restaurant:** The inn is open daily for lunch and dinner. Oliver's Restaurant, awarded two Rosettes by the AA, has built up a reputation for excellent food and fine wine, at affordable prices. Guests can dine in the restaurant, the oak beamed conservatory or the bar which offers delicious home-produced bar food and an excellent selection of real ales, premier beers, wines and spirits. A member of Hatton Group Hotels. **Nearby:** Castle Combe is ideally situated for exploring Bath, Bristol and the Cotswolds. Golf and motor racing are local sports. **Directions: Castle Combe is on the A420 south of the M4 at junction 17 from London, or junction 18 from South Wales.**

For hotel location, see maps on pages 180–186

YE OLDE NAGS HEAD HOTEL

CROSS STREET, CASTLETON, DERBYSHIRE S30 2WH
TEL: 01433 620248 FAX: 01433 621604

OWNERS: Carole and Graham Walker
CHEF: Carol Walker

S: £45–£65
D: £55–£85

Inn: The picturesque village of Castleton, at the heart of the Peak District National Park, is the setting for Ye Olde Nags Head, a 17th century coaching house. Castleton is a natural base for touring this area, yet is also well-positioned as a stopover spot for executives, being midway between Sheffield and Manchester. Attention to detail is evident in the bedrooms, each equipped with trouser press, hairdryer and tea-making facilities. Three rooms have four poster beds and one also has a spa bath. Gleaming brass and open fireplaces set the tone in the congenial public bar and lounge, where a selection of real ales, beers and lagers is served. **Restaurant:** Cut glass, silver and fresh flowers adorn the tables in the elegant dining room, which opens daily to residents and non-residents for lunch and dinner. Extensive table d'hôte, à la carte and flambé menus include traditional English roasts, local game, vegetarian dishes, fresh fish and seafood. Choose from a comprehensive list and, after the meal, relax in the coffee lounge. During licensing hours a wide choice of hot and cold bar meals is available. **Nearby:** Above Castleton's narrow, twisting street are the grey ruins of Peveril Castle. The area is renowned for its stunning limestone scenery – visit the Blue John Mine, Speedwell Cavern and Treak Cliff. Potholing, riding, climbing and golf can be enjoyed locally. **Directions: The village of Castleton lies on the A625. It is 16 miles from Sheffield and 28 miles from Manchester.**

For hotel location, see maps on pages 180–186

KINGSHEAD HOUSE RESTAURANT

BIRDLIP, GLOUCESTERSHIRE GL4 8JH
TEL: 01452 862299

OWNERS: Warren and Judy Knock
CHEF: Judy Knock

1 rms | 1 ens

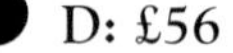

D: £56

Restaurant: Made of Cotswold stone, this 17th century former coaching inn is the home of Warren and Judy Knock. It is close to the Cotswold Path from where there are fine views over the Severn Valley. In the unpretentious oak-beamed restaurant, you can enjoy excellent English cooking prepared by chef-owner Judy. Her menu changes twice-weekly, offering up to four courses with perhaps five delicious choices for each course. Everything tastes admirably fresh – fish is delivered from Abergavenny, meat from the local butcher and vegetables come directly from a local farm. Main courses range from strips of fillet steak with celeriac, Stilton and walnuts to halibut in a herb crust with parsley butter, while for a starter there may be a delicious brandade of smoked haddock in puff pastry. Puddings are equally appealing, with such delights as Lord John Russell's iced pudding (a 'bombe' of an orange ice cream encased in a lemon ice cream). There is one en suite bedroom well proportioned and comfortably furnished. The restaurant opens for lunch Tuesday to Sunday and for dinner Tuesday to Saturday. Smoking is discouraged but not entirely banned. **Wine:** The wine list – expertly compiled by Warren Knock – offers a good selection of half-bottles. With over seventy different wines there is something to suit every palate. **Directions: Birdlip is situated just off the A417 on the B4070, 8 miles from Gloucester and Cheltenham.**

CHEF'S SPECIALS

•••••••

covered puff pastry tart
filled with a mixture of wild mushrooms & almonds, accompanied by button mushrooms in a cream and nutmeg sauce

rack of lamb
in a minted crust served with a green pea purée and a tomato butter sauce

fresh peaches and raspberries
in lime flower syrup with a sorbet of fromage blanc

For hotel location, see maps on pages 180–186

The Pheasant Inn

HIGHER BURWARDSLEY, TATTENHALL, CHESTER CH3 9PF
TEL: 01829 770434 FAX: 01829 771097

OWNERS: David and Valerie Greenhaugh
CHEF: David Boucker

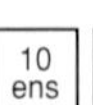

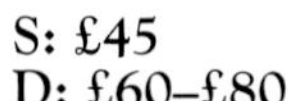

S: £45
D: £60–£80

Inn: This is a charming 300 year old inn, partly timbered, at the top of the Peckforton Hills looking out over the Cheshire Plains to Wales. The bar has a magnificent log fire and a resident parrot called Sailor. Recently a conservatory has been added which is used as an extension to the dining room at weekends. The bar is well stocked, there is an array of real ales and some fine wines to accompany meals. **Restaurant:** The Highland Room, popular with local inhabitants, has a daily menu chalked up, which includes a choice for vegetarians. At weekends there is a superb Sunday lunch menu for just £9.50, while on Saturday evenings they produce the most delicious four-course dinner for only £14. Eight of the ten en suite bedrooms are in converted barns, allowing peace and privacy – all rooms have modern amenities. For added interest the landlord keeps a herd of prize-winning Highland cattle which graze in surrounding fields. **Nearby:** Chester, Wrexham and Nantwich are within reach by car. Oulton Park motor racing is nearby. There is trout fishing and golf available and the health-giving Peckforton Hills are ideal for rambling. **Directions: A41 from Chester. After six miles turn left for Tattenhall then left again in village, signed Burwardsley. Top of hill, left at Post Office and hotel is higher still on left.**

For hotel location, see maps on pages 180–186

THE NOEL ARMS

CHIPPING CAMPDEN, GLOUCESTERSHIRE GL55 6AT
TEL: 01386 840317 FAX: 01386 841136

OWNER: Noel Hotels Ltd
GENERAL MANAGER: Neil John

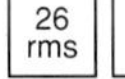

S: £60
D: £80

Inn: The Noel Arms, built as a coaching lodge in the 14th century, prides itself on its status as Chipping Campden's oldest inn. This superb building has a vivid history: old wool merchants resided here while on business from the Continent; and the future King Charles II took refuge here after the Battle of Worcester in 1651. Adorning the oak-panelled walls today is a gleaming array of armoury and muskets summoning up the building's august past. Guests can expect a level of service and comfort cultivated by centuries of hospitality. Bedrooms are located both in the original building and in the new wing – a respectful extension to the main structure. Some have four-poster beds, all offer modern facilities, including tea and coffee-making facilities. Downstairs, the friendly and relaxed atmosphere is continued in old oak beams and panelling, with an open fire in the lounge bar around which guests gather with drinks before dinner. **Restaurant:** In the Conservatory, or the Restaurant, a wide-ranging menu offers rosette quality cuisine based on produce from the nearby Vale of Evesham. Guests can choose vegetarian food, and pick from an extensive wine list. **Nearby:** walking country in Gloucestershire, Warwickshire and Worcestershire. Banbury, Tewkesbury, Worcester, and Moreton-in-Marsh. **Directions: From Oxford take the A34 to Chipping Norton, then A44 to Moreton-in-Marsh. Chipping Campden is signposted.**

For hotel location, see maps on pages 180–186

THE NEW INN

COLN ST-ALDWYNS, Nr.CIRENCESTER, GLOUCESTERSHIRE GL7 5AN
TEL: 01285 750651 FAX: 01285 750657

OWNERS: Brian and Sandra-Anne Evans
CHEF: Tony Robson-Burrell

11 rms | 11 ens

S: £50
D: £75

Inn: 'New', this fine old coaching inn is not. The thick, creeper-clad walls and open hearths have warmed and welcomed Cotswold travellers since Elizabeth I was queen. Set in the picture-book village of Coln St-Aldwyns, The New Inn offers a personal welcome to match the traditional props of stone flags, oak beams and hand-pumped real ales. The village meets in the fine old bar where the menu is only outdone by that in the restaurant. The rooms, beautifully and individually furnished, combine style with comfort. **Restaurant:** Here, the Inn lives up to its name, with new and exciting standards of cuisine. Though eclectic in inspiration, the accent is on both modern and old English dishes, made with fresh local ingredients and complemented by a wide-ranging wine list. Sunday lunch is justly popular. The 11 superbly appointed bedrooms offer flexibility – with excellent facilities for small conferences. All have en suite bath or shower and are enviably quiet. **Nearby:** The famous walking and riding country of the Cotswolds is on the doorstep, and within easy driving distance are the historic, sporting and cultural centres of Bath, Cheltenham and Oxford. **Directions: Leave A40 soon after Burford, taking B4425 towards Bibury and turning left after Aldsworth. Or leave A417 at Fairford heading for Aldsworth: Coln St-Aldwyn is midway between the two. The inn is in the centre of the village.**

For hotel location, see maps on pages 180–186

THE CRICKETERS

CLAVERING, NR SAFFRON WALDEN, ESSEX CB11 4QT
TEL: 01799 550442 FAX: 01799 550882

OWNERS: Trevor and Sally Oliver
MANAGER: Philip Waldron
CHEF: Christopher Hill

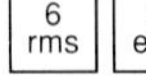

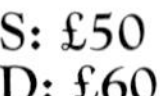

S: £50
D: £60

Inn: This attractive 16th century freehouse in the Essex countryside, just ten minutes from Stansted Airport, has enhanced its popularity and reputation for good food by purchasing an adjacent residence to provide accommodation. Known as The Pavilion, this house provides six charming bedrooms, two with four-posters – one on the ground floor suits those with mobility problems. All are en suite, colourful and well appointed. Breakfast is served in the main building. The oak-beamed bar, serving real ale, and restaurant have cricket memorabilia on the walls. There is a non-smoking area. Guests enjoy the big log fire in the winter and alfresco refreshments in the garden in summer. **Restaurant:** The Restaurant menu, changing seasonally, has ten appetizing starters and ten succulent main courses, interesting interpretations of classic English cooking and the puddings are of the same calibre. A salad bar pleases slimmers. The wine list is diverse, from house wines through to champagnes, European vineyards alongside many New World names, and many half-bottles. **Nearby:** Guests enjoy horse racing at Newmarket, or exploring Cambridge, Saffron Walden and Duxford Air Museum. **Directions: Leave M11 at junction 8, heading west, then right onto B1383, signed Newport and left at the B1038 to Clavering.**

The Crown at Hopton

HOPTON WAFERS, CLEOBURY MORTIMER, WORCESTERSHIRE DY14 0NB
TEL: 01299 270372 FAX: 01299 271127

OWNERS: John and Mavis Price

8 rms | 8 ens

S: £40
D: £70

Inn: This enticing 16th century inn is situated in a hamlet dating back to the Norman Conquest, surrounded by the lush farmland, tumbling streams and wooded valleys of South Shropshire. Exposed beams and wooden floors characterise the bedrooms, which are decorated in a welcoming cottage style. All are spacious and most attractive. The bar, which offers a selection of cask-conditioned beers, adjoins an open terrace and, like all the rooms, has many original features including an inglenook fireplace. **Restaurant:** Originally a 15th century smithy, the traditionally furnished restaurant – known as The Hopton Poacher – makes a fine setting in which to relax over dinner. There is a fixed-price menu offering a choice of imaginatively cooked dishes prepared from fresh, seasonal ingredients. The wine list is well compiled and dessert wines are available by the glass. A good selection of ports, cognacs and armagnacs is available. **Nearby:** Apart from exploring the beautiful countryside, guests can visit Stokesay Castle, many National Trust properties and historic Ludlow. Another option is to take a romantic trip aboard a steam locomotive on the Severn Valley Railway. Ironbridge Gorge Museum is about 30 minutes drive away. **Directions: The Crown Inn is by the A4117 between Ludlow and Kidderminster, two miles west of Cleobury Mortimer.**

For hotel location, see maps on pages 180–186

The Redfern Hotel

CLEOBURY MORTIMER, SHROPSHIRE DY14 8AA
TEL: 01299 270395 FAX: 01299 271011

OWNERS: Jon and Liz Redfern
CHEF: Richard Redfern

11 rms | 11 ens

S: £45–£60
D: £65–£80

Inn: This country town hotel provides good-value accommodation and a warm welcome in the heart of England. The Redfern Hotel stands in an attractive setting in Cleobury Mortimer – a market town dating back to the *Doomsday Book*. Crisply decorated bedrooms have white-painted walls and floral fabrics, in keeping with the country house style. Real ale is served in the cosy bar where memorabilia and pictures depicting the town's history are displayed. For parents' peace of mind, a baby-listening service is available. **Restaurant:** Redfern's English Kitchen Restaurant has a homely, welcoming atmosphere, with its home-cured hams and cider flagons hanging from the beams. The menu is changed daily to offer a variety of home-cooked dished such as Shropshire chicken stuffed with Lymeswold cheese and breadcrumbs, or fillet of pork in orange and ginger sauce. **Nearby:** Golf is available at a local course with concessionary green fees. For the more adventurous the Redfern also has its own canal narrowboat for hire. Local attractions include the Ironbridge Museum, famous for its archaelogical records of the Industrial Revolution. A trip on the Severn Valley Railway takes you on a scenic route through riverside towns. Other sights close by are Ludlow Castle and the beautiful countryside of the Welsh Marches. **Directions: Cleobury Mortimer is on the A4117 midway between Kidderminster and Ludlow, 11 miles from each.**

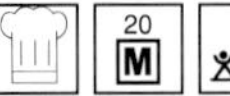

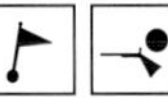

THE NOBODY INN

DODDISCOMBSLEIGH, NR EXETER, DEVON EX6 7PS
TEL: 01647 52394 FAX: 01647 52978

OWNER: Nick Borst-Smith

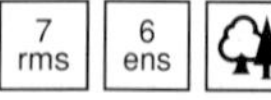

S: £30–£45
D: £50–£65

Inn: According to legend, a past owner of Nobody Inn once locked the doors against weary travellers seeking rest and refreshment. Upon receiving no answer to their knocking, they went on their way believing there was nobody in. "Nobody Inn" it has remained since then. Today's traveller, however, is assured of the warmest welcome from the owner of this renowned 16th century inn. Guests can stay either in the spacious bedrooms of the Georgian manor house 150 yards away, or in the smaller rooms of the inn, which are full of old world charm. All are very well equipped. The building's character has been well preserved, with huge inglenooks, oak beams and stained glass windows. **Restaurant:** The lovely dining room provides a relaxed atmosphere with dishes cooked from the finest, fresh, local ingredients. Food can also be enjoyed in the bar, which is a favourite spot in the winter months. The cellar ranks with the finest in the country. Traditionally brewed beer, local cider, 230 whiskies, 700 wines, fine ports and brandies, and home made mulled wine are all available. Accommodation can also be arranged for horses. **Nearby:** Dartmoor offers many country pursuits: riding, tuition in game shooting and fishing can all be arranged. England's oldest stained glass can be seen in the village church. **Directions: Turn left off Exeter–Plymouth road (A38) at the Devon and Exeter racecourse, signposted Dunchideock to Doddiscombsleigh.**

For hotel location, see maps on pages 180–186

THE GEORGE HOTEL

HIGH STREET, DORCHESTER-ON-THAMES, OX9 8HH
TEL: 01865 340404 FAX: 01865 341620

OWNER: Brian Griffin
MANAGER: Michael A.C. Roberts

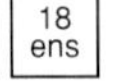

S: £60
D: £75–£95

Inn: Tucked away in the heart of the Thames Valley lies The George, one of the oldest inns in the country. In the days of the stage coach it provided a welcome haven for aristocrats like Sarah Churchill, the first Duchess of Marlborough, while more recent times have seen famous guests of a rather different hue such as author D. H. Lawrence. Luxurious and individually decorated bedrooms provide every modern amentity and there is a choice of splendidly grand rooms with four-poster beds or cosy rooms beneath oak beams. The sense of old world charm has been well preserved throughout The George by the carefully chosen furnishings and décor and by the many fine antiques. There are two rooms in a self-contained annexe which offer business organisers ideal surroundings in which to hold private meetings. **Restaurant:** The chef uses fresh seasonal produce and herbs from the hotel's own garden to produce delicious and imaginative cuisine. The elegant restaurant with its attractive water garden is the perfect setting in which to enjoy an excellent meal, complemented by friendly service. **Nearby:** The area is scattered with many fascinating towns, villages and historic homes. To the north lies the Cotswolds, Woodstock and Stratford-upon-Avon, to the south and east are Henley, Windsor and London. Oxford and Blenheim are a short drive away. **Directions: On A4074 nine miles south of Oxford.**

For hotel location, see maps on pages 180–186

MANOR HOUSE HOTEL AND RESTAURANT

10/15 HIGH STREET, OLD DRONFIELD, DERBYSHIRE SI8 6PY
TEL: 01246 413971

OWNERS: Janet and Andrew Coghlan

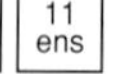

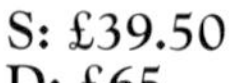

S: £39.50
D: £65

Inn: Situated in the heart of Old Dronfield, the Manor House offers a professional, yet relaxed environment for both business and social travellers. There are two suites and nine en suite bedrooms combining high standards of modern luxury with the charm and ambience of a building dating from 1540. The Piper-Heidsieck suite is a new addition to the hotel facilities. This opulently restored suite is designed to reflect Piper's long standing relationship with the stars on the big screen and includes complementary champagne Piper. Oak beams and Derbyshire stone are features carried throughout the building. **Restaurant:** The restaurant now enjoys an enviable reputation in the locality, serving new English classical cooking with influences from Europe and the Americas. Innovation of ideas and a light touch with sauces coupled with simple yet effective presentation of dishes ensure that the restaurant is often booked some weeks in advance and booking is recommended for weekend visits. Wines are treated with as much importance as food and the cellar is stocked with over 200 bins including some rare Mas De Daumas Gassac and some unusual Franconian, Mexican and Moldovan wines. **Nearby:** Chatsworth House, Haddon Hall, Bakewell and the Peak District, Blue John Mines, Chesterfield Spire and Dronfield Church. **Directions: Old Dronfield is three miles south of Sheffield, off the A61. The Manor House is in the centre of the village near the church.**

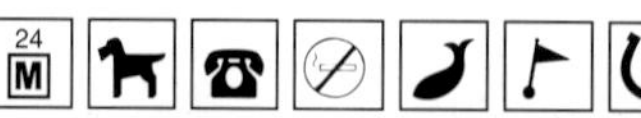

For hotel location, see maps on pages 180–186

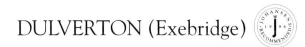

THE ANCHOR COUNTRY INN AND HOTEL

EXEBRIDGE, NR DULVERTON, SOMERSET TA22 9AZ
TEL: 01398 23433

OWNERS: John and Judy Phripp
CHEF: David Lynn

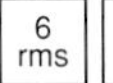

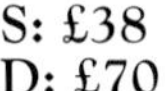

S: £38
D: £70

Inn: The Anchor Inn, a lovely 16th century coaching inn, is mentioned in R.D. Blackmore's *Lorna Doone*. It has been expertly modernised to provide the highest standards of comfort, while retaining its old world charm and atmosphere. A warm and sincere welcome awaits guests. There are six most attractive en suite bedrooms, all offering modern facilities and one boasting a four poster bed. The inn enjoys a superb location on the bank of the River Exe. The comfortably furnished residents' lounge looks towards it over the beautiful lawned gardens. **Restaurant:** The resident chef provides a delicious array of home cooked cuisine, with several local specialities including venison and trout. Vegetables are carefully selected from the best local suppliers. The superb quality and presentation of the food are complemented by first class service and an excellent selection of wines. Lighter meals are offered on the bar menu. **Nearby:** All year long brown trout swim under the bridge and in the deep pools alongside the Inn's gardens. Dry and wet fly fishing are available in season. Riding, shooting and golf can all be enjoyed locally and guided tours of the moor to see the elusive red deer can also be arranged. Walkers will enjoy Exmoor National Park, just 2 miles away, and there are many National Trust properties and gardens within 25 miles. **Directions: Exebridge is south of Dulverton on the B3222, just off the A396 Minehead–Tiverton road.**

For hotel location, see maps on pages 180–186

MOLE & CHICKEN

EASINGTON TERRACE, CHILTON ROAD, BUCKINGHAMSHIRE HP18 9EY
TEL: 01844 208387 FAX: 01844 208387

OWNERS: Johnny Chick and Alan Heather
MANAGER: Tracey Gardener
CHEF: Pedro Davies

Restaurant: Below the Chiltern Hills not far from the London–Oxford Road there is a restaurant that goes by the inviting name of Mole and Chicken housed in a building that was in Victorian times the village pub and store. The view from the terraced garden, overlooking some of Oxfordshire and Buckinghamshire's finest villages, is outstanding. The Mole & Chicken's menu offers a good variety of most tempting dishes, including calves 'liver cooked in a cream, mushroom and brandy sauce, turkey breast strips served with a blueberry sauce, chargrilled loin of pork steak with a Dijon and gruyere glace, Tandoori chicken with plain rice and an excellent house curry. A vegetarian dish, which changes weekly, is also always available. House specialities include half a whole shoulder of English lamb with a honey, rosemary and garlic sauce. and half a Norfolk duckling with 'the best orange sauce in the world.' The excellent cuisine is complemented by very friendly and efficient service. À la carte prices range from £5.95 to £11.50. **Nearby:** There are plenty of opportunities for guests of the Mole & Chicken to take advantage of leisure facilities in the vicinity, which include golf, fishing, shooting and boating.Henley, Waddesden Manor and Blenheim Palace are all within a short distance. **Directions: M40 junction 9, signposted Thame. Follow the signs to Long Crendon. Once out of the village take first right hand turn to Easington.**

CHEF'S SPECIALS

•••••••

monkfish and bacon salad
with a walnut and pesto dressing

the envy of india
chicken methi sahib with rice and poppadums

seafood platter
smoked salmon langoustine, crab meat and prawns with a salad of beef tomatoes and a corriander mayonnaise

For hotel location, see maps on pages 180–186

THE BLUE LION

EAST WITTON, NR LEYBURN, NORTH YORKSHIRE DL8 4SN
TEL: 01969 624273 FAX: 01969 624189

OWNERS: Paul and Helen Klein
CHEF: Chris Clarke

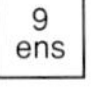

9 ens

Inn: Heather moorlands, waterfalls, limestone scars and remote valleys surround the picturesque village of East Witton – the gateway to Wensleydale and Coverdale. The Blue Lion, a 19th century coaching inn, has much to entice visitors to its doors – lovely individually furnished bedrooms, welcoming public rooms with original flag-stone floors and open fires, plus delicious food. Private functions for up to 45 people can be accommodated. **Restaurant:** A frequently changing menu provides an ample selection of well-compiled, innovative dishes. Some interesting choices such as red mullet, monkfish or wild boar served with a rich port wine sauce are regularly available. The wine list that accompanies the menus offers a vast array of excellent wines from all over the world. The dining room is attractively decorated with candle-light creating an intimate atmosphere. In the bar there is a fine selection of hand-pulled traditional beers as well as an extensive menu of freshly prepared meals served at lunchtime and dinner. **Nearby:** The spa towns of Ripon and Harrogate are within easy driving distance and well worth a visit. Jervaulx Abbey and many castles are in the area. There is an all-weather tennis court in village. **Directions: A6108, eight miles north of Masham and five miles south of Leyburn.**

For hotel location, see maps on pages 180–186

The Wheatsheaf Inn

EGTON, NR WHITBY, NORTH YORKSHIRE YO21 1TZ
TEL: 01947 895271 FAX: 01947 895271

OWNERS: Albert, Susan and Michael Latus

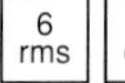

S: £35–£40
D: £40–£55

Inn: This traditional, stone-built inn is situated in a delightful part of North Yorkshire in the small village of Egton, just five miles from the sea. Proprietors of The Wheatsheaf, Albert and Susan Latus, create a welcoming atmosphere. With the emphasis on attentive service, guests receive good hospitality and excellent value for money. In the public rooms the original character has been maintained and the small, cosy bedrooms have been furnished in keeping with the style of an old country inn. **Restaurant:** Stone walls, oak beams and attractively laid tables are the setting for dinner. A varied à la carte menu offers a good selection of starters, including several seafood choices: herring, fresh sardines, fish pâté and smoked trout. Main courses range from country pies to international dishes such as Cajun chicken. A good selection of bar meals is available. There is also a special dish-of-the-day. **Nearby:** The surrounding North York Moors National Park provides ample scope for walking, fishing, riding, canoeing, sailing and trips on steam trains. Captain Cook's birthplace at Great Ayton, Robin Hood's Bay, Staithes and Whitby, with its abbey, are a short drive away. **Directions: Egton is close to Whitby. From Pickering, turn off the A169 to Grosmont and Egton.**

For hotel location, see maps on pages 180–186

THE ANCHOR INN

SUTTON GAULT, SUTTON, NR ELY, CAMBRIDGESHIRE CB6 2BD
TEL: 01353 778537 FAX: 01353 776180

OWNERS: Robin and Heather Moore
MANAGER: Amanda Corcoran
CHEF: Mark Corcoran

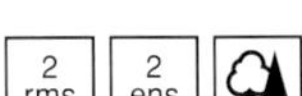

D: £55
Suite: £75

Inn: The Anchor was built around 1650 to provide lodgings for the men who had been conscripted to dig the Old and New Bedford Rivers, which began the transformation of watery tracts of swamp into the present day rich agricultural landscape of the Fens. The inn has evolved over the years and now offers every modern facility, while retaining its timeless charm and character. In 1995 it was voted 'UK Inn of the Year' by 'Les Routiers'. An intimate atmosphere is created by the pine tables which stand on gently undulating old floors, the antique prints, and the log fires that burn in the cooler months. Both the bedrooms, one a suite, are newly furnished and decorated and offer views across the Washes. **Restaurant:** The core of the menu provided is traditional British food, prepared using local produce. In the spring there are fresh handdressed crabs from Cromer, through the summer Bottisham smoked hams and Brancaster oysters and mussels, and in the winter, pheasant, pigeon and wild duck from the marshes. Also featured are French regional dishes and, occasionally, more exotic recipes from other parts of Europe and the Far East. **Nearby:** Less than half an hour's drive away are Ely, the Ouse Washes, the nature reserve of Wicken Fen and the university city of Cambridge. **Directions: North of Cambridge on the A14 take the B1050 at Bar Hill. At Earith turn onto the B1381 and Sutton Gault is signposted from Sutton High Street.**

THE CHRISTOPHER HOTEL

HIGH STREET, ETON, WINDSOR, BERKSHIRE SL4 6AN
TEL: 01753 852359 FAX: 01753 830914

OWNER: Mrs Carol Martin
CHEF: Christian Dallacosta

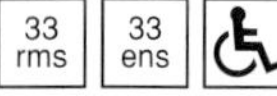

S: £66
D: £73–£82

Inn: Half way between Eton college and Windsor Bridge, in Eton's High Street, The Christopher Hotel is an old coaching inn which for many years enjoyed somewhat of a racy reputation. The hotel, which was built in 1511, has comfortable and elegantly furnished bedrooms in both the main building and courtyard. A range of modern amenities includes colour TV with cable channels, tea and coffee making facilities, trouser press, hairdryer and direct-dial telephone. Guests may choose between having a continental breakfast served in their room or taking a full traditional English breakfast in the restaurant. **Restaurant:** Excellent food, which has a good local reputation, can be enjoyed in the relaxed atmosphere of the hotel's welcoming restaurant. The cuisine is prepared from the freshest produce and complemented by a fine selection of wines to suit all pockets. A traditional atmosphere and friendly service are the hallmarks of the Victoria Bar, which offers a wide variety of bar food and a wide variety of drinks. **Nearby:** Windsor Castle and Cliveden; The many outdoor attractions available in the locality include trips on the Thames, golf at Sunningdale and the Berkshire, the Windsor Royal Horse Show and Driving Championships, Ascot races. **Directions: Leave M4 at junction 5 and follow signs to Eton. Hotel is in the High Street with its own car park through carriage entrance.**

For hotel location, see maps on pages 180–186

THE ACORN INN HOTEL

FORE STREET, EVERSHOT, NR DORCHESTER, DORSET DT2 0JW
TEL: 01935 83228

OWNERS: Keith and Denise Morley
CHEF: Keith Morley

S: from £52
D: from £90
(including dinner)

Inn: Nestling in an unspoilt and peaceful village amongst Dorset's rolling hills, this charming 16th century country inn was renamed the "Sow & Acorn" at Evershead by Thomas Hardy in his novel *Tess of the D'Urbevilles*. Beamed bars, original stone walls and open log fires add to the ambience and cosy atmosphere. The bedrooms range from small good value doubles to more spacious ones. Two of the rooms have four-posters and one with a Jacuzzi bath. **Restaurant:** Two candle-lit restaurants are available, one non-smoking. With the emphasis on choice, the à la carte menu offers a versatile range of dishes from plain and simple cooking to the diverse and unusual, with flambés a speciality. In addition, a separate fresh fish and seafood menu and vegetarian menu are offered. Hot bread baked on the premises is served with all starters. The four-course table d'hôte menu offers excellent value with extensive choices. The special bargain break package and 20% discount for five nights or more are well worth consideration. **Nearby:** Thomas Hardy's home near Dorchester, Cerne Abbas Giant, Parnham House, Ford Abbey, Sherborne Castle, Corfe Castle and the Fleet Air Arm Museum. Scenic walks lead from the village across rolling hills, while the Dorset coastline is a 20-minute drive. **Directions: Evershot is on the B732, off the A37, eight miles from Yeovil and twelve miles from Dorchester.**

For hotel location, see maps on pages 180–186

RIVERSIDE RESTAURANT AND HOTEL

THE PARKS, OFFENHAM ROAD, NR EVESHAM, WORCESTERSHIRE WR11 5JP
TEL: 01386 446200 FAX: 01386 40021

OWNERS: Vincent and Rosemary Willmott
CHEF: Rosemary Willmott

S: £60
D: £80

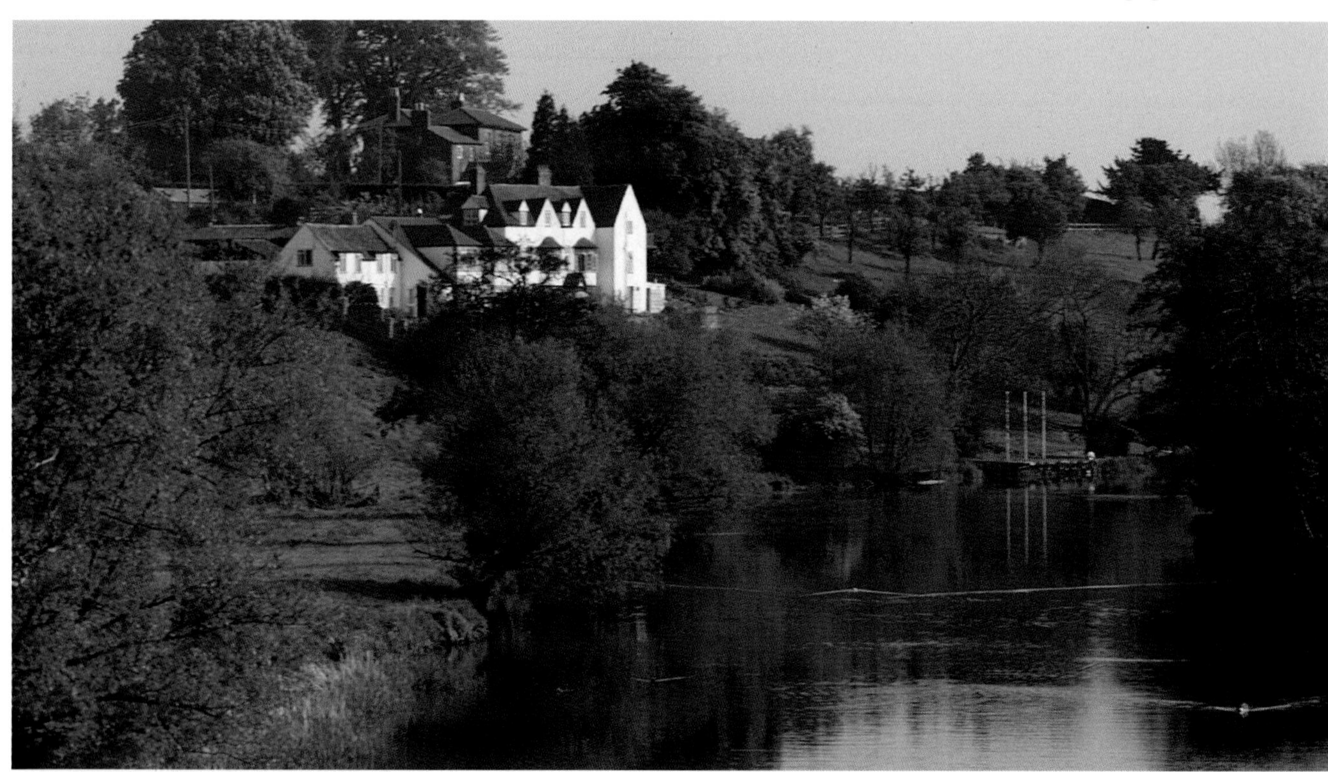

Inn: The Riverside may not be a big hotel, but it has great style and a superb position, being perched high above the River Avon in the original Evesham Abbey's 15th century deer park. Three cleverly converted 17th century cottages blend with the main house to create an elegant 1920's residence. There are just seven enchanting bedrooms, all thoughtfully appointed. Lovely chinz fabrics and views over the gardens to the river add to guests' pleasure on arrival. **Restaurant:** Having a Chef-Patronne, the restaurant is extremely important, and a designated non-smoking area. The three menus are reasonably priced for the exceptional choice offered. Interesting starters are followed by a selection of traditional and innovative dishes, including fresh monkfish and local pheasant. The tempting dessert list is shorter. The cellar holds 46 wines from £9 to £60. The restaurant is closed on Sunday evenings and all day Monday. The bar has big sofas, deep armchairs and large windows overlooking the river, the ambience being that of a country house drawing room. **Nearby:** Guests may fish in the Avon, take a small boat out or visit the Royal Worcester Porcelain factory, go to Stratford-upon-Avon, or relax watching county cricket at Worcester. **Directions: Take M5/ junction 7 or M40/junction 16 to Evesham and approach the hotel from the B4510 to Offenham down a private drive through market gardens.**

For hotel location, see maps on pages 180–186

THE CRIDFORD INN

TRUSHAM, NR NEWTON ABBOT, DEVON TQ13 0NR
TEL: 01626 853694

OWNERS: David and Sally Hesmondhalgh

S: £37.50
D: £55

Inn: Peacefully situated in the Teign Valley, this charming Devon longhouse was originally built in 1081 as a nunnery. Proprietors David and Sally Hesmondhalgh, previously owners of The Pheasant at Kirkby Lonsdale, have been working hard to restore the inn to its original glory. The interiors are characterised by slate-stone floors, exposed beams, natural stone walls, inglenook fireplaces and stained-glass windows. There are four bedrooms, all appropriately decorated with country-style furnishings: two have a shower en suite and two have a bath. **Restaurant:** The medieval dining room opened in August 1992, following a period of refurbishment: it is complete with a wood burner, inglenook fireplace, gleaming silverware and sparkling crystal. The reasonably priced menu has been chosen to reveal the best of local Devon food. Main course choices may include monkfish in a fresh lime brandy and cream sauce, or roast local duckling. Several vegetarian dishes and home-made pies, own-home smoked meats, fish and cheeses are on the lengthy bar menu, with desserts such as sticky toffee pudding and old-fashioned tipsy trifle. **Nearby:** Dartmoor, Exeter, the Elizabethan town of Totnes and the Devon coast. **Directions: Take the Teign Valley exit B3193 off A38; follow Trusham signs. The Cridford Inn is signposted about three miles along this road.**

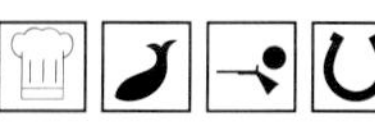

THE HIGHWAYMAN

EXLADE STREET, CHECKENDON, BERKSHIRE RG8 0UA
TEL: 01491 682020 FAX: 01491 682229

OWNERS: Roger and Carole Shippey
CHEF: Steven Foran

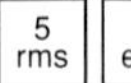

S: £45
D: £60
Cottage: £55–£65

Inn: This very attractive rambling 16th century inn is in the heart of the Chiltern hills, in a small village on the Berkshire/ Oxfordshire boundary, between Reading and Henley. It serves well-kept real ales, but also sensibly offers Pimms in the summer and mulled wine in winter. The comfortable bedrooms, all en-suite with showers, include a single room, and there is also a pretty self-contained cottage available, adjacent to the inn. All have television. The accommodation, however, is not suitable for children under five. **Restaurant:** An interesting range of bar food is served as well as an imaginative three-course dinner, prepared by a chef who shows special flair when preparing one of the inns specialities. Fresh seafood is always a popular dish. The wine list contains some interesting selections to accompany your meal. **Nearby:** Stonor Park is a local beauty spot and Oxford is a reasonable drive away. There is Cliveden to visit, and the enchanting riverside towns of Marlow and Henley. Riverside walks, perhaps near Pangbourne, are very pleasant, or hire a boat and cruise on the Thames. **Directions: Take the B4074 from Reading to Oxford, joining the B47074 and follow the sign to Exlade Street (the village name) just before reaching Checkendon.**

For hotel location, see maps on pages 180–186

The Royal Oak Inn

WINSFORD, EXMOOR NATIONAL PARK, SOMERSET TA24 7JE
TEL: 01643 851455 FAX: 01643 851388

OWNER: Charles Steven

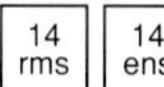

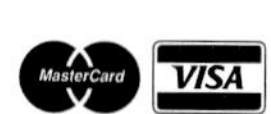

S: from £70
D: from £90

Inn: This world-famous picturesque thatched inn, dating from the 12th century, stands in the centre of an ancient riverside village on the edge of Exmoor National Park. Eight of the bedrooms are situated in the inn itself while a further six rooms have been created in the courtyard area. All are furnished to a high standard, some featuring four-posters. For relaxation the three lounges and two bars are all well appointed with open fires, chintz fabrics and oak beams. The inn is rated RAC 3 Stars with 2 Merit Awards and ETB 4 Crowns Highly Commended. Dogs can be accommodated at the owner's discretion. Special breaks are offered. **Restaurant:** Tables set with Wedgwood and fine glassware create an attractive setting for dinner. Only the freshest local produce is used to prepare traditional English country recipes to a consistently high standard. Everything, from hams and pies to pâtés and bread, is home-cooked. Table d'hôte and à la carte menus are changed daily. A good choice of light bar meals is available. **Nearby:** Proprietor Charles Steven can arrange many sporting pastimes for his guests, including riding, fishing, hunting, shooting, golf and adventure walking. The hotel also provides a comprehensive sightseeing list covering Exmoor National Park and beyond. **Directions: Leave M5 at junction 27 to Tiverton, take A396 Tiverton to Minehead road for 20 miles, then turn left to Winsford village.**

SCULTHORPE MILL

SCULTHORPE, NR FAKENHAM, NORFOLK NR21 9QG
TEL: 01328 856161/862675 FAX: 01328 856651

OWNERS: Mr and Mrs R. Crisp
MANAGER: Mrs Julie Bowers
CHEF: Peter Howard

S: £40
D: £60

Inn: This 18th century listed watermill straddles the banks of the River Wensum and enjoys an idyllic setting in six acres of water meadows. The building has recently undergone an extensive and sympathetic renovation programme which included the development of six en suite bedrooms. All of these offer both a full range of modern comforts and facilities, as well as superb views of the river, lawned gardens and the meadows. Sculthorpe Mill is the perfect place for guests seeking total relaxation. **Restaurant:** The oak-beamed, first floor restaurant overlooks the river and offers an extensive choice of traditional and vegetarian dishes, making full use of our surroundings using locally caught seafood, game when in season, fresh vegetables, and a wide selection of herbs from our kitchen garden. Select a meal from the blackboards, dishes of the day, to food from around the world, through to the Mill Mixed Grill, only for those with a healthy appetite, all topped off with a generous helping of home-made puddings or luxury ice-creams and sorbets. **Nearby:** The inn is an ideal base from which to explore the Norfolk coast. There are a number of stately homes in the area, including Sandringham, Blickling Hall and the magnificent Houghton Hall. Other attractions range from bird sanctuaries to the Steam Engine Museum at Thursford. A variety of golf courses are closeby. **Directions: The inn is on A148 two miles west of Fakenenham.**

For hotel location, see maps on pages 180–186

TRENGILLY WARTHA COUNTRY INN AND RESTAURANT

NANCENOY, CONSTANTINE, FALMOUTH, CORNWALL TR11 5RP
TEL: 01326 40332

OWNERS: The Logan and Maguire Families
CHEF: Michael Maguire

S: £32–£40
D: £46–£60

Inn: The name Trengilly Wartha literally means the settlement above the trees. Indeed, this popular inn lies in a wooded valley surrounded by acres of private gardens and meadows, in a designated area of outstanding natural beauty. The Logan and Maguire families offer visitors warm hospitality. Large fireplaces, stone walls, flag-stone floors and old beams are complemented by cottage-style decoration. The bedrooms are quiet and four have been refurbished with Laura Ashley fabrics. In addition to the bar, there is a comfortable lounge, games room and family room. **Restaurant:** The dining room has been designed to mirror the style of a French family hotel. Chef Michael Maguire has a great reputation locally for his imaginative cooking and fixed-price menus. These are frequently changed to take advantage of the best seasonal produce. A choice of over 180 labels is offered on the informative wine list. Bar meals available including the best of local seafood from the 'feast of fish' blackboard. **Nearby:** The Lizard Peninsula, the seal sanctuary at Gweek, Trebah Gardens and the Helford Estuary are within easy reach. Activities to be enjoyed locally include riding, sailing and surfing. **Directions: Take A39 towards Falmouth, then follow signs to Constantine on B3291. From Constantine follow signs to Trengilly Wartha.**

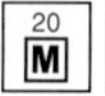

For hotel location, see maps on pages 180–186

The White Hart

FORD, CHIPPENHAM, WILTSHIRE SN14 8RP
TEL: 01249 782213

OWNERS: Chris and Jenny Phillips

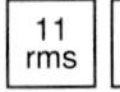

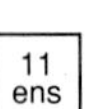

   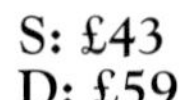

S: £43
D: £59

Inn: Believed to date back to 1553, the White Hart at Ford, listed for its architectural interest, is made of stone and prettily situated alongside the Bybrook River. The terrace overlooking the water is the ideal spot to eat and drink while looking out for kingfishers, herons and wagtails. Despite its rustic character, country lanes and riverside walks, the small village of Ford is within easy reach of the M4, Chippenham and Bath. Four of the bedrooms have four-poster beds and two have half-testers. Whether your room is located in the old stable block or main building, it will be comfortable and well-equipped. **Restaurant:** The White Hart is renowned for its delicious home cooking: all meals are freshly prepared, carefully presented and offer very good value. In the Riverside Restaurant the extensive à la carte menu typically includes venison casserole, herb-roasted grouse, supreme of chicken with a crab and saffron sauce and rack of lamb with chestnut and leek stuffing. The bar menu includes hearty soups, pies and ploughman's lunches. As well as traditional scrumpy, the bar offers one of Wiltshire's widest selection of real beers. The Good Pub Guide 'Pub of the Year' 1995. **Nearby:** Numerous country walks – you can walk through the Bybrook Valley to Castle Combe. Bath, Bowood House, Corsham Court and Lacock are nearby. **Directions: Leave the M4 at junction 17 or 18. Ford is situated off the A420 Bristol–Chippenham road.**

  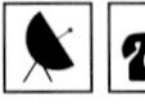  

For hotel location, see maps on pages 180–186

THE WOODFALLS INN

THE RIDGE, WOODFALLS, FORDINGBRIDGE, HAMPSHIRE SP5 2LN
TEL: 01725 513222 FAX: 01725 513220

OWNER: Michael Elvis
CHEF: Christian Lohez

10 rms | 10 ens

S: £37.50
D: £44–£70

Inn: This inn, named after its village, on the northern edge of the New Forest had a spell renamed The Bat & Ball Inn, when the local cricket ground was relocated next door! On the original route to Salisbury, it has offered refreshment to travellers since 1870, now often en route to the cross-channel ferries. Recent refurbishment has included additional bedrooms, all of which are named after flowers of the forest and some have four posters. Single rooms are also available. The spacious and attractive bar is extremely well stocked, and serves a wide selection of hand-pumped cask conditioned ales. There is a big open fire in winter. **Restaurant:** The Lovers' Restaurant buys its fish from the local harbours. There is an excellent table d'hôte menu in addition to the à la carte choice, and a full English breakfast starts the day for residents. More informal meals are served in the bar or conservatory. There is a moderately priced and varied wine list. Picnic baskets can also be arranged. **Nearby:** Walking and riding in the enchanting New Forest. Salisbury with its cathedral is in easy reach. Active guests can sail on the Solent or find excellent local golf. **Directions: From M27/junction 1 take B3079, fork left at Brook onto B3078, then fork right at Telegraph Corner onto B3080 for Woodfalls, just five miles from the motorway.**

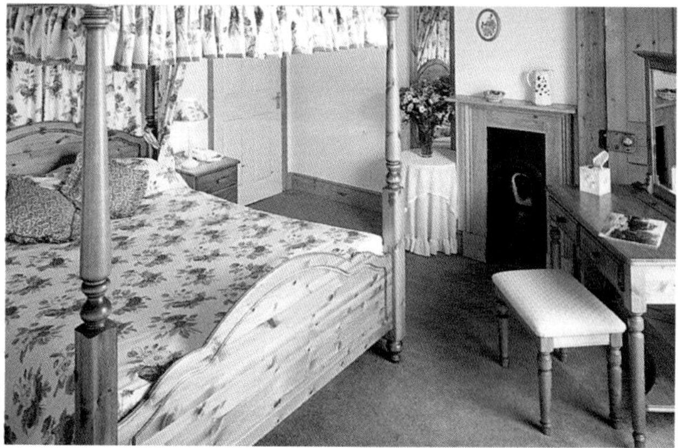

HARE & HOUNDS

THE GREEN, FULBECK, LINCOLNSHIRE NG32 3SS
TEL: 01400 272090 FAX: 01400 273663

OWNERS: The Riley and Freeman Families
CHEF: Michael Savil

  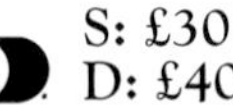

S: £30
D: £40

Inn: The Hare and Hounds, a Grade II listed 17th century building, was a maltings until 1910. It is set on one of the two greens in the village of Fulbeck on The Ridge and offers splendid views of Newark, nine miles away. The inn's new owners have undertaken an extensive refurbishment programme, improving the bedrooms' decor and furnishings and upgrading the public areas using attractive pine panelling. Open fires and fresh flowers create an attractive and inviting environment in which to relax and forget the cares of the world. **Restaurant:** Monthly changing menus offer good food, which is both freshly prepared and well presented. Sample the delights of 'fillet of pork rösti', pork fillet wrapped in a lattice potato shell with a stem ginger and piquant sauce, 'Tournados Rossini', fillet of beef steak topped with pâté and mushrooms and served on a crouton of bread with madeira sauce, or choose from an excellent range of fish dishes. The meals are complemented by a small but inexpensive wine list and those who enjoy real ale will be delighted to learn that the proprietors plan to build a mini brewery within the grounds of the inn. **Nearby:** The inn is ideally placed for guests wishing to expore Lincoln, Newark or Rutland Water. There is no shortage of interesting places in close proximity and they include Furbeck Hall, Belton House and Harlaxton Manor. **Directions: On the A607 between Grantham and Lincoln, near the point where A607 crosses A17.**

For hotel location, see maps on pages 180–186

THE MONCKTON ARMS HOTEL

GLASTON, NR UPPINGHAM, RUTLAND LE15 9BP
TEL: 01572 822326 FAX: 01572 821481

MANAGER: Spencer Dainton
CHEF: Mark Goode

10 rms | 10 ens

S: £32
D: £40

Inn: This attractive family run hotel has retained its old-world charm while meeting today's demands for service and comfort. It is a truly friendly rural inn, much enjoyed both by guests and local residents, supported by very efficient staff. The bar is the hub of the hotel, with log fires in the winter, and serving well-kept real ales, some from local breweries. Bar food is plentiful and freshly made to order, with an outside barbecue in the summer. **Restaurant:** The restaurant has a fine reputation, with daily specials added to the already extensive à la carte menu. A choice of vegetarian dishes is always available and there is a traditional grill selection, the meat coming from local farmers. The wine list is admirable. Breakfasts start early, at 7.30 am. All bedrooms are en suite with either bath or shower, and have the anticipated amenities. **Nearby:** The hotel is well placed for Uppingham School parents, and convenient for business meetings in Peterborough, Leicester or Corby. Rutland Water offers water sports and fishing. Burghley House, Rockingham Castle and the long viaduct at Seaton all deserve a visit. **Directions: Glaston is on the A47, halfway between Leicester and Peterborough. There is ample car-parking.**

MALLYAN SPOUT HOTEL

GOATHLAND, NR WHITBY, NORTH YORKSHIRE YO22 5AN
TEL: 01947 896486 FAX: 01947 896327

OWNERS: Peter and Judith Heslop
CHEFS: Peter Heslop and David Fletcher

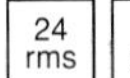

S: £45–£65
D: £65–£120

Inn: Set in excellent walking country, this is a perfect spot from which to explore the beautiful North York Moors National Park, cast for trout or salmon on the River Esk and enjoy many country pursuits such as riding. The hotel occupies a fine position in the picturesque village and takes its name from the waterfall flowing through the wooded valley, just a short walk away. Behind the stone-built, ivy-clad exterior are comfortable rooms with a relaxing atmosphere. Three spacious lounges command views of the two acre garden and Esk valley beyond. Cottage-style bedrooms, decorated with lovely fabrics, provide every convenience. Mini-breaks available all year. **Restaurant:** Chef-patron Peter Heslop takes pleasure in creating fine cuisine. An impressive table d'hôte menu offers guests an extensive choice of dishes, making it easy to see why this restaurant is so popular locally. Freshly caught seafood from Whitby is a house speciality. An AA Rosette has been awarded for cooking. **Nearby:** Take a scenic trip on the North York Moors Railway. Whitby Abbey – once a burial place for kings, Easby Abbey, a 12th century monastery. Magnificent Castle Howard is just 20 miles away. **Directions: The hotel is situated nine miles from Whitby and 38 miles from York. From the A169 Pickering–Whitby road, turn off to Goathland. The nearest B.R. station is Whitby.**

For hotel location, see maps on pages 180–186

Inn On The Lake

OCKFORD ROAD, GODALMING, SURREY GU7 1RH
TEL: 01483 415575 FAX: 01483 860445

OWNERS: Martin and Joy Cummings
MANAGER: Clive Cummings
CHEF: Neale O'Brien

19 rms 19 ens

S: from £50
D: from £75–£85

Inn: Part Tudor, part Georgian, part modern, this country house inn stands in two acres of landscaped gardens overlooking a reed-fringed lake. Proprietors Martin and Joy Cummings make the comfort of guests their priority, and as a result were recipients of the Innkeeper of the Year Award 1987. The warmth of welcome visitors receive here is matched by the efficient service provided by the staff. The fully equipped bedrooms are individually designed and furnished to a high standard. The comfortable public rooms include a cosy real ale bar and several rooms for conferences and functions. **Restaurant:** Seasonal A la Carte and weekly Table d'Hote menus providing superb international dishes are offered in the attractively decorated Lake View Restaurant which has been awarded 2 AA Rosettes. The wine list, although modest, seeks to represent the classic wine regions of Europe. For private functions, quotations can be given for outside catering. **Nearby:** The Royal Horticultural Society headquarters at Wisley is a short drive away, as is the Winkworth Arboretum. Several historic houses can be found in the vicinity while the North Surrey Downs are good for walks. Three theatres, six museums and an art gallery are all within easy reach. **Directions: Take the A3 Guilford–Portsmouth road from London. Then A283 towards Milford. At Milford, turn left at the lights on the A3100. Go under the railway bridge; the inn is situated on the right, beside the mini-roundabout.**

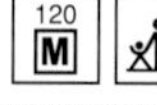  

For hotel location, see maps on pages 180–186

THE LEATHERNE BOTTEL RIVERSIDE INN & RESTAURANT

THE BRIDLEWAY, GORING-ON-THAMES, BERKSHIRE RG8 0HS
TEL: 01491 872667

OWNERS: Keith Read and Annie Bonnet
CHEFS: Keith Read and Clive O'Connor

Dinner for Two including Wine: £60–£80

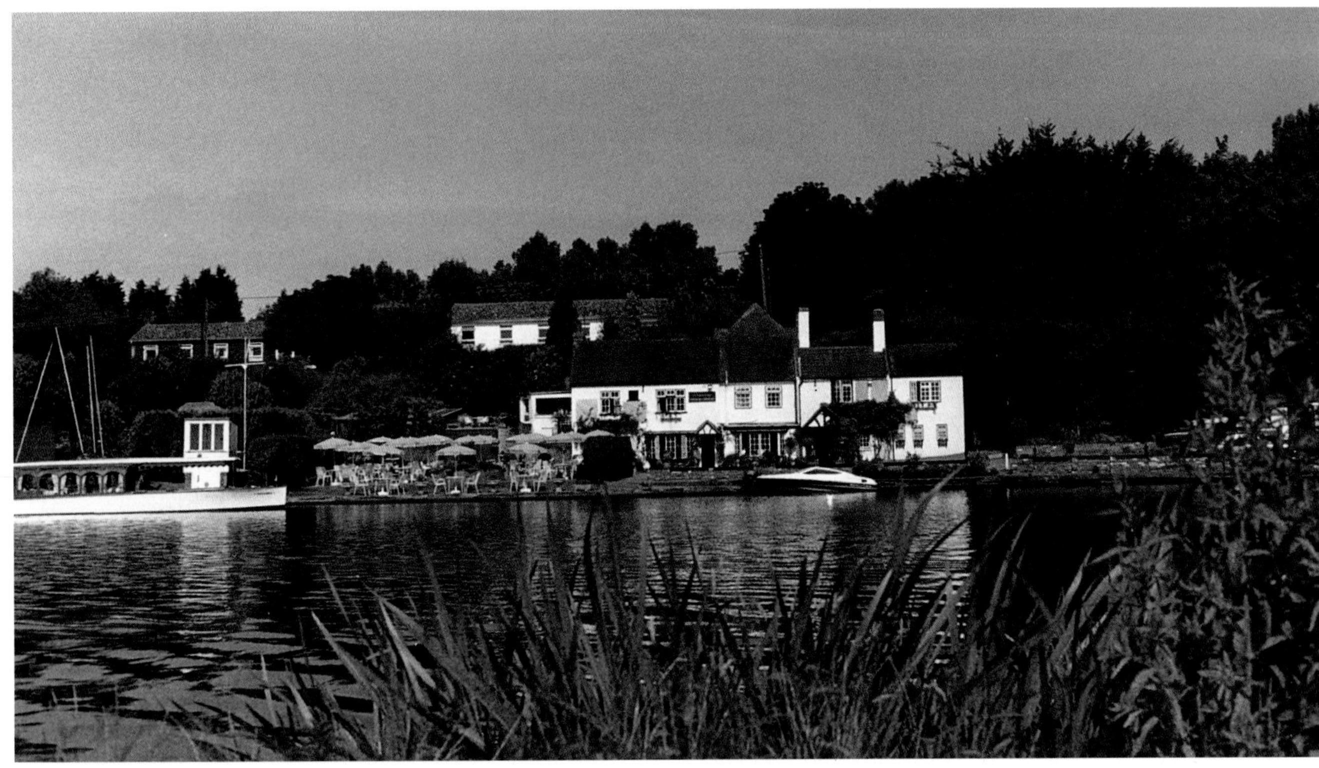

Food: Quite simply, this is a most excellent restaurant. The setting is unique, on the banks of the Thames in a nature conservation area, overlooking water meadows and the Berkshire Downs. Self-taught chef-patron Keith Read together with Clive O'Connor, has become widely acclaimed. *TheTimes* has awarded him a six-star rating and includes him among today's most accomplished chefs. *Egon Ronay* describes him as unpretentious and imaginative, relying on fresh, quality produce. In summer, dine in the riverside terrace garden, which is ablaze with colour and scented with wild herbs. The menu may include sea bass with virgin olive oil, samphire and sweet ginger, or tuna with apple mint and a stew of plum tomatoes and basil. In winter huge log fires glow and the smell of simmering game stock fills the air. Local pheasant flavoured with lemon thyme and pancetta, or local wood pigeon with red chilli, chick peas and coriander, are among the choices. Puddings are simple and mouthwatering: ginger brandy snap baskets full of summer berries, or steaming cappuchino pudding with Mount Gay sauce. The two dining rooms reflect the style and taste of the owners: strong colours, fresh flowers and faultless yet relaxed service. Each table has a view of the river and the bar is filled with cookery books and exquisite marble sculptures. **Directions: Signposted off the B4009 Goring-on-Thames–Wallingford road. From M4 junction 12: 15 minutes; from M40 junction 6: 15 minutes. Oxford is 30 minutes drive and London 60 minutes.**

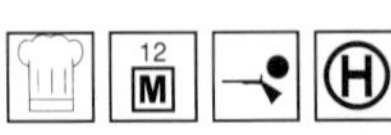

For hotel location, see maps on pages 180–186

THE STARR RESTAURANT WITH ROOMS

MARKET PLACE, GREAT DUNMOW, ESSEX CM16 1AX
TEL: 01371 874321 FAX: 01371 876337

OWNERS: Brian and Vanessa Jones
MANAGER: Terry and Louise George
CHEF: Mark Fisher

S: £55
D: £85–£100

Inn: The Starr is an attractive whitewashed building situated in the Essex village of Great Dunmow. The eight bedrooms are situated in the converted stable block at the rear of the main building. The personal touch is very much in evidence. All bedrooms are furnished and decorated to a high standard, yet no two are the same. With names such as the Oak Room, the Brass Room, the Blue Room and the Poppy Room, the bedrooms ensure that the atmosphere is a far cry from the standardised approach of many hotels. All rooms have en suite bathroom, colour TV and telephone. There are two elegant rooms available for private luncheons or dinners for meetings. Closed 2–9 January. **Restaurant:** The Starr Restaurant combines the charm of a traditional beamed English setting with food prepared to a high standard. A varied menu offers cooking that is essentially English but with a distinct French accent. A light luncheon menu is also available for those who may prefer an omelette and a glass of wine. Large comprehensive wine list available. **Nearby:** Audley End near Saffron Walden, Gosfield Hall, Mountfitchet Castle and Thaxted. **Directions: From M11 junction 8 take A120 towards Colchester. In Great Dunmow the market place is directly off the High Street. London Stansted Airport is just 15 minutes' drive away.**

THE BLACK HORSE INN

GRIMSTHORPE, BOURNE, LINCOLNSHIRE PE10 0OY
TEL: 01778 591247

OWNERS: Robert and Gillian Hodgson

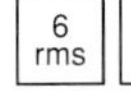

S: £45
D: £55
Suite: £80

Inn: The Black Horse, quite a short detour for drivers on the A1, has benefited from the ideas of its new owners, who, while preserving the charm of the old inn, have carried out skilful restoration work that now enables them to offer the very best modern hospitality. Open fireplaces have been maintained and the beer cellar with its two streams keeping ale temperatures in peak condition is back in full use, bringing traditional ale to the comfortable bar. The dining room still has its beams and stone walls, while the Pheasantry, a cosy lounge, has a changed character and with it new furniture and pretty fabrics. Guests are enchanted with the bedrooms, with lovely coloured chinzes, and little extras in the bathroom. The delightful new honeymoon or, for the unromantic, the executive suite has its own small sitting room and a spa bath. **Restaurant:** The handsome restaurant offers its own delicious interpretation of English cooking, and the 'Fine Wine List' is very reasonably priced. **Nearby:** Very close by is Grimsthorpe Castle, with its attractive park and nature trail around the lake. Other stately homes nearby include Burghley House, famous for its horse trials, Belvoir Castle and Belton House. Golf, fishing and swimming are 20 minutes drive away. **Directions: Leave A1 between Grantham and Stamford, taking A51 at Colsterworth heading through Grimsthorpe towards Bourne.**

CHEFS' SPECIALITIES

•••••••

Black Horse pate
a coarse country style pate served with a warm cottage loaf & salad

salmon steak
cooked in champagne & cream sauce served with pink & green peppercorns

raspberry trifle
home-made with raspberries & fresh cream to a secret recipe

For hotel location, see maps on pages 180–186

THE MAYNARD ARMS

MAIN ROAD, GRINDLEFORD, DERBYSHIRE S30 1HP
TEL: 01433 630321 FAX: 01433 630445

OWNERS: Bob and Thelma Graham
MANAGERS: James and Christina Lamb
CHEF: Brian Holloway

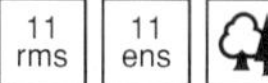

S: £49
D: £65

Inn: The new owners of this Victorian inn have, following extensive refurbishment, transformed its ambience and image – guests now finding a very stylish small hostelry at this superb location overlooking the beautiful Derbyshire Peak National Park. The en suite bedrooms are charming, comfortable and well equipped. Guests booking Friday and Saturday nights may stay in their room free on the Sunday night (except before Bank Holidays). **Restaurant:** The excellent restaurant offers a cosmopolitan dinner menu also featuring local game when in season, together with reasonably priced wines. An extensive range of bar food is served at lunchtime and in the evenings in the Longshaw Bar – the busy hub of the inn. The second, quieter, bar is ideal for a drink before dinner, and the peaceful lounge, with a view of the pretty garden has a big log fire in winter months. **Nearby:** Chatsworth, Haddon Hall and Castleton are spectacular reminders of the architectural heritage of the region. The market town of Bakewell is fascinating. Walkers have an endless choice of directions to take, fishing is on the Derwent. Golf, ponytrekking, even gliding can be arranged locally. Regional theatres abound. **Directions: Leaving Sheffield on the A625, The Maynard Arms is on the left just before reaching Grindleford.**

For hotel location, see maps on pages 180–186

THE ROCK INN HOTEL

HOLYWELL GREEN, HALIFAX, WEST YORKSHIRE HX4 9BS
TEL: 01422 379721 FAX: 01422 379110

OWNER: Robert Vinsen
MANAGER: Ervis Trujillo
CHEF: James Pardon

S: £38–£72
D: £55–£85

Inn: Situated in a tranquil valley, yet mid-way between the commercial centres of Halifax/Huddersfield and Manchester/Leeds, this superb hostelry offers all the attractions of a traditional wayside inn as well as the sophistication of a first-class hotel. AA, Egon Ronay and Les Routiers recommended, ETB 4 Crowns commended, all double-glazed bedrooms are equipped to luxurious standards being en suite with baths and showers, remote-control satellite TV, mini-bar and tea/coffee making facilities. The Victoriana-style bar serves a range of hand-pulled ales and is open all day, every day for meals and drinks. Superb conference facilities are available for up to 200 persons. **Restaurant:** Churchill's is a spacious restaurant, with a dance floor and a light and airy conservatory, opening out on to a large patio, overlooking a delightful rural aspect, where one can dine 'alfresco'. A variety of menus is available all day in any of the dining areas including the two conservatories, ranging from snacks to an 'East meets West' selection and daily black-board specials. **Nearby:** Romantic Brontë country and the spectacular Yorkshire countryside. The award-winning Eureka! Museum is a great favourite with families and the immediate area is a golfer's paradise. **Directions: Take junction 24 off M62 and follow signs for Blackley for approximately one mile, at the crossroads turn left for Holywell Green. The hotel is 1/2 mile along on the left.**

For hotel location, see maps on pages 180–186

THE CHEQUERS AT SLAUGHAM

SLAUGHAM, NR HANDCROSS, WEST SUSSEX RH17 6AQ
TEL: 01444 400239/400996 FAX: 01444 400400

OWNERS: Paul and Sue Graham
CHEF: Wayne Hall

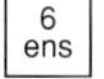

S: £49–£60
D: £61–£71

Inn: Situated in a conservation village, The Chequers at Slaugham is a delightful hostelry offering a good welcome, superior accommodation and acclaimed cooking. All six of the de luxe guest rooms are appointed to a high standard, each with a host of amenities that include remote-control television, trouser press, radio alarm, hairdryer and refreshments. The en suite bathrooms are a particular feature and the four-poster suites have either a spa or double bath. The public rooms are given over mainly to dining areas, however, there is a comfortable residents' lounge. **Restaurants:** The Chequers' culinary reputation has gone from strength to strength. The menu caters for all tastes but it reflects a special emphasis on seafood dishes as proprietor Paul Graham purchases fresh fish from Billingsgate Market. Depending upon availability, the menu may include wing of skate, halibut, monkfish, fresh crab, plaice, lemon sole, scollops, salmon and richly flavoured fish soups. A wide bar menu is available throughout the week. During the summer the guests can dine alfresco in the Terrace Restaurant. **Nearby:** The Chequers is conveniently located just a few minutes from Gatwick and is easily accessible from London. It is also well placed for visiting the stately homes and gardens of Surrey and Sussex. **Directions: From the main London–Gatwick–Brighton road (A23), exit one mile south of Handcross.**

For hotel location, see maps on pages 180–186

The George Hotel

MARKET STREET, HATHERLEIGH, DEVON EX20 3JN
TEL: 01837 810454 FAX: 01837 810901

OWNERS: John Dunbar-Ainley and Veronica Devereux
CHEF: Rafael Aunon

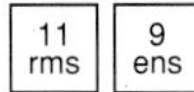

S: £35–£60
D: £48–£90

Inn: A century prior to the Reformation, The George Hotel was a rest house and sanctuary for monks of Tavistock, then in later years it served as a brewery, tavern, law court and coaching inn, its structure having been virtually unchanged over the passage of time, The George Inn has an atmosphere of English heritage which guests will sense upon arrival. The thatched roof, blackened beams and huge open fireplaces all add to the inn's character, while the bedrooms – which vary in size – have been attractively decorated in keeping with the period style. As well as the three bars, there is a well-furnished residents' lounge upstairs. Among the facilities, the inn has a games room plus an outdoor swimming-pool.

Restaurant: Whether choosing from the à la carte menu, savouring a bar snack or enjoying cream tea, guests will be presented with Devon's finest produce. The à la carte menu features Cornish seafood, prime local beef and fresh garden vegetables, prepared with flair and finesse. On the bar menu traditional dishes like steak and kidney pie appear next to vegetarian choices such as Mediterranean pasta bake. **Nearby:** Ideal for Dartmoor and the coastlines of Devon and Cornwall. Riding, tennis, golf and the newly completed Tarka Trail are all nearby. **Directions: Approaching the area from the A30 Exeter road, turn right at Okehampton on to the A386 signposted to Hatherleigh.**

For hotel location, see maps on pages 180–186

RED LION INN

HAWKSHEAD, AMBLESIDE, CUMBRIA LA22 0MV
TEL: 015394 36213 FAX: 015394 36747

OWNER: John Winter Smith
MANAGER: Roy Wilson

10 rms 10 ens

S: £40–£45
D: £60–£70

Inn: This 15th century village centre coaching inn, bearing the arms of John of Gaunt, is the oldest hostelry in Hawkshead, originally founded by horsemen in the 10th century. Hawkshead itself is steeped in history with winding cobbled streets and a cluster of whitewashed cottages around two picturesque squares overlooked by a parish church. William Wordsworth was a pupil at the local grammar school, whilst the 15th century courthouse is now a museum of rural life and the Beatrix Potter Gallery won a civic award in 1990 for the high standards attained during its restoration. Cars are not allowed in the village, but the inn has a small car park. All the bedrooms were refurbished in 1993 and are small, cosy and are all en suite. The bars are warm and welcoming with open fires and old oak beams. **Restaurant:** There is a full à la carte menu and a daily changing table d'hôte menu or, for those who prefer it, bar meals are served at lunch and dinner times. **Nearby:** Lake Windermere is 10 minutes away. The 9,000 acre Grizedale Forest and park includes a sculpture trail and has a unique theatre in the forest itself. **Directions: M6 junction 36 onto A591 through Windermere to Ambleside – follow A593 towards Coniston and turn left on B5285 to Hawkshead – the Red Lion is in the centre of the village.**

For hotel location, see maps on pages 180–186

Old White Lion Hotel

HAWORTH, KEIGHLEY, WEST YORKSHIRE BD22 8DU
TEL: 01535 642313 FAX: 01535 646222

OWNERS: Paul and Christopher Bradford

14 rms | 14 ens

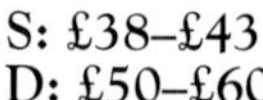

S: £38–£43
D: £50–£60

Inn: Situated on the cobbled main street in the village of Haworth, famous for being the home of the Brontë family, The Old White Lion is a 300-year-old inn. Resident owners Paul and Chris extend a warm and friendly welcome to guests. Relax in the oak-panelled residents' lounge or enjoy a drink in one of the two cocktail bars, which also serve a wide range of home-made hot and cold bar snacks, as well as an extensive range of real ales. There are 14 comfortable bedrooms with en suite facilities, including some family rooms. Most have magnificent views over the surrounding countryside. There is a self-contained function room which seats up to 100 people, with private bar and dance area. Special weekend breaks are available. **Restaurant:** Featured in many of the food guides, the candle-lit restaurant offers an extensive à la carte menu as well as a good-value table d'hôte. All meals are freshly cooked to order. **Nearby:** Scenes of *Jane Ayre* and *Wuthering Heights*, Brontë Museum, Parsonage and Church; Keighley and Worth Valley Railway, Bradford, National Museum of Film and Photography. Ideal for exploring the Yorkshire Moors and Dales, including the medieval city of York and the beautiful English Lake District, ten golf courses within 10 miles. **Directions: Leave the M62 at junction 24, then take the A629 through Halifax towards Keighley. Follow signs to Haworth.**

For hotel location, see maps on pages 180–186

Rhydspence Inn

WHITNEY-ON-WYE, NR HAY-ON-WYE, HEREFORDSHIRE HR3 6EU
TEL: 01497 831262

OWNERS: Peter and Pamela Glover
CHEF: James Lord and Michael Everleigh

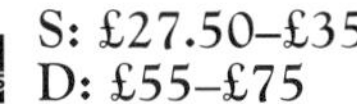

S: £27.50–£35
D: £55–£75

Inn: This 14th century manor house is set in the heart of Kilvert country and features several times in the works of the celebrated diarist. A striking half-timbered building, it has been tastefully extended to create an attractive dining room overlooking a well-kept garden. The bedrooms are individually furnished in time honoured style and all afford scenic views of the Wye Valley and the Black Mountains. The two welcoming bars have exposed beams and open fires typical of traditional inns and both serve draught ale and cider on tap. Closed for two weeks in January. **Restaurant:** An exceptionally well-balanced à la carte menu offers the best of country fare and international cuisine. Advantage is taken of the abundance of fresh local produce – Hereford beef, Welsh lamb, fresh fish and seasonally available game are among the choices on the frequently changing menu. The sweet trolley offers a delicious array of puddings. Snacks, both the traditional and more unusual, are served in the bar. Private parties can be catered for. **Nearby:** The area is a paradise for nature lovers. Riding, pony-trekking, caving, wind-surfing and canoeing on the River Wye are all available and Hay-on-Wye, famous for its second-hand bookshops, is close by. For walkers Offa's Dyke Path passes near to the inn. **Directions: The Rhydspence stands above – and is well protected from – the A438 Brecon–Hereford road. OS map reference 243472.**

For hotel location, see maps on pages 180–186

THE WALTZING WEASEL

NEW MILLS ROAD, BIRCH VALE, DERBYSHIRE SK12 5BT
TEL: 01663 743402 FAX: 01663 743402

OWNERS: Lynda and Michael Atkinson
CHEF: George Benham

8 rms | 8 ens

S: £45–£75
D: £65–£95

Inn: The Waltzing Weasel is a traditional country inn which, as its distinctive name suggests, offers a welcome alternative to the anonymous urban hotel. It is set within the heart of the Peak District, yet is only 40 minutes from Manchester and its international airport, Sheffield and Stockport. With its log fires, relaxed rustic character and country antiques, this is a civilised retreat for those looking for a welcome break, be they tired executives, hardy walkers or confirmed slouches. They are guaranteed no jukeboxes nor fruit-machines here. Individually styled bedrooms offer comfortable accommodation and most of the rooms enjoy lovely views over the surrounding countryside. **Restaurant:** Acclaimed chef George Benham provides good, honest food in the intimate restaurant which overlooks the garden towards the dramatic landscape of Kinder Scout. Starters such as seafood pancakes, fresh asparagus and gravadlax promise good things to come. Main courses may include poached Scotch salmon, roast duck in tangy orange sauce and chicken cooked to order in white wine, tomatoes, mushrooms and crevettes. Excellent bar meals are served at lunchtime. **Nearby:** Shooting, fishing and golfing facilities are within easy reach, as are Chatsworth, Haddon Hall, Castleton, Bakewell and Buxton with its opera house. **Directions: The Waltzing Weasel is located on the A6015 New Mills–Hayfield road, 1/2 mile from Hayfield.**

For hotel location, see maps on pages 180–186

THE FEVERSHAM ARMS HOTEL

HELMSLEY, NORTH YORKSHIRE YO6 5AG
TEL: 01439 770766 FAX: 01439 770346

OWNERS: Gonzalo Aragues y Gaston and Rowan Bowie de Aragues
CHEFS: Martin Steele and Linda Barker

S: £55–£65
D: £70–£80

Inn: This historic coaching inn, rebuilt in 1855 of mellow Yorkshire stone by the Earl of Feversham, has been owned and managed by the Aragues family since 1967. Set in two acres of walled gardens, The Feversham Arms has been updated to a high standard to offer every modern convenience, while special care has been taken to preserve the character and charm of the older parts of the hostelry. The bedrooms are individually furnished and some have special features such as four-poster beds and de luxe bathrooms. Open fires blaze in the winter months. Dogs can be accommodated by arrangement. **Restaurant:** The attractive candle-lit Goya Restaurant serves English, French and Spanish cooking and, by relying on fresh local produce, offers seasonal variety. There is a delicious fish and seafood menu. To accompany dinner, an extenive wine list includes a wide selection of Spanish wines and clarets. **Nearby:** Situated in the North York Moors National Park and close to many golf courses, this comfortable and welcoming hotel is ideal for sporting pursuits as well as for touring the moors, dales, east coast and the medieval city of York. The ruins of Rievaulx in Ryedale ($2^1/_2$ miles) should not be missed. Special Bonanza Breaks available. **Directions: From the A1 take the A64, then take the York north bypass (A1237) and then the B1363. Alternatively, from the A1 take the A168 signposted Thirsk, then the A170.**

For hotel location, see maps on pages 180–186

THE FOX COUNTRY HOTEL

IBSTONE, NR HIGH WYCOMBE, BUCKINGHAMSHIRE HP14 3GG
TEL: 01491 638289 FAX: 01491 638873

OWNERS: David and Ann Banks

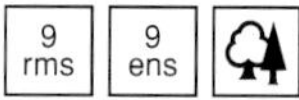

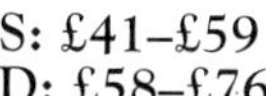

S: £41–£59
D: £58–£76

Inn: This attractive inn, in a woodland setting and dating back to the 17th century, if off the Chilterns Ridgeway. It is a haven for local businessmen from the busy High Wycombe area and equally much enjoyed at the weekend by those seeking a genuine country 'pub'. It is privately owned, and the pride of the proprietors is reflected throughout – first sight being the pretty hanging baskets enhancing the exterior – and once inside guests are instantly aware of the friendly ambience. There are nine charming pine-furnished bedrooms, all with en-suite showers, looking out over the countryside. The bars are traditional, with oak beams and log fires. Well kept real ale is served. In summer guests enjoy their drinks on the patio and in the flower-filled garden. **Restaurant:** The restaurant is very inviting, with its fresh flowers and crisp table linen. Fish is a speciality on the appetizing menu and the wines have been carefully chosen. Excellent informal meals can be enjoyed in the lounge bar, which has a dedicated non-smoking area. **Nearby:** National Trust places to visit include Cliveden, and there is even a small vineyard and brewery in the valley. Families will enjoy Beckonskot Model Village or taking out a boat on the Thames at Henley or Marlow. **Directions: Leave the M40 at Junction 5, for Ibstone, and after one mile the hotel is on the left down a country lane. It is just 45 minutes from London and a useful stopover for Heathrow.**

For hotel location, see maps on pages 180–186

BARNACLES RESTAURANT

WATLING STREET, NR HINCKLEY, LEICESTERSHIRE LE10 3JA
TEL: 01455 633220 FAX: 01455 250861

OWNER: David Freeman
CHEF: Carl Shardlow

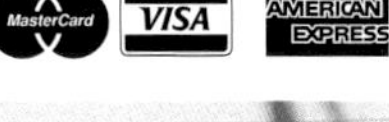

Cuisine: The name of this excellent restaurant gives prospective guests a clue that fish plays an important part on the menu. It has its own smokery and trout lake in two acres of walled garden – an oasis for local business men and women, being open for both lunch and dinner, although closed all day Sunday and Monday lunchtime. The brick-walled restaurant is elegantly furnished and has a stylish small bar in which to enjoy apéritifs while studying the fascinating menu which gives translations for lobster, scallops and snappers in many languages! The selection of grilled fish includes tuna and 'house' trout, while the whole baked turbot and brill is a triumph. Carnivores enjoy specialities such as Carpet Bagger steaks, home-grown venison and roast Gressingham duck. The sweet dishes are exciting variations of traditional dishes, the bread and butter pudding served with honey ice cream and crème brûlée is accompanied by cherries in Kirsch! There are over 70 wines listed, including a good range of half bottles. House wines and dessert wines may be had by the glass, and the prices are very reasonable, with a choice at under £10-a-bottle through to premier cru white burgundy below £30. **Directions: Leave the M69 at junction 1, taking the exit A5 south after leaving roundabout 100 yards on right hand side.**

CHEF'S SPECIALS

•••••••

pan fried baby red mullet
cooked and served with herb butter

tail of monkfish
grilled and finished in the oven with Pernod and caviar butter

roast Gressingham duck
half roast duck pan fried and served with cherry jus

steam toffee and apple sponge
with sticky toffee sauce and clotted cream

HOME FARM HOTEL

WILMINGTON, NR HONITON, DEVON EX14 9JR
TEL: 01404 831278 FAX: 01404 831411

OWNERS: Jim and Libby Cressy

12 rms | 12 ens

S: £30
D: £56

Inn: Home Farm is an attractive thatched farmhouse, set in four acres of beautiful grounds. A small hotel since 1950, the owners are just completing a refurbishing programme to create charming and relaxing ambience. The staff are friendly, the spotless rooms have big bowls of flowers in summer and big log fires in the winter. Children are made welcome. The target is to offer value for money. The Residents Lounge is comfortable, and there is a cosy, well-stocked bar serving light bar meals, draught beer and lager. **Restaurant:** The restaurant, oak-beamed and with an inglenook fireplace, offers a marvellous à la carte choice as well as a reasonable 'home cooking' table d'hôte menu using local produce. The wine list is good. Bedrooms are in the main building or across a cobbled courtyard. All have private bathroom, telephone, colour television, hairdryer, radio alarm and tea/coffee making facilities. **Nearby:** Wilmington is in the heart of 25 National Trust properties and there are six golf courses within 15 miles. Riding, water sports and fishing can be arranged. Honiton is known for its lace, as is Axminster for its carpets. **Directions: Take the A303 to Honiton, join the A35 signposted to Axminster. Wilmington is three miles on and Home Farm is set back off the main road on the right.**

For hotel location, see maps on pages 180–186

MARSTON FARM HOTEL

BODYMOOR HEATH, SUTTON COLDFIELD, WARWICKSHIRE B76 9JD
TEL: 01827 872133 FAX: 01827 875043

OWNERS: Wimpole Hotels Ltd
MANAGER: Peter Dann
CHEF: Robert Taylor

S: £37.50–£75
D: £75–£95

Inn: Sir Robert Peel and Lord Norton were both previous owners of the lovely 17th century farmhouse building which is now Marston Farm Hotel. Set amid nine acres of meadowland, the grounds are bordered by the Birmingham Fazeley canal which bustles with bright coloured barges and upon which the hotel has six moorings. Within the grounds are mature gardens, a tennis court, croquet lawn and well-stocked fishing lake. Inside, discreet, subtle décor, deep armchairs, inglenook fireplaces and cosy snugs combine to create an intimate, welcoming atmosphere. The service and personal attention offered to all guests is in keeping with English country house tradition. The bedrooms are well-designed and quite spacious: those in the main house have beams, and four poster beds are available. Some rooms are specially equipped for the lady guest. Remote-control teletext, satellite TV, direct-dial telephones, tea/coffee facilities, hairdryer and trouser press are provided. There are conference and banqueting facilities with syndicate rooms and audio-visual equipment. Weekend, Christmas and speciality breaks available. **Restaurant:** The Bracebridge Room, overlooking the original farm courtyard, makes a relaxed setting in which to savour succulent country fare. **Nearby:** Belfry Golf Centre, Middleton Hall and Drayton Manor Park. **Directions: Junction 9, M42 follow signs to Tamworth; Kingsbury Water Park.**

For hotel location, see maps on pages 180–186

The Pheasant Inn

CASTERTON, KIRKBY LONSDALE, CUMBRIA LA26 2RX
TEL: 015242 71230

OWNERS: Melvin and May Mackie
CHEF: David Mason

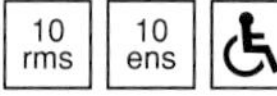

S: £40–£44
D: £64–£68

Inn: The Pheasant is Lunesdale's oldest inn, yet it offers all the comforts expected by today's traveller. A friendly welcome is extended to all by owner-managers Melvin and May Mackie, whether your visit is for a drink, dinner or to enjoy a short break in pleasant surroundings. Convenient for those with children at Sedbergh or Casterton School. Each ensuite bedroom is equipped with colour TV, direct-dial telephone and tea-making facilities. A log fire burns merrily in the bar and there is a lounge for residents. Truly an 'inn for all seasons', The Pheasant is a good choice for a break at any time of year. In spring the nearby woods are filled with daffodils and bluebells, while during autumn and winter a stroll over the Lunesdale Fells is an exhilarating way to blow away the cobwebs. **Restaurant:** In the dining room guests can choose from the à la carte menu, with daily changing specials prepared from fresh local produce. Starters include game terrine, black pudding and mustard sauce, followed by main courses such as casserole of venison, local lamb and fresh fish served with a difference. A wide selection of hearty bar meals is available. **Nearby:** Levens Hall and Sizergh Castle (N.T.), the Settle to Carlisle railway, the Yorkshire Dales and Trough of Bowland. **Directions: Leave M6 at junction 36. Follow A65 towards Skipton. After Kirkby Lonsdale, turn left onto A683 Sedbergh–Casterton road. The inn is one mile ahead on left.**

For hotel location, see maps on pages 180–186

THE SNOOTY FOX

MAIN STREET, KIRKBY LONSDALE, CUMBRIA LA6 2AH
TEL: 015242 71308 FAX: 015242 72642

OWNERS: Jack and Maura Shone
MANAGERS: Gordon and Joanne Cartwright

9 rms 9 ens

S: £26–£28
D: £46–£52

Inn: Situated in the picturesque market town of Kirkby Lonsdale, this Grade II listed Jacobean coaching inn offers comfortable accommodation, excellent food and a warm welcome. The nine cosy bedrooms, all of which have been recently refurbished, provide a range of modern comforts. Eight have en suite shower rooms and one offers both a bath and shower room. They are all non smoking. **Restaurant:** The inn has established a fine reputation for offering a first rate bill of fare, which is served either at the bar or in the oak-panelled restaurant. The chef, Gordon Cartwright, was trained by the Roux brothers and was formerly at Sharrow Bay. Sample the delights of roast best end of Herdwick lamb, topped with a mustard and herb crust and presented with a pan jus flavoured with roast garlic and rosemary, or try the salade tiède of freshly smoked halibut, served with oyster mushrooms and a creamed red pimento sauce. The two whitewashed and stone walled traditional bars, warmed by open fires in the cooler months, sell hand pumped ale. **Nearby:** Local attractions include Sizerigh Castle and Levens Hall. The area is ideal for walking enthusiasts and there are also opportunities golf, shooting, fishing and riding. **Directions: From M6 junction 36 take the A65 to Kirkby Lonsdale. Turn left into the town centre the Snooty Fox is just off the square in the mains street. The car park is at the rear of the inn.**

30 M

WHOOP HALL INN

BURROW-WITH-BURROW, KIRKBY LONSDALE, CUMBRIA LA6 2HP
TEL: 015242 71284 FAX: 015242 72154

OWNERS: John and Dorothy Parr
MANAGER: Elaine Eccleston
CHEF: Sharon Elders

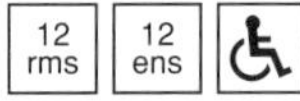

S: £45–£48
D: £65–£85

Inn: Over 350 years old, this 17th century coaching inn is a welcoming retreat for all guests – there are facilities here for families with children and for visitors with disabilities. Roaring log fires in the cooler months, oak beams and traditional hand-pulled beers make this a popular place to soak up the friendly atmosphere or perhaps enjoy a quiet game of darts or dominoes. Guests are offered all the modern comforts of a well-equipped en suite bedroom. Ten of the twelve bedrooms are in a converted barn and stable block, two of them on the ground floor and can accommodate disabled guests, and most rooms have good views down the Lune Valley or over the Barbon Fells. **Restaurant:** The galleried restaurant is in the old barn. The menus provide something for all tastes: specialities include freshly caught seafoods, crisply roasted duckling with orange and a variety of game in season. All dishes are cooked to order and a reasonably priced wine list includes over 30 bins. Lighter meals are served in the 40-seater buttery. In warm weather guests can savour an alfresco barbecue meal on the patio and orchard beer garden where there is a play area for children. **Nearby:** Whoop Hall Inn is well placed for trips to the Dales and the Lake District. It is a mile outside Kirkby Lonsdale with its traditional Thursday market and 18-hole golf course. Ingleton waterfalls and caves and Leighton Hall are also close by. **Directions: Leave M6 at junction 36 and take the A65; the hotel is ½ mile east of Kirkby Lonsdale.**

For hotel location, see maps on pages 180–186

THE GEORGE & DRAGON HOTEL

MARKET PLACE, KIRKBYMOORSIDE, NORTH YORKSHIRE YO6 6AA
TEL & FAX: 01751 433334

OWNERS: Stephen and Frances Colling
CHEF: Hilary Snowden

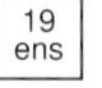

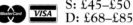

S: £45–£50
D: £68–£85

Inn: Situated on the cobbled market square of the North Yorkshire village of Kirkbymoorside, The George & Dragon Hotel is housed in an ancient building reputed to date back to the 13th century. Its old-world charm – there are oak beams in many of the rooms – is combined with the comfort and service of a modern hotel. Artistically decorated ensuite bedrooms overlook a private courtyard or the beautiful garden. The bar – the hub of every good hostelry – has a cosy atmosphere, with an open fire on chilly days. There is an excellent selection of hand-pumped beers, wines and spirits. A blackboard bistro menu offers home-made wholesome food including vegetarian choices. There are no fruit machines, no juke boxes nor pool tables, instead the civilised murmur of conversation to a background of classical music or traditional jazz, amidst a wealth of sporting memorabilia. For guests who enjoy sporting pursuits, golf, shooting, gliding and off-road driving can all be arranged nearby. Special breaks available. **Restaurant:** Once the Old Brewhouse, the attractive dining room offers freshly cooked English dishes from an à la carte menu that changes weekly. **Nearby:** Castle Howard, Helmsley Castle, Rievaulx Abbey, North York Moors Railway, North Yorkshire Moors National Park, York and the Coast. **Directions: The hotel is in the centre of Kirkbymoorside, off the A170 Thirsk–Scarborough road midway between Helmsley and Pickering.**

For hotel location, see maps on pages 180–186

Longview Hotel and Restaurant

51/55 MANCHESTER ROAD, KNUTSFORD, CHESHIRE WA16 0LX
TEL: 01565 632119 FAX: 01565 652402

OWNERS: Stephen and Pauline West
CHEF: James F. Falconer-Flint

23 rms | 23 ens

  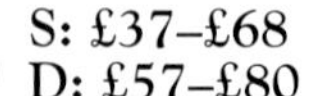

S: £37–£68
D: £57–£80

Inn: This delightful house, once the home of a Victorian merchant, has been thoughtfully restored to create an elegant small friendly hotel a few minutes walk from the centre of this little market town, so accessible from Manchester and the airport. The house has been furnished to reflect its era, with well polished antiques, flesh flowers and pretty chintzes. The bedrooms are very pretty, decorated in floral cottons and benefit from hairdriers, television and a hot drinks tray, as well as Victorian pin cushions! Ten bedrooms are in the modernised 19th century house next door. There are also six luxury service apartments in a house nearby and all overlook 'The Heath'. **Restaurant:** There is a well stocked cosy cellar bar where you can relax before being seated in the comfortable period restaurant. Noted for its cuisine throughout the area, we are sure that you will enjoy such delights as roast beef and Cheshire puddings made with a home-made horseradish mixture or Tatton Estate venison fillet. There are superb vegetarian dishes. Last of all treat yourself to some lovely desserts or some delicious home-made ice cream The wine list is international, and includes very reasonable house wines. **Nearby:** There are beautiful country house gardens to visit, and Tatton Park just round corner. Chester is within reasonable driving distance. **Directions: Leave M6 at junction 19 on A556 westbound towards Chester. Left at lights, left at roundabout in Knutsford and the hotel is 300 yards on the right.**

For hotel location, see maps on pages 180–186

FEATHERS HOTEL

HIGH STREET, LEDBURY, HEREFORDSHIRE HR8 1DS
TEL: 01531 635266 FAX: 01531 632001

OWNER: David Elliston
CHEF: John Capaldi

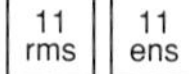

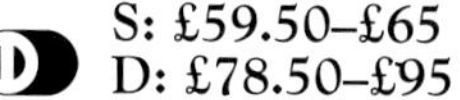

S: £59.50–£65
D: £78.50–£95

Inn: The black and white timbered exterior of the Feathers Hotel stands out very clearly in Ledbury's main street. This traditional coaching inn, which dates back to the 1560s, is impressive even by the high standards of the area. The bedrooms retain their quaint character, with beamed walls and ceilings, yet are comfortably appointed. There are two bars and a comfortable lounge area in which to relax, all with log fires. Up to 150 people can be seated in the ballroom and conference suite, making it a popular venue for wedding receptions and private functions. Within the premises are two squash courts which guests can use. **Restaurant:** The Feathers' cooking has earned an AA Rosette and a great reputation in the area. The main restaurant offers an à la carte menu with appetising dishes, many of which are prepared simply, to maximise the flavour of the ingredients. More informal meals are served in Fuggles, a bistro-style bar where hops hang from the rafters. A wide range of ales and over 60 international wines is offered, to accompany dishes such as spaghetti carbonara and grilled fresh salmon. **Nearby:** Ledbury, with its narrow lanes and cobblestone streets, is ideally placed for the Malvern Hills, Hereford, Worcester and Gloucester. Also close are Eastnor Castle and Falconry Centre at Newent. **Directions: Leave the M50 at junction 2 and take the A417 towards Hereford. The Feathers Hotel is in Ledbury High Street.**

For hotel location, see maps on pages 180–186

THE THREE HORSESHOES INN & RESTAURANT

BUXTON ROAD, BLACKSHAW MOOR, NR LEEK, STAFFORDSHIRE
TEL: 01538 300296 FAX: 01538 300320

OWNERS: William and Jill Kirk
CHEFS: Paul Knight and Chris Gordon

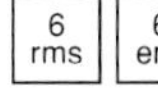

S: £42
D: £50

Inn: A homely family–run hostelry situated in the beautiful Staffordshire Moorlands on the edge of the Peak District National Park, the Three Horseshoes is a traditional farmhouse style inn providing comfortable accommodation and excellent food. It stands in its own large and beautiful garden, with patios, terraces and a childrens' play area. The six en suite cottage style bedrooms have been recently redecorated and furnished. **Restaurant:** Affording superb views, the restaurant serves fine food, fresh vegetables and a choice of over 200 wines. In the evening, candlelight and romantic music combine to create a peaceful and relaxing atmosphere. A Bar Carvery provides home cooked traditional dishes, as well as a roast of the day, accompanied by fresh market vegetables. On Saturday nights there is a dinner and dance with a cabaret and à la carte menu offering an extensive choice of food. The inn is closed from Christmas through to the New Year. **Nearby:** The area around the inn includes Rudyard Lake for sailing and walks (from which Kipling took his name),Tittesworth Reservoir for fishing, walking and bird watching, and the Roaches for climbing and walking. About 15 minutes away are the Manifold Valley, Dovedale, Berrisford Dale, Hartington, Alstonefield and Butterton. Alton Towers and Chatsworth are is just 20 minutes away. **Directions: Inn is on the A53 road to Buxton, easily reached by the M6 via the Potteries and the M1 via Derby.**

WHEELBARROW CASTLE

STOKE PRIOR, LEOMINSTER, HEREFORDSHIRE HR6 0NB
TEL: 01568 612219

OWNERS: Bryan and Valerie Gardiner
CHEF: Valerie Birchley

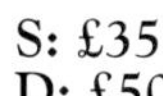

S: £35
D: £50

Inn: This has to be one of England's most pleasant inns, a 17th century grand farmhouse, surrounded by beautiful countryside. The front terrace and enclosed courtyard are lovely places to sit, if not seeking a shady spot in the pretty gardens. There are six comfortable double rooms, either with bathrooms or showers en-suite and television. **Restaurant:** The kitchen is a family affair with chef Valerie Birchley being ably assisted by her daughter, Emma Sheppard. À la carte lunch and dinner are served in the very pleasant restaurant, a traditional Sunday lunch is offered and there is an extensive bar menu. A set price menu, changing daily, now has become a regular feature. Conferences and private parties are catered for in a separate function room with its own bar. The inn has its own smokery, specialising in smoked fish, so guests may take home a delicious souvenir of their stay! **Nearby:** Hereford Cathedral and Hay-on-Wye, famous for its bookshops are nearby. Active guests may enjoy the heated outdoor pool, play golf at Leominster, attend Chepstow Races or walk down to the River Lugg. **Directions: One mile south-east of Leominster signed at a lane between the A44 and A49.**

THE COUNTRYMEN

THE GREEN, LONG MELFORD, SUFFOLK CO10 9DN
TEL: 01787 312356 FAX: 01787 374557

OWNERS: Stephen and Janet Errington
CHEF: Stephen Errington

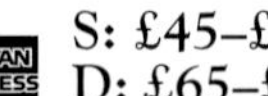

S: £45–£55
D: £65–£85

Inn: Overlooking Melford's magnificent green, the Countrymen has received wide acclaim for its superb food and splendid accommodation. Recognised by all major guides, the Countrymen is enjoyed by visitors and locals alike. Stephen and Janet have earned much praise for their enthusiastic and generous hospitality. The bedrooms, individually furnished with country antiques, offer every modern amenity. If you are lucky you could be sleeping in one of the four-posters or in an antique brass bedstead in a room with panoramic views over Melford. The comfortable lounge leading out to an attractive walled courtyard garden offers scope to enjoy the many books and games. **Restaurant:** Classically influenced, Dorchester trained Stephen creates dishes to tempt even the most jaded palate. The Countrymen has several fixed price menus as well as full à la carte fare. All menus change regularly to reflect seasonal dishes and Stephen's specialities. Adding another string to their bow Janet and Stephen have now opened a delightful bistro and wine bar, offering a selection of old and new world wines in an informal relaxed atmosphere. **Nearby:** Melford Hall, Kentwell Hall and a plethora of antique shops; Gainsborough's birthplace, historic Bury St Edmunds, Lavenham, Newmarket and Cambridge. **Directions: On the village green on the A1092 and the A134.**

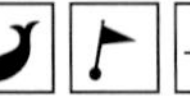

For hotel location, see maps on pages 180–186

THE GREYHOUND

MARKET STREET, LUTTERWORTH, LEICESTERSHIRE LE17 4EJ
TEL: 01455 553307 FAX: 01455 554558

OWNERS: Robert and Janet Eggleston
CHEF: Steve Dennis

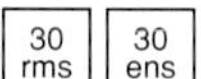

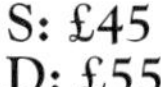

S: £45
D: £55

Inn: The Greyhound was built in 1720 as a coaching and posting inn and is now a Grade II listed building which has been extensively renovated and refurbished to a high standard by owner-managers Robert and Janet Eggleston. Standing near the old market place, The Greyhound offers a relaxing individuality for the discerning traveller, whether on a business trip or pleasure bound. The focal point of the inn is the 18th century courtyard around which the old stables and rooms were built. Whether an inexpensive single or plush suite, all the bedrooms have been decorated to a high specification. All of the bedrooms are well-equipped and two ground-floor rooms are suitable for disabled visitors. **Restaurant:** In the dining room, the menus range from creative English cooking to international cuisine. The old arched cellars of the inn have been renovated in a simple, plain style to form the Bistro. Comprehensive conference and banqueting facilities can be provided, and as there are also three syndicate rooms, flexible arrangements can be made to cater for a variety of functions. **Nearby:** Within easy reach of many famous places, such as Coventry Cathedral, Warwick Castle, Coombe Abbey, Stratford-upon-Avon, Bosworth Battlefield and Belvoir Castle. **Directions: From M1 junction 20 turn into Lutterworth. The Greyhound is at the top of the hill on the left-hand side. Junction 1 of the M6 is also nearby.**

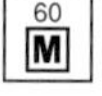

THE RISING SUN

HARBOURSIDE, LYNMOUTH, DEVON EX35 6EQ
TEL: 01598 753223 FAX: 01598 753480

OWNERS: Hugo and Pamela Jeune
CHEF: David Lamprell

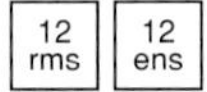

S: £45
D: £79–£99.50

Inn: Recommended in every way, this 14th century thatched smugglers' inn is perfectly positioned on the picturesque harbour overlooking East Lyn River. The building is steeped in history: *Lorna Doone* was partly written here and the inn's adjacent cottage – now luxuriously equipped for guests' use and pictured below – was once the honeymoon retreat for the poet Shelley. The best of the inn's medieval character has been preserved: oak panelling, uneven floors, open fires and crooked ceilings, all enhanced by tasteful furnishings and modern comforts. The bedrooms lack nothing and, like the terraced gardens, have splendid views. Parking in Lynmouth can be difficult at the height of the season. **Restaurant:** The food served in the oak-panelled restaurant is of excellent quality. Classic modern English, French and vegetarian cuisine is provided on both the table d'hôte and à la carte menus, which also feature local specialities such as freshly caught lobster and salmon. All this is accompanied by a superb wine list. Good value bar meals are also available. **Nearby:** The inn owns a $^1/_2$ mile stretch of river for salmon fishing and there are opportunities for sea angling. The hills and combes of Exmoor National Park, the North Devon coastline and the hunting country of Doone Valley are also near. **Directions: Leave the M5 at junction 23 (signposted Minehead) and follow the A39 to Lynmouth. Or take the A361, exit 27 (Tiverton) to South Molton, then the B3226 in the direction of Ilfracombe and then the A39 at Blackmoore Gate to Lynmouth.**

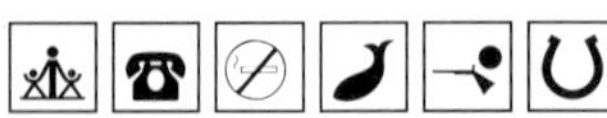

For hotel location, see maps on pages 180–186

Boulters Lock Hotel

BOULTERS ISLAND, MAIDENHEAD, BERKSHIRE SL6 8PE
TEL: 01628 21291 FAX: 01628 26048

OWNER: Joe Hazelton
MANAGER: John Smith
CHEF: David Jones

19 rms 19 ens

S: £95
D: £115

Inn: Originally built as a millers house in 1726, this privately owned hotel stands on its own island, next to the famous Boulters Lock, which is the longest, deepest and for many the loveliest lock on the River Thames. Where E.J. Gregory painted his famous picture "Boulters Lock – Sunday Afternoon 1895". There are panoramic views from both the Riverside Restaurant and Terrace Bar. The bedrooms are in converted lock-keepers cottages, and have been individually designed and furnished, some with authentic Victorian baths and ornate showers. The honeymoon suite has a carved four-poster bed. **Restaurant:** The food is classically French with seasonal English dishes. It features local fresh produce and fresh fish delivered daily. Dinner dances are organised on some Saturday nights throughout the year and traditional Sunday lunch is served from 12.00 noon until 3.00pm. Dining also in in the Terrace Bar from a Bistro menu. **Nearby:** Windsor Castle (five miles). Cliveden, former home of Nancy Astor, Cookham and Burnham Beeches are nearby. **Directions: Leave M4 at exit 7, take A4 to Maidenhead, over bridge turn right at mini roundabout into Ray Mead Road, signposted Cookham, under a mile to Boulters Lock Hotel.**

For hotel location, see maps on pages 180–186

THE HARROW AT WARREN STREET

WARREN STREET, NEAR LENHAM, KENT ME17 2ED
TEL: 01622 858727 FAX: 01622 850026

OWNERS: Alan Cole and Sheila Burns
CHEF: Richard Arter

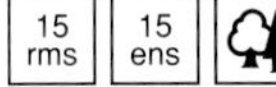

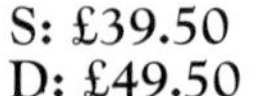

S: £39.50
D: £49.50

Inn: High on the North Downs of Kent stands this attractive hostelry, amid rolling farmland in the hamlet of Warren Street. Once the forge and rest house for travellers en route to Canterbury via the nearby Pilgrims' Way, it has now been converted into a comfortable country inn. Refurbishments have ensured that all the guest accommodation is designed to a high standard. For guests who wish to enjoy a leisurely lie-in, a Continental breakfast can be brought to the bedroom. The traditional character and atmosphere of the public rooms are enhanced by open log fires in the winter and exposed oak beams. **Restaurant:** The Harrow enjoys a reputation locally for its good cooking. There is a superb conservatory restaurant with views over a delightful floodlit water garden and patio. The à la carte menu features a delicious choice of seasonal dishes. For an appetiser perhaps try the *terrine de poireaux* – a terrine of leeks and langoustines served with tarragon vinaigrette, followed by pot-roasted guinea fowl with Madeira sauce. An excellent range of meals is also presented on the bar menus. The inn's facilities can be tailored to accommodate special functions. **Nearby:** Convenient for Canterbury, Maidstone and the Cinque Port of Rye. Leeds Castle is just 10 minutes' drive. **Directions: Leave the M20 at junction 8 or 9. Warren Street is signed from the A20 between Harrietsham and Charing.**

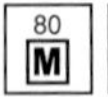

For hotel location, see maps on pages 180–186

RINGLESTONE INN

'TWIXT' HARRIETSHAM AND WORMSHILL, NR MAIDSTONE, KENT ME17 1NX
TEL: 01622 859900 FAX: 01622 859966

OWNER: Michael Millington-Buck

Restaurant: Step back in time into this unspoilt, medieval, lamplit tavern. 'A Ryghte Joyouse and welcome greetynge to ye all' proclaims the inscription carved in 1632 on the impressive English oak sideboard – a sentiment much echoed by today's Ringlestone Inn. Built in 1533, the Ringlestone was originally used as a hospice for monks, but became one of the early 'Ale Houses' around 1615. With its original brick and flint walls and floors, oak beams, inglenooks and English oak furniture, little of the inn has changed since then. Even in the later addition of the dining room, the tables were made from the timbers of an 18th century Thames barge. The Ringlestone has featured in many food guides over the last decade and it has established a reputation for excellent lunch and evening menus. A help yourself hot and cold lunchtime buffet offers a seasonal variety of country recipes. A candlelit supper could start with crab pâté or smoked mackerel follow by fresh trout, expertly filleted and baked with butter, lemon, almonds and oatmeal. The sweet selection is always a delight, with tempting pies, tarts and puddings in pools of fresh local cream. **Wine:** A wide range of English country fruit wines is available, along with wines from Europe and the New World. **Nearby:** Leeds Castle. **Directions: From M20, junction 8, travel north through Hollingbourne on B2163, then turn right at water tower crossroads.**

CHEFS' SPECIALITIES

•••••••

mussels provençale
served in tangy tomato, garlic and sherry sauce

game pie
duck, rabbit and pheasant simmered in redcurrant wine

fresh trout
filleted and baked with butter, lemon, almonds and oatmeal

THE HORSE AND GROOM INN

CHARLTON, NEAR MALMESBURY, WILTSHIRE SN16 9DL
TEL: 01666 823904 FAX: 01666 823390

OWNER: Sellcover Ltd
MANAGERS: Nichola King and Philip Gilder
CHEF: Philip Gilder

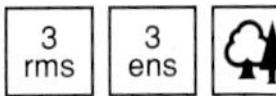

S: £55
D: £69.50

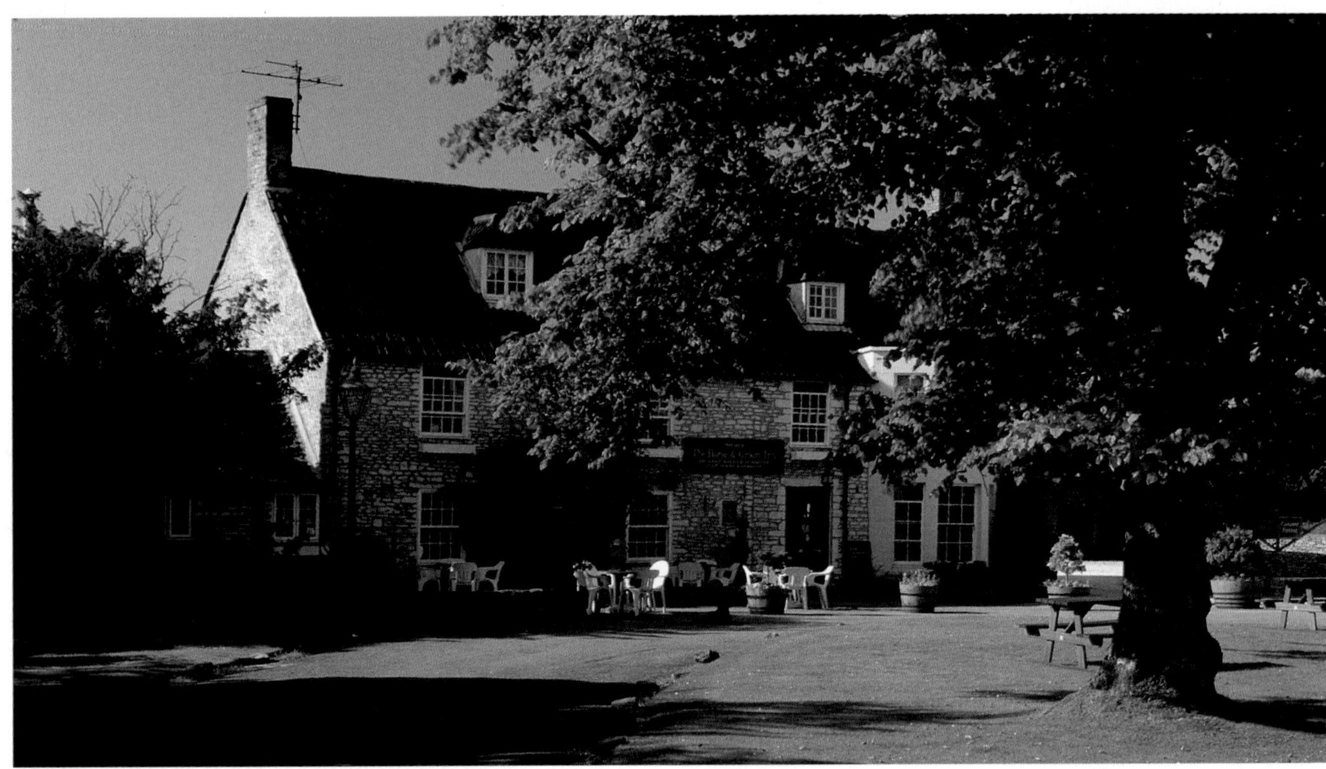

Inn: In the small village of Charlton in the heart of Cotswold country, the Horse & Groom Inn possesses a unique rustic charm. Inside, this 16th century coaching inn has been sensitively reinterpreted, with no loss of its period atmosphere; careful thought and attention has been invested in each of the three bedrooms, resulting in peaceful, relaxing rooms with all modern conveniences (plus extra touches like mineral water, fresh fruit, flowers and bathrobes). Décor is muted, in elegant shades like sage green, jasmine and peach; windows look out over the beautiful Cotswold countryside. A full English breakfast is included in the tariff. **Restaurant:** The Horse & Groom has a fine reputation for its cuisine, which has attracted the attention (and recommendation) of such connoisseurs as Egon Ronay. There are simple bar snacks such as ploughman's lunches and jacket potatoes, and full à la carte menus featuring freshly roasted duck breast with caramalised oranges & Grand Marnier, sea bass supreme and an imaginative range of salads. Locally caught trout is another popular choice. The Horse & Groom is a free house serving real ales from Wiltshire breweries. In summer, drinks and meals may be enjoyed in the private garden. In winter guests choose to relax by log fires crackling in the grates. **Nearby:** Bath, Cotswolds, Malmesbury. **Directions: Exit M4 junction 17. Horse & Groom is two miles east of Malmesbury on B4040.**

For hotel location, see maps on pages 180–186

THE GREEN MAN

MARKET STREET, MALTON, NORTH YORKSHIRE YO17 0LY
TEL: 01653 600370 FAX: 01653 696006

OWNERS: English Rose Hotels
MANAGER: Valerie Gardner
CHEF: Ian Couch

26 rms | 26 ens

S: £55
D: £110
Suite: £120

Inn: For over a century a famous meeting place 'The Green Man' has been at the heart of the North Yorkshire market town of Malton. In 1993 this historic hotel was beautifully restored and refurbished from top to toe with rich colour schemes, fine fabrics, English oak furniture and panelling, yet carefully preserving those features that are uniquely the Green Man's, such as the magnificent stone fireplace in the hall surrounded by gleaming copper artifacts where in autumn and winter there is always a blazing log fire and in summer a blaze of flowers. Also the lovely pieces of Mouseman furniture made by Robert Thompson of Kilburn, now restored to the Oak Lounge Bar. The en suite bedrooms are all individually furnished and designed.

Restaurant: The Green Man Lot15 restaurant is so named after Malton's many auction houses and market day sales that surround the hotel. At lunch time a carvery is offered as well as a selection of Yorkshire fayre. At dinner making a play of the restraurants name, 15 lots of everything will be discovered on the bill of fare. The selections of starters and main courses include well cooked and presented Yorkshire dishes with a choice of vegetarian and fresh locally caught fish. The desserts, all home-made, are a must. **Nearby:** York with its minster, races and Jorvik centre, Eden Camp Miltary Exibition, North York Moors National Park and Castle Howard. **Directions: Take the A64, Malton is between York and Scarborough.**

THE MASONS ARMS

MEYSEY HAMPTON, NR CIRENCESTER, GLOUCESTERSHIRE GL7 5JT
TEL: 01285 850164 FAX: 01285 850164

OWNERS: Andrew and Deborah Gent

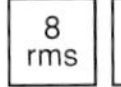 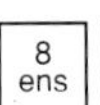 

S: £30
D: £49

Inn: Located beside the village green, this 17th century inn is situated on the southern edge of the Cotswolds. It provides a perfect haven for travellers or holidaymakers seeking peace and tranquility. There are eight comfortable and individually decorated bedrooms and all offer en suite facilities, tea and coffee trays and remote control colour TVs. The heart of the Masons is the bar, still a centre of village life where locals and guests enjoy a convivial atmosphere. Golf, fishing, windsurfing and jet skiing are all available locally, with cycle routes and nature walks ensuring that there is something for every guest to enjoy. **Restaurant:** Excellent home cooked food is served in the separate dining room or the bar. The menus are varied and interesting and include daily 'specials' catering for all tastes. Why not try chicken with a light mustard sauce, rump steak with a black bean sauce or Barnsley lamb chop with a herb crust? Or perhaps more traditional fayre such as homemade steak and kidney pie or fisherman's pie. **Nearby:** Cirencester, originally the centre of Roman Britain, is six miles to the west and Bibury, with its famous Arlington Row, four miles to the north. **Directions: Meysey Hampton is six miles east of Cirencester on the A417. Nearest motorway M4, junction 15.**

For hotel location, see maps on pages 180–186

THE RAGGED COT

HYDE, MINCHINHAMPTON, NR STROUD, GLOUCESTERSHIRE GL6 8PE
TEL: 01453 884643/731333 FAX: 01453 731166

OWNERS: Margaret and Mike Case

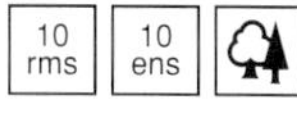

S: from £48
D: £60–£75

Inn: This delightful 'Old Worlde' inn is set deep in the heart of the Cotswolds, surrounded by a wealth of picturesque villages and 580 acres of National Trust grassland on which cattle roam freely. The charmingly decorated bedrooms are all equipped with a teletext colour TV, telephone and hospitality tray, while the Bridal Suite boasts a traditional four-poster bed. **Restaurant:** A cosy, intimate atmosphere, efficient service and excellent cuisine at realistic prices are all features of The Ragged Cot's restaurant. An à la carte menu offers a good variety of attractively presented dishes, all prepared from the freshest market produce. A bar menu is available for guests who prefer a quick meal during the day. The characterful bar is warm and friendly and provides the ideal environment in which to relax and enjoy a quiet drink. **Nearby:** The extraordinary Rococo Garden at Painswick, Roman Cirencester, Lechlade Garden and Fuchsia Centre, Barnsley House Gardens, Cotswold Wild Life Park, Littledean Hall, Arlington Mill Country Museum and The Chestnut Gallery. There are also local opportunities for guests to enjoy gliding, fishing, watersports, riding and golf. Badminton is 15 miles away and the spa town of Cheltenham is 16 miles. **Directions: From M5 junction 13 take the A4173. Pass through the village of Minchinhampton into Hyde; the Ragged Cot is on the main road on the left.**

For hotel location, see maps on pages 180–186

In association with MasterCard

The Kings Arms Inn & Restaurant

MONTACUTE, SOMERSET TA15 6UU
TEL: 01935 822513 FAX: 01935 826549

OWNERS: Jonathan and Karen Arthur
CHEF: Graham Page

13 rms 13 ens

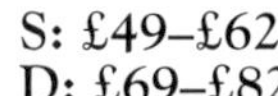

S: £49–£62
D: £69–£82

Inn: This charming inn, found in one of Somerset's loveliest villages, is built in mellowed local stone. It dates back to the 16th century and discreet modernisation has preserved the mullioned windows and stone walls. The bedrooms are delightfully decorated in muted floral fabrics and comfortably furnished – one with a four-poster. They are en suite and meet the needs of today's exacting travellers. The traditional Pickwick Bar, with a roaring log fire serving real ale from nearby breweries, is frequented by the locals and offers informal lunch and supper menus during the week. **Restaurant:** The Abbey Room has built up a fine reputation for its modern English cooking with a rosette award. Salmon mousse is studded with truffles and pistachio nuts, while pork fillet is served with a cumin and coriander potato timbale. Asparagus, goats' cheese and mushroom strudel with a red and green pepper sauce will appeal to vegetarians and non-vegetarians alike. The wine list has been selected with great care, to meet all tastes and pockets. Special mini-break offers and room upgrades are available. **Nearby:** Montacute House, a fine example of Elizabethan architecture, Sherborne Castle and Abbey, Yeovil Air Museum, Cricket St Thomas Wildlife Park and a butterfly farm at Nether Compton. It is wonderful walking country. **Directions: Just off the A303; on the A3088 head towards Yeovil. Montacute clearly marked. The inn is in the centre of the village by the church.**

For hotel location, see maps on pages 180–186

THE SWAN HOTEL

NEWBY BRIDGE, NR ULVERSTON, CUMBRIA LA12 8NB
TEL: 015395 31681 FAX: 015395 31917

OWNER: Swan Hotel (Newby Bridge) Ltd
MANAGER: James Bertlin
CHEF: Philip Gorton

36 rms | 36 ens

S: £59–£80
D: £90–£120
Suite: £136

Inn: At the southern end of Lake Windermere, The Swan Hotel undoubtedly has one of the most picturesque locations in the whole of the Lake District, with superb views over the water and surrounding countryside. Comfort is the declared first priority of the management. The 36 en suite bedrooms, ranging from suites and deluxe doubles to high standard doubles and singles, are traditional in character yet offer every modern amenity. The public rooms are attractively decorated, with comfortable bars as well as an elegant lounge which adjoins the restaurant. **Restaurant:** Choose from the traditional Tithe Barn (non-smoking) or less formal Mailcoach. Imaginative menus are complemented by a carefully compiled wine list. Local produce such as potted Morecambe Bay shrimps, Lakeland char and poached Esthwaite trout are freshly cooked to order. Special diets can be catered for. A special children's menu is available. Smaller conferences may be accommodated and special breaks are available. ETB 4 Crowns Highly Commended and AA 3 stars. **Nearby:** The Lake District National Park, Holker Hall and Stott Park. There are facilities for many sports close by and the hotel has its own fishing rights and boat moorings. **Directions: Newby Bridge is on the A590. Leave the M6 at junction 36 and follow the A590 to Barrow. The Swan is just across the bridge at Newby Bridge.**

For hotel location, see maps on pages 180–186

THE GARDEN HOUSE HOTEL

SALHOUSE ROAD, RACKHEATH, NORWICH, NORFOLK NR13 6AA
TEL: 01603 720007 FAX: 01603 720019

OWNERS: John and Jill Smart

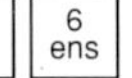

S: £35
D: £50

Inn: This small modern, family owned, hotel, with its reputation for extremely good food, falls into the category, long recognised in France, of a restaurant with rooms. Its name is justified, nonetheless, as it has extensive and well-kept gardens, guests appreciating the mass of colour in the summer. The lounge has large windows, big inviting chairs, and a small bar which is available only to residents and those dining that evening. The light bedrooms are immaculate and extremely comfortable, the double rooms en suite and the singles with private shower rooms. **Restaurant:** The very popular restaurant consists of two dining rooms, one overlooking the gardens. The fixed price menu offers a wide choice. It always includes locally caught fish, seasonal game and shellfish. Extremely fresh vegetables, delicious tarts and puddings all emphasise the quality of the ingredients used. The wine list is small but well balanced and reasonably priced. **Nearby:** The Norfolk Broads for boating, and the coast with its bird sanctuaries. Norwich City has its cathedral and museum and The Garden House is an ideal base for exploring the county's fascinating villages, historic houses and parks. **Directions: From Norwich take the A1151 for Wroxham. At Rackheath turn right at sign for Salhouse Station. On reaching T-junction turn right and Garden House is mile on the left.**

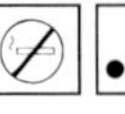

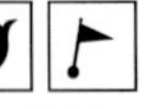

For hotel location, see maps on pages 180–186

Hotel Des Clos

OLD LENTON LANE, NOTTINGHAM, NOTTINGHAMSHIRE NG7 2SA
TEL: 0115 9866566 FAX: 0115 9860343

OWNERS: John and Rosemary Abbey
CHEFS: John Abbey and Louise Hurst

10 rms 10 ens

S: £69.50
D: £75
Suite: £110–£125

Inn: An attractive conversion of Victorian farm buildings, this family-run hotel retains the atmosphere of its origins while offering guests every modern comfort. The hotel benefits from its location on the banks of the River Trent, yet its close proximity to Nottingham and the motorway network ensures its convenience for the traveller. Each designed around an individual theme, the en suite bedrooms are well-equipped with colour TV, trouser press and refreshment facilities. Conference facilities enable executives to stage small meetings and a wide choice of weekend breaks is also on offer. **Restaurant:** Since the opening of the French restaurant in 1990, chef-proprietor John Abbey has established a reputation for cuisine and fine wines. A choice of lunch and evening menus is presented and during the summer guests may dine alfresco in the courtyard garden. An admirable list of French wines includes vintage clarets, over 60 half-bottles and 72 different Chablis labels. **Nearby:** The city of Nottingham is home to the National Watersports Centre, Trent Bridge Cricket Ground and a large market. Other notable landmarks are Nottingham Castle, Sherwood Forest and Southwell Minster. **Directions: Take exit 24 from M1 and take A453 signposted Nottingham (10 miles). Cross River Trent and follow signs to Lenton. Turn left at roundabout and immediately left again, down the lane to the river.**

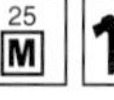

THE OXENHAM ARMS

SOUTH ZEAL, NR OKEHAMPTON, DEVON EX20 2JT
TEL: 01837 840244/577 FAX: 01837 840791

OWNERS: James and Patricia Henry
CHEF: Jamie Henry

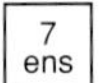

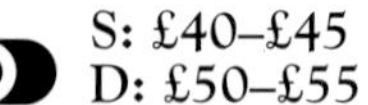

Inn: Thought to have been built by monks in the 12th century, the inn is a designated ancient monument, constructed around a 5,000 year old monolith. The bedrooms, lounge and bar retain plenty of the original characteristics, such as timbered ceilings, granite fireplaces, flagstone floors, arches and old doorways. Unobtrusive restoration and modernisation have been carried out to ensure the provision of up-to-date convenience and comfort. Some of the bedrooms overlook the hills of Dartmoor. To the rear of the house is a pretty walled garden. **Restaurant:** In the cosy dining room, guests can choose from a menu that changes daily. Traditional English recipes such as country-style roast duckling are offered alongside more cosmopolitan dishes like pork hongroise, which is cooked with sherry, paprika, shallots, mushrooms and cream. House specialities include local salmon, trout, beef and poultry. **Nearby:** Situated at the foot of Cawsand Beacon, surrounded by splendid walking country, this is a good base for exploring Dartmoor and the Devon coast. Castle Drogo, many National Trust properties and good facilities for riding, fishing and wind-surfing can all be found locally. **Directions: Leave the A30 17 miles west of Exeter at Whiddon Down roundabout. South Zeal is signposted after 1½ miles. The Oxenham Arms is in the centre of the village.**

For hotel location, see maps on pages 180–186

THE WHEATSHEAF INN AT ONNELEY AND LA PUERTA DEL SOL – RESTAURANTE ESPAÑOL

BARHILL ROAD, ONNELEY, STAFFORDSHIRE CW3 9QF
TEL: 01782 751581 FAX: 01782 751499

OWNERS: Mark and Milagros Bittner
CHEF: Milagros Bittner

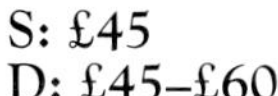

S: £45
D: £45–£60

Inn: This traditional inn, located in the North Staffordshire countryside – yet close to the Potteries, welcomes business travellers and tourists alike. Attractively refurbished and professionally run by the congenial resident proprietors, The Wheatsheaf Inn offers many comforts and facilities. Furnishings and décor are of a high standard throughout, and special touches like a basket of fruit on arrival and a complimentary morning paper add to the welcome. Popular Champagne Breaks and Golfing Breaks (using the amenities of the adjoining Onneley Golf Club) offer excellent value for money. **Restaurant:** Recently refurbished, the hotel's restaurant, La Puerta del Sol, offers the best traditional Spanish cooking – prepared by authentic methods – along with a wide range of popular English dishes. Guests are given a choice from the extensive à la carte menu and daily three-course table d'hôte menu. **Nearby:** The Wheatsheaf Inn at Onneley is just a short drive from the Potteries, the heart of Britain's ceramic industry. Also nearby are Bridgemere Garden World, Stapeley Water Gardens, the Dorothy Clive Gardens and the University of Keele. Alton Towers and Chester can be easily reached by car. **Directions: Located on the main A525 between the villages of Madeley and Woore just a 10 minute drive from Newcastle-under-Lyme and 15 minutes from Crewe, Nantwich, Market Drayton and Stoke-on-Trent. Easy access to the M6 motorway is available at junctions 15 and 16.**

For hotel location, see maps on pages 180–186

HOLCOMBE HOTEL

HIGH STREET, DEDDINGTON, OXFORDSHIRE OX15 0SL
TEL: 01869 338274 FAX: 01869 337167

OWNERS: Carol and Chedly Mahfoudh
HEAD CHEF: Alan Marshall

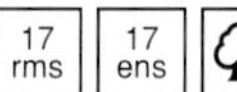

S: £58–£70
D: £84–£92.50

Inn: This delightful 17th century high quality hotel is family run and set in a pretty Cotswold village. It offers personalised attention and traditional hospitality and has a relaxed and friendly atmosphere. Each of the 17 tastefully appointed bedrooms has its own distinctive character and one boasts a water bed. Every amenity, including ionisers, is provided for the comfort of guests. **Restaurant:** Holcombe Hotel is known locally for its superb French, classical and traditional English cuisine. It is highly recommended and is recognised with an AA Red Rossette and RAC awards. Great care is taken in creating original and beautifully presented food. Real ale and excellent bar meals are served in the oakbeamed cottage bar. The Holcombe has been in the ownership of Chedley and Carol Mahfoudh since 1988, during which time they have received 5 awards, including the AA Courtesy and Care Award 1993, one of only 15 hotels out of 4,000. **Nearby:** The Cotswolds, Stratford-upon-Avon, Blenheim Palace, Woodstock and Oxford are among the region's many attractions. Golf can be arranged at an excellent, 18-hole, par 71 course 7 miles away. **Directions: Deddington is situated on the A4260, 15 miles north of Oxford and 6 miles from the M40 (junction 11). Follow sign to A4260 Adderbury; hotel is on the right at traffic lights.**

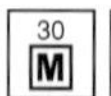

For hotel location, see maps on pages 180–186

THE JERSEY ARMS

MIDDLETON STONEY, OXFORDSHIRE OX6 8SE
TEL: 01869 343234 FAX: 01869 343565

OWNER: Donald Livingston

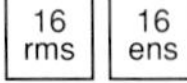

16 rms 16 ens

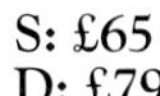

S: £65
D: £79

Inn: Near the city of dreaming spires, in the country of sparkling streams and gentle green pastures, The Jersey Arms occupies a site rich in history. As far back as 1241, the inn was listed as providing William Longsword 'for 25 men of Middleton, necessaries as food and drink'. It thrived in the days of coach-and-horse long-distance travel, and in 1823 was a key posting house for cross-country traffic. Today, The Jersey Arms has been honed into a retreat of comfort and peace. An informal air is created with old beams, antique flintlocks and simple, elegant furnishings. Bedrooms, all with private access, vary in size, while blending the charm of the past with modern décor. Facilities include hairdryers, colour TV and telephone. **Restaurant:** Cuisine of exceptional quality is prepared from the freshest local ingredients, and the menu is changed seasonally. Diners can sit in the Bar or Restaurant or, in fine weather, in the secluded courtyard garden. Relax first with an apéritif in the elegant lounge. **Nearby:** Oxford, Woodstock, Blenheim Palace with its gardens, Towcester and Cheltenham racecourses and Silverstone Racetrack. Heathrow airport is an hour away by car. **Directions: Between junctions 9 & 10 of the M40 on the B430 10 miles north of Oxford. From junction 9 take the Oxford Road, Middleton Stoney is signposted 1 mile down. From junction 10 Middleton Stoney is signposted as you leave the slip road.**

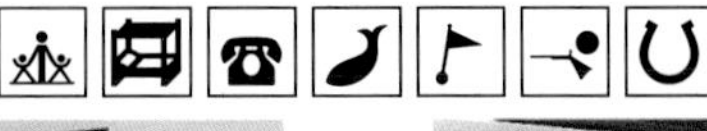

For hotel location, see maps on pages 180–186

The Mill and Old Swan

MINSTER LOVELL, OXFORDSHIRE OX8 5RN
TEL: 01993 774441 FAX: 01993 702002

OWNERS: Style Conferences
MANAGER: Peter Woollard

60 rms 60 ens

S: £50–£80
D: £80–£140

Inn: The Minster Lovell Mill stands on the edge of the village Minster Lovell, a small Oxfordshire village nesting in the valley of the River Windrush, on the edge of the Cotswolds. According to the *Doomsday Book*, three mills were at Minster Lovell, two of which existed on the present site and now constitute part of the historic properties. A wealth of oak beams, glowing fires, four-poster beds and antique furnishings welcome you to The Mill and Old Swan, which has been carefully restored to luxury standards. Attached to The Old Swan is The Mill which rambles over a 60 acre estate divided by the River Windrush. It is a charming location for relaxing, walking through the gardens or enjoying a choice of sporting activities including tennis, punting and fly-fishing which are all available to guests of The Old Swan. **Directions: From the A40 (Oxford/Burford road), take B4047 signposted to Minster Lovell. Once in the village follow signs for Minster Lovell Hall.**

For hotel location, see maps on pages 180–186

THE TALKHOUSE

WHEATLEY ROAD, STANTON-ST-JOHN, OXFORDSHIRE OX33 1EX
TEL: 01865 351648

OWNERS: Johnny Chick and Alan Heather
MANAGER: Dave Benson
CHEF: Mark Skidmore

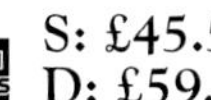

S: £45.50
D: £59.50

Inn: The Talkhouse is a 17th century inn which once housed the village blacksmith. Lying on the outskirts of Oxford, it has been carefully and tastefully refurbished under its new owners, Johnny Chick and Alan Heather, who also own the Mole & Chicken near Thame. A friendly and courteous staff are happy to attend to their guests' every need. **Restaurant:** An extensive and interesting menu is provided in the restaurant. For a starter try a chicken breast satay with garlic bread and chilli dip, or perhaps a plate of the best smoked Scottish salmon. Follow with home made steak and kidney pie, grilled calves' liver with bacon and sage or chargrilled chicken breast with a delicious five-spice sauce. The house speciality is chicken piri piri, a whole chargrilled chicken with exotic spices on a bed of salad and served with shoestring chips. Irresistible puddings include fresh banana crêpes with orange sauce and cream and Talkhouse upside down apple pie with cream. **Nearby:** The Talkhouse is ideally situated for guests who wish to visit the famous university city of Oxford. There are six premier golf courses within a 20 minute drive, along with opportunities locally for fishing, shooting and walking. Blenheim Palace, William Kent's garden at Rousham house, Cliveden, the Cotswolds, Henley and Silverstone are all within easy reach. **Directions: M40 junction 8, then the A40 to Wheatley and pick up the B4027.**

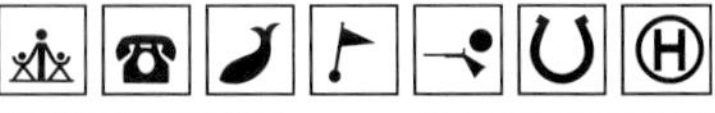

THE OLD CUSTOM HOUSE HOTEL

SOUTH QUAY, PADSTOW, CORNWALL PL28 8ED
TEL: 01841 532359 FAX: 01841 533372

OWNERS: St Austell Brewery & Co Ltd
MANAGER: Linda Allen
CHEF: Guy Pompa

24 rms | 24 ens

S: £45–£64
D: £52–£84

Inn: Miles of golden sands, rugged cliffs topped with wild flowers and numerous old harbours make Cornwall's north coast one of Britain's most scenic areas. Padstow, a town of narrow, crooked streets lined with quaint inns and shops, is an ideal touring base. Originally built in the 1800s as the Customs and Excise building, this listed house occupies a fine position on Padstow's quayside. Most of the bedrooms overlook the harbour and the Camel estuary; all are decorated and equipped to a high standard. The bars have been refurbished in keeping with the building's character, and there is also a pleasant conservatory lounge.

Restaurant: Situated in the old grain warehouse, the dining room offers à la carte and table d'hôte menus. Lunch and evening meals are served in the public bar, where children are welcome in a large family area. **Nearby:** Guests can walk the Coastal Path which passes through Padstow, discover the legend of King Arthur at Tintagel or visit the beautiful stately homes and gardens in the vicinity. Water sports can be enjoyed locally including golf at Trevose and St Enodoc, surfing at Polzeath and sailing in the estuary. **Directions: Entering Padstow, follow the signs for the quay.**

For hotel location, see maps on pages 180–186

JUBILEE INN

PELYNT, NR LOOE, CORNWALL PL13 2JZ
TEL: 01503 220312 FAX: 01503 220920

OWNERS: Tim and Judith Williams
P.A: Pam Dawson
HEAD CHEF & GENERAL MANAGER: Peter Catnach

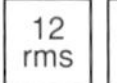  

S: £33–£35
D: £56–£60

Inn: The Jubilee has been an inn since the 16th century, changing its name from The Axe in 1887 to mark the 50th anniversary of Queen Victoria's accession. The low beamed ceilings, open hearths and old prints create an air of tradition and charm throughout. The bedrooms are tastefully furnished in a cottage style; three are for families and one is a bridal suite with a spiral staircase designed by a well-known West Country artist. With a residents' lounge, three bars, a beer garden, plus a large garden with a children's play area and volley-ball net, there are plenty of places to relax. Barbecues are held in the summer. Special breaks arranged. **Restaurant:** An impressive à la carte menu and friendly, professional service are offered in the dining room. The inn's speciality is fish and shellfish, which come straight off the boats in nearby Looe. An extensive bar menu and traditional Sunday lunches are also on offer. **Nearby:** The Duchy of Cornwall nurseries, several National Trust Properties and Dobwalls Adventure Park and Monley Sanctuary are just a selection of the many interesting places to visit. Bodmin Moor, numerous picturesque villages and beautiful coastline are all to be explored. **Directions: From Plymouth, cross Tamar Bridge and follow the main road to Looe. Leave Looe on the Polperro road and turn right for Pelynt.**

For hotel location, see maps on pages 180–186

THE WHITE HORSE INN

SUTTON, NR PULBOROUGH, WEST SUSSEX RH20 1PS
TEL: 01798 869221 FAX: 01798 869291

OWNERS: Howard and Susie Macnamara
MANAGERS: Joss and Val Maude

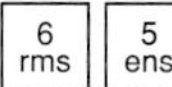

6 rms 5 ens

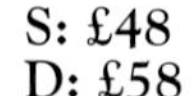

S: £48
D: £58

Inn: This privately owned inn has offered rest and comfort to both travellers and locals since 1746. Howard and Susie MacNamara have restored the traditions of the inn by making available six pretty rooms which are comfortably furnished and appointed with modern amenities. The double-bedded rooms have king-size beds and most of the rooms have spacious en suite bathrooms. All bedrooms have tea and coffee making facilities and colour TV. There is also an attractive garden cottage; however, unlike the other bedrooms this does not have a direct-dial telephone. Managers Joss and Val Maude are always on hand to offer a warm and friendly welcome.

Restaurant: The White Horse is a popular place to eat, both with locals and patrons from further afield. Fresh wholesome food is always featured on the menu. The three-course table d'hôte dinner with coffee is very reasonably priced. **Nearby:** Amberley Chalk Pits, horseracing at Goodwood, the harbour town of Chichester, Arundel Castle, Petworth House, Parham House and Gardens, and the Roman Villa at Bignor. **Directions: Sutton is a little hamlet situated between A29 (Pulborough to Arundel road) and A285 (Petworth to Chichester road). Look for brown sign to Roman Villa at Bignor – Sutton is a mile further west.**

For hotel location, see maps on pages 180–186

THE WHITE SWAN

THE MARKET PLACE, PICKERING, NORTH YORKSHIRE YO18 7AA
TEL: 01751 472288 FAX: 01751 472288

OWNER: Deirdre Buchanan

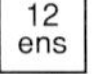

S: £55–£58
D: £76–£80
Suite: £98

Inn: Deirdre Buchanan and her staff will welcome you warmly into this charming small hotel. The well-appointed bedrooms are presented to a high standard with attractive fabrics and colour co-ordinated soft furnishings. The Ryedale Suite features a half-tester bed, Edwardian furnishings and an air-bath to help induce a feeling of contentment after a busy day. The décor throughout the inn is in country cottage style: there are frilled drapes and cushion coverings in the public rooms, and numerous brass tankards hanging from the beamed ceiling of the bar. Here guests can settle in front of the open log fire and peruse the menu at leisure. **Restaurant:** Deirdre Buchanan is a *Dame de la Jurande de Saint Emilion*, so the wines are guaranteed to be of exceptional quality. There are over 200 bins on the wine list including 70 St Emilions. Fresh market produce forms the basis of the menus which are changed daily. The new Bistro is open at lunch and dinner time for a more informal meal. It is an ideal venue for small business meetings. Special two and three day breaks, Christmas shopping breaks and wine, golf and bridge weekends available. **Nearby:** The North York Moors Railway, Beck Isle Museum, which contains an exhibition of local history and folk culture, and golf at Kirkbymoorside. **Directions: From York: take the A64 from the Malton bypass to Pickering. From the A1 North (or the A19), go via the A170 from Thirsk (up Sutton Bank).**

For hotel location, see maps on pages 180–186

THE PORT GAVERNE HOTEL

NR PORT ISAAC, NORTH CORNWALL PL29 3SQ
TEL: 01208 880244 FAX: 01208 880151 FREEPHONE 0500 657867

OWNER: Midge Ross

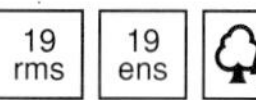

S: £45–£49
D: £90–£98

Inn: Port Gaverne Hotel is situated on the North Cornwall Coastal Path in a secluded cove half a mile from the old fishing village of Port Isaac. Much of the surrounding area is supervised by the National Trust. The 350-year-old hotel is owned and managed by Midge Ross and its character owes as much to the skills and materials of local tradesmen as it does to the dedication of its proprietress. Bedrooms are cosy and well appointed, with direct dial telephone and TV. The residents' lounge never fails to woo guests with its old-world personality. **Restaurant:** At Port Gaverne Hotel chef Ian Brodey and his staff have built up an international reputation for fine cuisine with delicious seafood dishes and a vegetarian menu. It was recently awarded an AA rosette. The hotel is also noted for its 'Breather' weekends in autumn and winter and its self-contained 18th century cottages. **Nearby:** Walk the coastal path in either direction for National Trust countryside in abundance. There is safe, sheltered swimming within seconds of the hotel door. Visit: Delabole Slate Quarry, Boscastle, Tintagel, Bodmin and Polzeath. **Directions: Port Gaverne is signposted from the B3314 south of Delabole and is reached along the B3267. Follow the signs for Port Gaverne only (not Port Isaac).**

For hotel location, see maps on pages 180–186

The Harbour Inn

COMMERCIAL ROAD, PORTHLEVEN, NR HELSTON, CORNWALL TR13 9JD
TEL: 01326 573876

OWNERS: St Austell Brewery & Co Ltd
MANAGERS: David and Wendy Morton
CHEF: Brian Mortimore

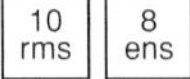

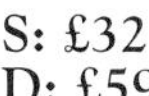

S: £32
D: £59

Inn: Overlooking Porthleven's picturesque quayside, The Harbour Inn is popular with locals and visitors alike. Characterised by flag-stoned floors, beams and wood panelling, the bar retains the atmosphere of an old fishermen's pub. Good-value accommodation, friendly service and traditional surroundings are assured. Most bedrooms overlook the harbour and all have pastel décor with stripped pine furnishings. On the first floor there is a comfortable lounge. ETB 3 Crowns Commended, AA 2 Stars. **Restaurant:** Not surprisingly, imaginative seafood dishes are a speciality of the à la carte menus. Starters include squid, king prawns and poached scallops, followed by main courses such as swordfish, sharksteak or monkfish flamed with brandy in a cream sauce. All meals are well presented and complemented by a good choice of wines and ales. Bar meals are also available. Live entertainment most Saturdays. **Nearby:** Fine beaches, open moorland, wooded estuaries, undulating sand dunes and rugged cliffs can all be found in the area. For skin-divers King Arthur's sword is said to be lying at the bottom of Loe Pool near Penrose. Penzance, Falmouth, the north coast and the beauty spots of The Lizard peninsula are a short car journey away. Facilities for riding, tennis, fishing and many types of water sport are nearby. **Directions: Via Truro take the A39 to Falmouth, then follow signs to Helston. Porthleven is signposted.**

For hotel location, see maps on pages 180–186

YE HORN'S INN

HORN'S LANE, GOOSNARGH, NR PRESTON, LANCASHIRE PR3 2FJ
TEL: 01772 865230 FAX: 01772 864299

OWNERS: Mark Woods and Elizabeth Jones

6 rms | 6 ens

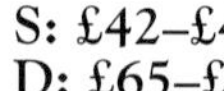

S: £42–£45
D: £65–£70

Inn: A striking black-and-white timbered building standing at a crossroads in lovely rolling countryside, Ye Horn's radiates charm and atmosphere. Built in 1782 as a coaching inn, the hotel has been run by the Woods family for 40 years. Today it is expertly managed by Elizabeth Jones, her brother Mark Woods and his wife Denise, offering first-rate accommodation for both business visitors and the holiday-maker. The 6 spacious bedrooms, all en suite, are in the adjoining barn – a recent conversion – and are stylishly furnished as well as spotlessly clean. All offer tea and coffee-making facilities, trouser press and hairdryer. Oak beams, sumptuous carpets and, in winter, open fires, combine to create a mood of cosy, relaxed hospitality throughout.

Restaurant: The restaurant has earned a fine reputation for its delicious traditional cuisine, prepared wherever possible from fresh, local produce and served in the main dining room or the 'snug' next to it. Specialities include home-made soup, roast duckling, roast pheasant and a truly addictive sticky toffee pudding. Full English or Continental breakfasts are also available daily. **Nearby:** Chingle Hall, a haunted house, Beacon Fell Country Park, the Ribble Valley, the Forest of Bowland and Blackpool. **Directions: Exit M6 junction 32, take A6 north to first traffic lights. Turn right onto the B5269 signposted Longridge, to just past Goosnargh village shops. Where the road veers sharply right, continue: the hotel is signposted after a few minutes.**

For hotel location, see maps on pages 180–186

Quorn Grange

88 WOOD LANE, QUORN, LEICESTERSHIRE LE12 8DB
TEL: 01509 412167 FAX: 01509 415621

OWNER: Jeremy Lord
MANAGER: Gary Bland
CHEF: Gerard Stacey-Midgley

S: £60–£75
D: £75–£90

Inn: Ivy-clad Quorn Grange, built in the 1880s as a family residence, is now owned and run as a country house hotel and restaurant by the Lord family of Queniborough Hall. In keeping with the public rooms, the bedrooms are decorated in excellent taste, and many have fine, countryside views. For guests' relaxation, the hotel has a spacious conservatory furnished with cane, plus a beautifully landscaped garden. Superb facilities are available for private parties and banquets, ranging from the intimate Oak Panel Room to the Goodacre Suite seating up to 130 guests. **Restaurant:** Quorn Grange has a reputation for providing relaxed, efficient service and good, modern English cuisine. Chef Gerard Stacey-Midgley changes his à la carte menu every month, always creating innovative dishes using fresh, seasonal produce. The cellar is well stocked with many fine wines. **Nearby:** With Charnwood Forest and the rolling Leicestershire countryside there is plenty to explore. Nottingham and Belvoir Castles, Nottingham itself and the old Roman city of Leicester are easily accessible. Many activites, such as riding, can be arranged for guests. **Directions: Situated off the old A6 road between the university towns of Loughborough and Leicester. Some maps still describe Quorn as Quorndon.**

For hotel location, see maps on pages 180–186

THE MILBURN ARMS HOTEL

ROSEDALE ABBEY, PICKERING, NORTH YORKSHIRE YO18 8RA
TEL: 01751 417312 FAX: 01751 417312

OWNERS: Terry and Joan Bentley
CHEF: Andrew Pern

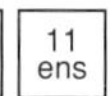

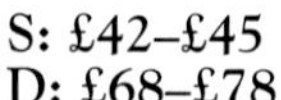

S: £42–£45
D: £68–£78

Inn: Situated in the village of Rosedale Abbey amid superb scenery in the heart of the North Yorks National Park, The Milburn Arms is a stone-built hotel dating back to the 14th century. Owners Terry and Joan Bentley provide a friendly welcome for their guests. Low beams, log fires and comfortable sofas make for a cosy atmosphere in the public rooms and there is an interesting collection of books. The 11 individually designed bedrooms, some exceptionally spacious, are prettily decorated and all have en suite bathrooms with complimentary toiletries. Facing the village green is a large front garden with lawns, flower beds and mature trees and from the patio at the back there are views of Rosedale and the surrounding hills. **Restaurant:** Terry and Joan appreciate the importance of fine food and wine as part of an enjoyable stay and the restaurant has won 2 AA Rosettes for its excellent cuisine. The à la carte menu changes monthly and uses fresh fish from Whitby and local game in season, and there is a carefully selected wine list. In addition, excellent bar meals are available every lunchtime and evening. Special breaks available. **Nearby:** The moors are literally on the doorstep, and the city of York and the coast not far away. Historic sites worth a visit include Rievaulx Abbey and Castle Howard. **Directions: From the A170 Thirsk– Scarborough road turn north at Wrelton following signs to Rosedale Abbey. The village is seven miles further; the hotel is in the centre of the village.**

For hotel location, see maps on pages 180–186

The Golden Lion Inn Of Easenhall

EASENHALL, NR RUGBY, WARWICKSHIRE CV23 0JA
TEL: 01788 832265 FAX: 01788 832878

OWNERS: James and Claudia Austin
CHEF:Mark Turner

4 rms 4 ens

S: £36–£38.50
D: £44–£48.50

Inn: The Golden Lion, dating back to the 16th century, is set back from the main road through Easenhall, a delightful English village not far from Rugby, and ideal for parents visiting the celebrated boarding school. It has low oak beamed ceilings, narrow doorways and uneven floors which all add to its charm, and guests receive a traditional warm welcome. The small bar is proud of its best ales, fine wines and wide range of spirits. Delicious snacks are available both at lunchtime and in the evening. The bedrooms are extremely comfortable, quite spacious, with attractive cottage furniture. There are also kennels for visiting dogs.

Restaurant: The restaurant is divided into two rooms and specialises in country cooking. In summer guests can eat al fresco in the garden and patio, where barbecues are often held, sometimes joined by the pet donkey. **Nearby:** Guests can enjoy village cricket or go further afield to Coventry Cathedral, Coombe Abbey or Warwick Castle. The NEC Birmingham and Stoneleigh Agricultural Centre are in easy reach too. There are excellent golf courses in the neighbourhood. **Directions: Easenhall is reached from the M6 junctions 1/2, taking the B4112 off the A426 for Rugby or the A427 from the Coventry by-pass.**

For hotel location, see maps on pages 180–186

THE MERMAID INN

MERMAID STREET, RYE, EAST SUSSEX TN31 7EU
TEL: 01797 223065 FAX: 01797 225069

OWNERS: The Mermaid Inn Ltd
MANAGER: Robert Pinwill
CHEF: Brian Murray

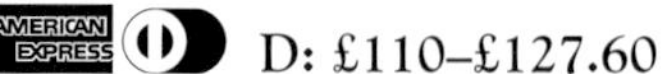

D: £110–£127.60

Inn: A smugglers' inn, rebuilt in 1420, which won the 1973 Queen's Award to Industry for Export Achievements. The Mermaid, one of England's oldest and loveliest inns, stands in a cobbled street in Rye, a town full of history, a member of the famous Cinque Ports since 1156, and more recently visited by H.M The Queen Mother. The inn is flourishing under new ownership and benefiting from discreet modernisation, merging modern comfort and high standards with timbered rooms and roaring fires in the winter! Five of the bedrooms, with mullioned windows overlooking the town, have four-poster beds. All are en suite or have private bathrooms and include six family; rooms. There are two pleasant lounges for residents' use. **Restaurant:** The delectable restaurant menu is based on fresh local food, especially the fish, fruit and vegetables. Fine wines are available while the bar sells draught traditional beers. **Nearby:** There are many famous golf courses in the area; fishing, water sports, tennis and riding are available. Ypres Tower is a short walk away, while Battle, Bodiam and Hastings are within driving distance. **Directions: Rye is located east of Hastings on the A259. From London or M25 take the A21 south then A268. Mermaid Street is at the centre of the ancient town.**

For hotel location, see maps on pages 180–186

The White Hart Hotel

CHURCH STREET, ST AUSTELL, CORNWALL PL25 4AT
TEL: 01726 72100 FAX: 01726 74705

OWNERS: St Austell Brewery & Co Ltd
MANAGERS: David and Christina Walker
CHEF: Geoffrey Mansfield

18 rms | 18 ens

S: £40–£45
D: £65–£70

Inn: The White Hart Hotel has stood in Church Street since 1735. Visitors in the early part of this century included the Duke and Duchess of Cornwall in 1909, and later King George V and Queen Mary, who were touring the West Country. Although it has seen many changes over the years, The White Hart continues a tradition of good food, comfortable accommodation and a friendly welcome. The bedrooms are well furnished and the lounges spacious with plenty of room to relax with friends. St Austell Ales are served at the bar – they are known for a fresh, clean, well-fermented taste. Special breaks are available out of season. Ample parking nearby. **Restaurant:** A reasonably price table d'hôte menu is served between 7pm and 9pm. The choice includes a roast of the day, fresh locally caught fish as available and vegetarian dishes. A separate bar menu is available daily. Buffet menus can be provided for business lunches and private parties – a large conference room is available for such functions. **Nearby:** Charlestown (TV locations for *The Onedin Line and Poldak*), Whealmartyn Museum, Mevagissey and the Cornish coast with its fishing villages and sandy bays. Sea and river fishing, a variety of water-sports and riding can be arranged locally. **Directions: Approach St Austell on the A390. At the third roundabout follow the town centre exit which will take you to the rear of the hotel.**

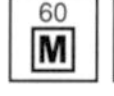

The Rising Sun

THE SQUARE, ST MAWES, CORNWALL TR2 5DJ
TEL: 01326 270233

OWNER: St Austell Brewery & Co Ltd
MANAGERS: Colin and Jacqui Phillips

S: £54–£71
D: £76–£91

Inn: At the Rising Sun, guests can enjoy a waterside location overlooking the harbour in the heart of St Mawes. The bedrooms offer comfortable accommodation and the sea-facing rooms command fine views. With two choices of bar – a conservatory lounge bar and a public bar – and a cosy residential lounge, The Rising Sun has plenty of places for relaxation. Special Christmas and New year breaks are available. **Restaurant:** Wild woodland mushrooms with garlic and herbs, and a tresse of salmon and turbot on a saffron sauce are samples of the delicious dishes offered for dinner. The chef makes good use of the area's rich supply of seafood when compiling the à la carte or table d'hôte menu. Lunchtime snacks and evening meals are also available from the bar menu. An extensive wine list carries a varied selection of French, German and New World wines. **Nearby:** St Mawes is situated on the tip of the picturesque Roseland Peninsula, overlooking the estuary of the River Fal. The Rising Sun makes a good base for exploring Cornwall's dramatic coastline and picturesque villages. **Directions: Take A30, then follow signs to Truro via A39 when leaving Fraddon. Soon after joining A390 turn left to A3078 to St Mawes.**

For hotel location, see maps on pages 180–186

The Old Bell Inn Hotel

HUDDERSFIELD ROAD, DELPH, NR OLDHAM, SADDLEWORTH, GREATER MANCHESTER OL3 5EG
TEL: 01457 870130 FAX: 01457 876597

OWNERS: Philip and Judith Grew
MANAGER: Susan Doherty

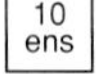

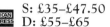

S: £35–£47.50
D: £55–£65

Inn: Many famous figures from the past, including Queen Victoria and Charles Dickens, have visited this stone-built, 18th century inn, which acquired its current name under the tenancy of William Bell. Today's guests are offered attractive accommodation in furnished and well-equipped bedrooms. A number of rooms have four-poster beds – perfect for a romantic weekend. Old beams, open fires and lead lattice windows create a cosy atmosphere in the bar and comfortable residents' lounge. Private parties for up to 40 can be catered for. **Restaurant:** An imaginative menu is changed seasonally to offer plenty of choice and variety. Guests can try, for example, venison steak with black cherry and purée of chestnut sauce. A separate vegetarian menu is always provided. For less formal occasions, meals are also served in the bar. **Nearby:** The village of Delph, with its weavers, cottages and cobbled side-streets still a reminder of its cloth-making history, lies on the edge of the Peak District National Park and Saddleworth Moor – an area of great natural beauty. Places to visit include Castle Shaw Roman Fort, Huddersfield canal where boat trips can be taken, Dovestones Reservoir with its watersports and the art and craft centre at Uppermill. Various golf courses are nearby. Special weekend rates are available on request. **Directions: The Old Bell Inn is on the A62 Oldham–Huddersfield road, in the village of Delph.**

For hotel location, see maps on pages 180–186

MILFORD HALL HOTEL AND RESTAURANT

206 CASTLE STREET, SALISBURY, WILTSHIRE SP1 3TE
TEL: 01722 417411 FAX: 01722 419444

OWNERS: Graham Fitch and Pamela Bruford
MANAGER: Mark Robertson-Walker
CHEF: William Culley

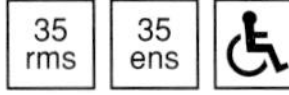

S: £42.50–£45
D: £55–£67.50

Inn: A thoughtful mix of old and new is the distinguishing feature of Milford Hall, a Georgian house built in the 1780s. This family run hotel has been sensitively restored and extended to create an intimate ambience. The warmth and comfort of traditional English hospitality awaits its guests and the proprietors pride themselves on offering both every modern facility and also value for money. There are four pretty bedrooms in the main house, while the remainder are situated in the modern extension with two designed with the disabled guest in mind. All offer a full range of facilities. The gardens of the old house have been re-landscaped to blend the established avenues of limes with newly planted lawns, shrubberies and flower beds. **Restaurant:** Guests can enjoy three types of cuisine at Milford Hall: à la carte, tablé d'hôte or barmeals. The food is very good, AA Rosette for cuisine gained, the surroundings elegant and the prices realistic. **Nearby:** Salisbury is an ideal centre for touring Wiltshire's sweeping downlands and Hampshire's New Forest, for visiting historic houses such as Wilton and Longleat, and ancient monuments such as Stonehenge, Avebury and Old Sarum. **Directions: Milford Hall is a few hundred yards from the conjunction of Castle Street, the main A30 ring road around Salisbury and the A345 Amesbury Road.**

For hotel location, see maps on pages 180–186

EAST AYTON LODGE COUNTRY HOTEL & RESTAURANT

MOOR LANE, FORGE VALLEY, EAST AYTON, SCARBOROUGH, NORTH YORKSHIRE YO13 9EW
TEL: 01723 864227 FAX: 01723 862680

OWNERS: Brian and Karry Gardner
CHEF: Brian Gardner

S: £40–£50
D: £55–£90

Inn: This small elegant hotel stands in its own three acres of well kept gardens, in the North Yorkshire Moors National Park, close to the River Derwent. The chef-patron and his fellow proprietor have created a beautifully appointed hotel, lovingly furnished and decorated, overlooking the spectacular countryside. The reception rooms include a charming residents' lounge and a most attractive bar, very well-stocked, serving a good selection of bar snacks. Morning coffee is available. The bedrooms range from four-poster honeymoon suites to family rooms. All are en suite and thoughtfully equipped. **Restaurant:** The three dining rooms make private functions possible without intruding on diners enjoying the excellent table d'hote menu or spoiling themselves with the superb à la carte choice. Vegetarians get a choice of eight dishes each day! The wine list extends from reasonably priced house wine through to a marvellous vintage château collection. **Nearby:** There are eight golf courses nearby, and forest trails for walkers. Troutsdale, Langdale and the Forge Valley, while a short drive leads to Castle Howard, historic York and pretty Thornton-le-Dale. **Directions: East Ayton is on the A170 Scarborough–Pickering road. The hotel is 1/4 mile up the Forge Valley road.**

For hotel location, see maps on pages 180–186

THE WALNUT TREE

WEST CAMEL, NR SHERBORNE, SOMERSET BA22 7QW
TEL: 01935 851292 FAX: 01935 851292

OWNERS: Peter and Georgina Ball

S: £45
D: £60

Inn: In a delightful Somerset village with it's tranquil setting stands The Walnut Tree. The charming newly renovated en suite bedrooms will satisfy the demanding criteria of todays traveller, with finishing touches of toiletries, hairdryers, trouser-presses, colour TV and telephones. There are three new bedrooms to be completed by the end of the year. **Restaurant:** Imaginative food is served in the charming candle-lit dining room, which has a marvellous ambience. Alternatively, relax and eat in the delightful lounge bar. The Walnut Tree has a fine reputation for its cuisine and has been n the Egon Ronay's guide for two successive years. Also in the 'Which' book for inns. For the discerning walker the 'Leyland Trail' passes through the village of West Camel. For the golfer there are six courses within the area. There are plenty of places to visit locally. The Fleet Air Arm Museum at Yeovilton, Hayes Motor Museum at Sparkford and historic the town of Sherborne and its Abbey. **Nearby:** Cheddar Gorge, Wookey Hole, Longleat House Safari Park, Glastonbury, Stourhead Gardens, the ancient city of Wells, Montacute House, Stonehenge and Cricket St Thomas' Wildlife Park. The Inn is also very convenient for both the coasts of Weymouth and Lyme Regis. **Directions: Follow A303 past Sherborne turnoff (A359) West Camel is between the Sparkford roundabout and the turning signed for the Yeovilton Airbase.**

For hotel location, see maps on pages 180–186

THE LAMB INN

SHIPTON-UNDER-WYCHWOOD, OXFORDSHIRE OX7 6DQ
TEL/FAX: 01993 830465

OWNERS: Luciano and Vivien Valenta
MANAGER: Robert Ansell
CHEF: Robin Bancroft

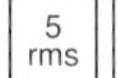  

S: £58
D: £75

Inn: Although it has been a hostelry for several hundred years, this inviting inn has lost none of its charm. It is situated on the outskirts of a delightful Cotswold village and has much to recommend it. The Lamb Bar has log fires and serves real ales, a carefully selected range of single malted whiskies, plus a choice of apéritifs and liqueurs. Bar meals are served during the day and evenings, and there is a lunchtime buffet. The bedrooms, which offer every comfort, are tastefully furnished with character in traditional period style. The proprietors offer everyone a friendly welcome, making this a most pleasant place to stay. **Restaurant:** Chef Robin Bancroft has a fastidious approach to quality and presentation. The restaurant offers fresh fish from Cornwall, ducks from Minster Lovell, seasonally available game and carefully chosen beef, lamb and fresh vegetables. Specialities include Wychwood chicken – boned chicken stuffed with asparagus, sliced and served with tarragon mayonnaise. There is a wine list of over 50 bins. Private parties and receptions for up to 30 people can be accommodated. Closed on Mondays. **Nearby:** The Cotswolds, Blenheim Palace, Oxford and Cheltenham are just a few of the places to see. **Directions: The Lamb is on the A361 near Shipton-under-Wychwood, between Burford and Chipping Norton.**

THE SHAVEN CROWN HOTEL

HIGH STREET, SHIPTON-UNDER-WYCHWOOD, OXFORDSHIRE OX7 6BA
TEL: 01993 830330 FAX: 01993 830330

OWNERS: Mr and Mrs J. Brookes
MANAGER: Justin Brookes

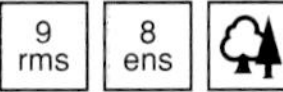

S: £33
D: £66–£82

Inn: Built of honey-coloured stone around an attractive central courtyard, The Shaven Crown Hotel dates back to the 14th century, when it served as a monks' hospice. The proprietors, the Brookes family, have preserved the inn's many historic features, such as the medieval hall with its ancient timbered roof. This is now the residents' lounge. Each of the bedrooms has en suite facilities and has been sympathetically furnished in a style befitting its own unique character. Rooms of various style and sizes are available, includeing a huge family room and ground-floor accommodation. **Restaurant:** Dining in thr intimate, candle-lit room is an enjoyable experience, with meals served at the tables beautifully laid with fine accessories. The best ingredients are combined to create original dishes with a cosmopolitan flair. The table d'hôte menu offers a wide and eclectic choice with a daily vegetarian dish amoung the specialities. An imaginative selection of dishes is offered every lunchtime and evening in the buttery bar. **Nearby:** The Shaven Crown is ideal for day trips to the Cotswolds, Oxford, Stratford-upon-Avon and Bath. There are three golf courses and tennis courts close by. Trout fishing and antiques hunting are popular activities in the area. **Directions: Take the A40 Oxford–Cheltenham road. At Burford follow the A361 towards Chipping Norton. The inn is situated directly opposite the village green in Shipton-under-Wychwood.**

For hotel location, see maps on pages 180–186

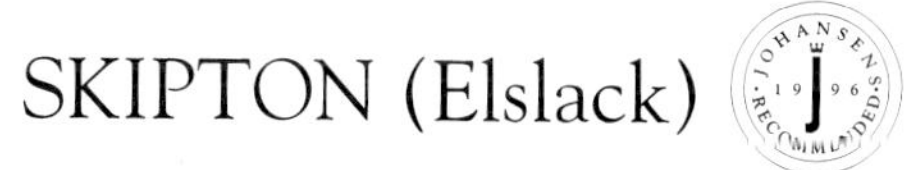

The Tempest Arms

ELSLACK, NR SKIPTON, NORTH YORKSHIRE BD23 3AY
TEL: 01282 842450 FAX: 01282 843331

OWNERS: Francis and Patricia Boulongne
MANAGERS: Jez and Helen Phipps
CHEF: Diane Thompson

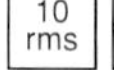

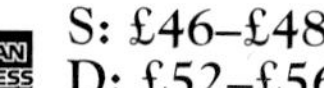

S: £46–£48
D: £52–£56

Inn: A 200-year-old Yorkshire-stone building, The Tempest Arms is situated between the old market towns of Skipton and Earby, surrounded by glorious open countryside and bordered by a stream. The atmosphere of the hotel is welcoming and relaxed, with a bar that is popular with both residents and locals. A hobby of the French owner is to collect 'frogs' and now he has over 500 featured around the hotel. Guest accommodation comprises ten bedrooms, offering a choice of double, family and twin-bedded rooms, all furnished to a high standard. Each room is equipped with en suite bathroom and shower, telephone, TV and tea and coffee making facilities. **Restaurant:** The à la carte Bonaparte Restaurant has earned a reputation for serving food that is delicious and varied. Fresh fish is a particular speciality, imaginatively cooked and well presented. Bar meals are available every lunch and dinnertime. Meetings, weddings and private functions can be catered for in the Pickhill Barn with its own garden. **Nearby:** The Yorkshire Dales, Pennine Way, Bolton Abbey, Ilkley Moor, Brontë country and York are an easy drive from the hotel. Hot-air ballooning is among the activities that can be arranged for guests. Two nights or more Yorkshire special breaks available. **Directions: Located on the A56, five miles equidistant between Skipton and Earby. Turn left from A56 to Elslack; hotel is just over the bridge.**

For hotel location, see maps on pages 180–186

TREE TOPS COUNTRY HOUSE RESTAURANT AND HOTEL

SOUTHPORT OLD ROAD, FORMBY, NR SOUTHPORT, MERSEYSIDE L37 0AB
TEL: 01704 879651 FAX: 01704 879651

OWNER: Mrs Lesley Winsland
MANAGER: John Barrington-Fortune
CHEF: David Oaks

S: £44–£60
D: £60–£78

Inn: The Former Dower House of Formby Hall, Tree Tops still retains all the elegance of a bygone age, set in five acres of lawns and woods. Over the last 11 years, the Winsland family have restored the house to its true glory and have installed all the modern conveniences sought after by today's visitor. Spacious accommodation is available in well-appointed en suite lodges with all the facilities a discerning guest would expect. An outdoor-heated swimming pool has direct access to the sumptuously decorated Cocktail Lounge. Rich, dark leather seating, oynx-and-gilt tables, and subtle lighting all contribute to the overall ambience, complemented by a truly welcoming and friendly staff. **Restaurant:** Highly polished Regency furnishings, silver tableware and crystal chandeliers set the scene for culinary delights involving. Using only the finest fresh ingredients. The new conservatory resturant has a totally relaxed atmosphere with a superb new à la carte menu serving modern and interesting dishes together with a special snack selection. **Nearby:** Tree Tops is only seven minutes' drive from Southport with its sweeping sands, and 20 minutes from Liverpool. Ten golf courses can be found within a five mile radius, including six championship courses. **Directions: From the M6 take the M58 and follow to its end. At roundabout follow signs to Bootle, then Formby. Follow A565 towards Southport, bypassing Formby, turn right at bollards to Tree Tops.**

For hotel location, see maps on pages 180–186

THE STONOR ARMS

STONOR, NR HENLEY-ON-THAMES, OXFORDSHIRE RG9 6HE
TEL: 01491 638345 FAX: 01491 638863

OWNERS: Stonor Hotels Ltd
MANAGER: Stephen Frost

S: £85
D: £95
Suite: £130–£140

Inn: This small hotel is not too far from London, and perfectly located for those going to Henley or Ascot. It is in a pretty village on the edge of Stonor Park and restoration has not diminished its 18th century elegance. The interior of the house has been beautifully decorated in the style of that era, combining grace with comfort. The bedrooms are enchanting, very spacious, furnished with French and English antiques and colourful yet harmonious fabrics. There is also a luxurious suite with its own sitting room. **Restaurant:** For a hotel of this size, guests have the extravagant choice of two dining-rooms. Formal dining takes place in the exquisitely furnished Stonor Restaurant which offers sophisticated English dishes and a distinguished wine list but does not allow pipes or cigars. Lunch and supper can be enjoyed in the more relaxed Blades Conservatory Restaurant, which encompasses the flagstoned bar lounge. Rowing memorabilia on the walls is appropriate to its name. This menu is light-hearted and imaginative, served in the conservatory or even in the garden on warm days. **Nearby:** Windsor and Oxford are easily accessible and sporting activities nearby include boating and golf or walking in the countryside. **Directions: Leave the M40 at junction 6, following B4009 to Watlington, then turn left onto B480 through Stonor.**

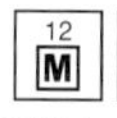

THE KINGS HEAD INN & RESTAURANT

THE GREEN, BLEDINGTON, NR KINGHAM, OXFORDSHIRE OX7 6HD
TEL: 01608 658365 FAX: 01608 658902

OWNERS: Michael and Annette Royce
CHEF: Stephen Coots-Williams

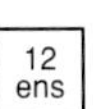

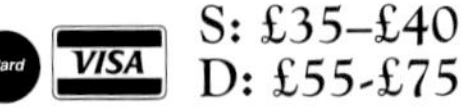

S: £35–£40
D: £55-£75

Inn: The Kings Head Inn and Restaurant is peacefully located beside a traditional village green, complete with a babbling brook inhabited by friendly ducks. During the summer months Morris dancers and musicians can regularly be seen in action on the green performing the Bledington Dances. The building has always served as a hostelry and much of its medieval character remains. With its exposed stone walls, original beams, inglenook fireplace and old settles, the Kings Head fulfils everyone's anticipations of a traditional English inn. The attractive timbered bedrooms, are well furnished to complement the full facilities. **Restaurant:** Activities in the kitchen are supervised by Annette Royce, who has earned the reputation for superbly prepared English and Continental dishes with the 'personal' touch. The carefully compiled à la carte menu is changed daily and is backed up by a selection of fine wines. Excellent inventive bar food is served at lunchtimes and in the evenings together with a changing selection of real ales. **Nearby:** The Kings Head Inn is situated in the heart of the Cotswolds, within easy reach of Oxford, Stratford-upon-Avon, Cheltenham and Blenheim. **Directions: Take the A44 Oxford–Woodstock road to Chipping Norton, then the B4450 to Bledington; or take the Oxford–Burford road to Stow-on-the-Wold and join the B4450. Nearest motorway M40 junction 11.**

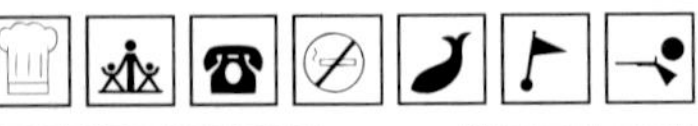

For hotel location, see maps on pages 180–186

THE ROYALIST HOTEL

DIGBETH STREET, STOW-ON-THE-WOLD, GLOUCESTERSHIRE GL54 1BN
TEL: 01451 830670 FAX: 01451 870048

OWNERS: Matthew and Celia Fagg

S: £45–£55
D: £60–£85

Inn: Reputed to be the oldest building in Stow-on-the-Wold, The Royalist Hotel, Grade II* listed, constructed in AD 947, is also credited in the Guinness Book of Records as being the Oldest Inn in England. The original oak framework is still there behind the 17th-century Jacobean façade (carbon-dating testing has established the timbers to be over 1,000 years old) and the 'houris' frieze from Crusading times is one of only two left in the UK. Within this venerable exterior, modern comforts have been judiciously introduced. The hotel is family run and service is friendly and helpful. It is excellent value for money. Bedrooms are spotless, comfortable and centrally heated. Glowing log fires in winter entice guests into the cosy hotel bar to relax over tasty homemade cuisine. There is also a coffee shop on the premises which serves food all day. There is a good choice of restaurants within a few minutes walk from The Royalist Hotel. **Nearby:** the Cotswolds countryside offers year-round opportunities for walking and hiking. Also visit Blenheim Castle, Woodstock, Bourton-on-the-Water, Cirencester and Sudeley and Warwick Castles. **Directions: Stow-on-the-Wold is where the A436, A429 and A424 all intersect. Approaching from Chipping Norton on the A436, the Royalist is on the right in the village centre.**

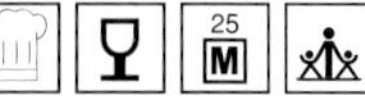

For hotel location, see maps on pages 180–186

BARASET BARN RESTAURANT

PIMLICO LANE, ALVESTON, STRATFORD-UPON-AVON, WARWICKSHIRE CV37 7RE
TEL: 01789 295510 FAX: 01789 292961

PROPRIETORS: Romano Biglirdi and Ermanno Pancaldi

Restaurant: This family-run restaurant, in a brilliant barn conversion overlooking beautiful gardens, is something very special. It is has wooden beams and arches and brick walls. The main restaurant is spacious, so tables are not crowded together, making it perfect for business entertaining. It is overlooked by a superb gallery which can be used for special occasions and which is reached by a carved staircase. The central charcoal grill is in keeping with the ambience. An elegant and original thought is the individual sealed fresh menu for each guest, demonstrating a strong Italian influence in the kitchen. There are set-price meals at lunchtime and in the evening, as well as an extensive à la carte choice. Various pastas feature in the starters, along with international favourites such as gravadlax and escargots. The à la carte menu lists the best of fish dishes – lobster and Dover sole – as well as Tournedos steaks, liver as cooked in Venice, chicken cooked with tarragon and lamb with rosemary. Homemade ice creams follow and five varieties of coffee! The set price meals are excellent value, containing a choice of fish and meat dishes. It is closed on Sunday nights and all day Monday. Lunch is 12.30–2.00 pm and dinner is 7.30–10.00 pm. Convenient for the heatre at Stratford-upon-Avon. **Nearby:** Shakespeare's birthplace and Anne Hathaway's Cottage. **Directions: Leave M40 at Exit 15. Take A429 to Wellesbourne, turn right into B4086.**

CHEF'S SPECIALS

ravioli
with fresh crab filling

fillets of sole à l'americaine
in lobster, cream and brandy sauce

escalopes of veal in Porcini
with wild mushrooms

For restaurant location, see maps on pages 180–186

THE BLUE BOAR INN

TEMPLE GRAFTON, ALCESTER, WARWICKSHIRE B49 6NR
TEL: 01789 750010

Food: The village of Temple Grafton – where William Shakespeare married Anne Hathaway – enjoys a rural setting midway between Stratford-upon-Avon and Alcester. The oldest part of The Blue Boar dates from the early 1600s and records show that it has been an ale house since that time. The onset of the cooler autumn days brings to life the three real log fires in the bar and restaurant area, where as the arrival of spring heralds alfresco meals in the patio garden. Renowned for its fine food, The Blue Boar has a wide-ranging à la carte and international menu catering for all tastes – including vegetarian. A good selection of pub bar meals is served in the bar areas. Produce is delivered daily and prepared in the kitchen to high standards by a team of chefs. The sweet menu changes daily, with all desserts prepared on the morning of service to ensure a home-made flavour. **Wine:** A wide selection of fine wines is available to provide quality and choice in all price ranges. About 40 labels are stocked. Traditional cask-conditioned ales are always available in the bar. **Price:** Full bar lunches and dinners: £15 for two. In the restaurant: lunch £20 for two, dinner £30 for two. **Directions: Three miles from Stratford-upon-Avon, 1/2 mile off the A46 to Alcester. From M40 junction 15 take A46 Stratford bypass (eight miles) and travel towards Alcester. Turn left to Temple Grafton.**

CHEF'S SPECIALS

fillet of stilton
fillet steak with stilton and red wine sauce

vegetable stroganoff
fresh vegetables in a brandy and cream sauce, with parsley and onions served on a bed of rice

chocolate whisky pudding
a rich sweet with chocolate, cherries, walnuts and biscuits, flavoured with whisky

TELFORD (Norton)

THE HUNDRED HOUSE HOTEL

BRIDGNORTH ROAD, NORTON, NR SHIFNAL, TELFORD, SHROPSHIRE TF11 9EE
TEL: 01952 730353 FAX: 01952 730355

OWNERS: The Phillips family

9 rms | 9 ens

S: £59
D: £69–£88

Inn: Character, charm and a warm, friendly atmosphere are guaranteed at this family-run, award-winning inn, situated only 45 minutes' drive from Birmingham International Airport. The bedrooms are attractively furnished with antiques and feature country-style patchwork bed linen and drapes; all guest rooms are fully equipped. There are pretty gardens with a pond, gazebo and herb garden. A special tariff is offered for mid-week and weekend breaks and extra accommodation is available in two cottages in the Ironbridge Gorge. **Restaurants:** The inn enjoys a growing reputation for its varied, interesting à la carte and table d'hôte menus. Home-made English fare such as steak pies and game is offered alongside continental dishes, and sweets range from delicate sorbets to traditional favourites like treacle tart. Bar meals are served daily, alongside a number of real ales. Early booking is recommended as the restaurant is very popular locally. **Nearby:** Severn Valley Railway, Midland Motor Museum, Weston Park, Ironbridge Gorge and Telford are within easy reach. Shifnal's cottages inspired Charles Dickens's *Old Curiosity Shop*. **Directions: Norton is on the A442 Bridgnorth–Telford road.**

For hotel location, see maps on pages 180–186

THE BELL HOTEL

CHURCH STREET, TEWKESBURY, GLOUCESTERSHIRE GL20 5SA
TEL: 01684 293293 FAX: 01684 295938

OWNERS: Peter and Gillian Hands
CHEF: Jason Aldous

25 rms 25 ens

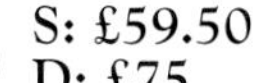
S: £59.50
D: £75

Inn: This half-timbered Inn is a splendid sight as one approaches the centre of the town. It stands opposite Tewkesbury Abbey,and has a long history of offering hospitality right back to the 15th century. Big log fires, oak beams and comfortable furniture welcome guests. The bedrooms have been thoughtfully equipped to meet the demands of the modern traveller and there is a superb Penthouse Suite. The large bar is attractive, with panelled walls and well stocked. It provides an oppportunity for travellers to mingle with the locals. **Restaurant:** The handsome Priory Restaurant has earned its wide reputation for imaginative interpretations of traditional English dishes. There are some 40 wines listed, and six different filter coffees. Designated a non-smoking area, it is open in the evenings and for Sunday lunch. The Chef's Pantry provides informal meals and snacks throughout the day, which are enjoyed in the garden in fine weather. **Nearby:** Tewkesbury has many historic buildings to explore, including the Norman Abbey. Not far away are Sudeley Castle with its lovely gardens and the Saxon walled town of Winchcombe. The Cotswold Hills are wonderful walking country, with views across to the Welsh Mountains and the Bristol Channel. **Directions: Leave the M5 at junction 9, signed Tewkesbury. The hotel is in the town centre and has good car parking.**

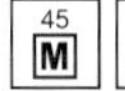

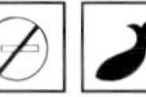

Thatchers Inn

29–30 LOWER HIGH STREET, THAME, OXFORDSHIRE OX9 2AA
TEL: 0184421 2146 FAX: 0184421 7413

CHEF/PATRON: Granville Wood
MANAGER: Kathy Robinson
HEAD CHEF: Jason Berridge

10 rms | 10 ens

S: £49.50–£59.50
D: £70–£85

Inn: A registered, historic Elizabethan building dating from the 1550's located in the market place of Thame in beautiful Oxfordshire. The original main building is a thatched cottage with beamed ceilings, inglenook fireplaces and a wealth of character. The ten uniquely different rooms, all en suite, feature four poster beds and period furnishings. The courtyard, with koi pond, offers a quiet relaxing spot to soothe the travelers soul and revive his spirits. other amenities for relaxation are a Californian style hot tub with Jacuzzi and a sauna. Combine this with first class, friendly, efficient service and you have an oasis in the heart of the country.**Restaurant:** Thatchers offers some of the best fare you will find anywhere in England. The kitchen produces seasonal menus utilising only the freshest of locally raised items. The cuisine is best described as modern English American. A traditional English breakfast is included in your stay or you may choose from the à la carte menu. Lunch is served Monday through Friday with brunch offered on Sunday. The evening menu reflects the true creativity of the chef as he prepares outstanding dishes all at reasonable prices. Patio dining is available during the summer months. **Nearby:** Oxford is just 25 minutes away as are Blenheim Palace and the Rothchilds' estate. Golf, hot-air ballooning, rally driving, fishing and hunting are all at hand. **Directions: Easy access from M40 and the Oxford–Aylesbury road.**

For hotel location, see maps on pages 180–186

Thelbridge Cross Inn

THELBRIDGE, NR WITHERIDGE, DEVON EX17 4SQ
TEL: 01884 860316 FAX: 01884 860316

OWNERS: Bill and Ria Ball
CHEF: Ria Ball

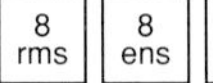

S: £35
D: £60–£75

Inn: An attractive, picturesque family run, country inn situated in glorious mid-Devon. Built of stone and cob with oak beams and log fires it is the perfect base for exploring the Devonshire countryside, Exmoor and Dartmoor are only a short drive away. For those of you who are hopelessy romantic, this inn will definitely appeal. Rumor has it that Lorna Doone passed through Thelbridge in her carriage after being shipwrecked at Porlock. As a former coaching inn, it still fulfils that role today, for it is the only inn left where the original Lorna Doone stage coach still calls, with passengers who stop off to savour Ria's outstanding cuisine. The accommodation is in eight en suite bedrooms all of which are extremely clean and comfortable. The inn boasts wonderful views over both Exmoor and Dartmoor, and for walkers is only a short distance away from the famous Two Moors Way. **Restaurant:** First-time diners soon recognise the reason for the restaurant's popularity, and why it is recommended by Egon Ronay. **Nearby:** From the front of the inn there are views towards Dartmoor while from the rear Exmoor can be seen in the distance. Many outdoor activities can be arranged locally. **Directions: Thelbridge Cross Inn is two miles west of Witheridge on the B3042, reached from M5 junction 27 via A361 and B3137.**

For hotel location, see maps on pages 180–186

GREEN FARM RESTAURANT AND HOTEL

NORTH WALSHAM ROAD, THORPE MARKET, NORFOLK NR11 8TH
TEL: 01263 833602 FAX: 01263 833163

OWNERS: Philip and Dee Dee Lomax

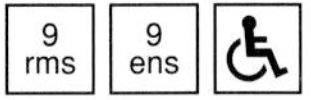

Inn: Green Farm is a delightful 16th century farmhouse inn. A warm, friendly welcome awaits all guests from proprietors Philip and Dee Dee Lomax and their staff. All rooms are en suite and guests will find colour TV, tea and coffee facilities, fresh fruit, flowers and home made chocolates provided for their comfort. Some of the rooms on the ground floor are suitable for disabled guests. **Restaurant:** Bar meals for lunch and dinner are served every day and there is a non-smoking dining room available. Chef-patron Philip Lomax has built up an excellent reputation locally. Many of his dishes are unique to Green Farm: subtle variations on well-loved themes. Try the brie wrapped in filo pastry, deep fried and served with apple and peppercorn sauce, or roast poussin with celery and lemon stuffing with sultana and redcurrant sauce. Many more dishes depend on local produce, such as Cromer crab, shellfish, sea trout and Holkham venison. Weddings can be catered for in the fully lined terraced marquee. Speciality evenings are held monthly at Green Farm and include "Old Time Music Hall" and champagne tasting. **Nearby:** Green Farm is an excellent base for golfers, birdwatchers and those wishing to explore historical Norwich, North Norfolk and its coast and broads. Other attractions include the National Trust properties of Felbrigg, Blickling and Sheringham Park, and the Bure Valley Railway. **Directions: On the A149 four miles from Cromer and from North Walsham.**

For hotel location, see maps on pages 180–186

THE BARN OWL INN

ALLER MILLS, KINGSKERSWELL, TORQUAY, DEVON TQ12 5AN
TEL: 01803 872130 FAX: 01803 875279

OWNERS: Derek and Margaret Warner
CHEF: Denis Le Jette

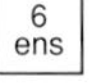
6 rms 6 ens

S: £47.50
D: £60–£75

Inn: The Barn Owl Inn has been converted from a farmhouse into a very good value inn. Although the building dates back to the 16th century, it has modern facilities and services, while retaining many original features, including an inglenook fireplace, an ornate plaster ceiling in the largest bar and a sizeable black-leaded range. Hand-crafted furniture can be found in the cottage-style bedrooms, complimentary bottles of spring water and baskets of fruit. **Restaurant:** The restaurant reflects the talents and eagle eye of French chef, Denis Le Jette. Selecting one's meal from the fascinating menu is a challenge, and the excellent but modestly priced wine list complements the superb dishes. Service is immaculate and the ambience is perfect. There is also a very good bar that serves real ale and excellent food. **Nearby:** Torquay is a holiday town par excellence, and the neighbouring seaside towns of Paignton and Brixham are in easy reach. Local places of interest include Compton Castle, once the home of Sir Walter Raleigh, Dartmoor and the underground caves in Kent's Cavern. Tennis and riding can be enjoyed locally. **Directions: Take the M5 to Exeter, then follow the A380 signposted Torquay. Drive one mile past the Penn Inn traffic lights, and the inn is on the right, signposted Aller Mills.**

THE SEA TROUT INN

STAVERTON, NR TOTNES, DEVON TQ9 6PA
TEL: 01803 762274 FAX: 01803 762506

OWNERS: Andrew and Pym Mogford
CHEF: Iain Baillie

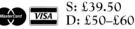

S: £39.50
D: £50–£60

Inn: High in the hills of the Dart Valley, The Sea Trout Inn dates from the 15th century. It was named by a previous landlord who caught such a fish in the nearby River Dart. Several specimens of the prize fish now adorn the inn in showcases. The two bars retain much of their period charm, with uneven floors, exposed oak beams, brass fittings and log fires. The bedrooms are decorated in an attractive cottage style, while the public rooms are cosy and inviting. Angling permits for trout, sea trout and salmon are available and the inn offers special fishing breaks with tuition, as well as Dart weekends. **Restaurant:** The inn's restaurant is highly acclaimed locally and has been mentioned in several guides. Chef Iain Baillie's finely balanced menus are based on the best seasonal produce from local suppliers. Both table d'hôte (£17.50 for three courses including coffee) and à la carte menus are available. **Nearby:** Dartmoor is excellent for walking, fishing and pony-trekking. Local attractions include the Devon coast, the Dart Valley Railway, Buckfast Abbey and Dartington Hall. **Directions: Turn off the A38 on to the A384 at Buckfastleigh (Dartbridge) and follow the signs to Staverton.**

For hotel location, see maps on pages 180–186

The Mortal Man Hotel

TROUTBECK, NR WINDERMERE, CUMBRIA LA23 1PL
TEL: 015394 33193 FAX: 015394 31261

OWNERS: Christopher and Annette Poulsom
CHEF: Frank Nash

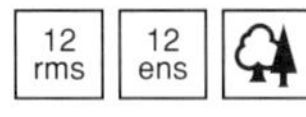

S: £55–£65
D: £110–£125
(including dinner)

Inn: Few country inns can match the spectacular Lakeland position of this 300-year-old hostelry. Lake Windermere is in view from the foot of the Troutbeck Valley, while Grasmere – the home of Wordsworth – and Coniston, where Ruskin lived, are just slightly further away. The inn is an ideal retreat, offering old-fashioned, friendly service in highly traditional surroundings. The interiors have an abundance of beautiful oak beams, panelling, open fires and solid furniture. All of the bedrooms have stunning views of the surrounding countryside and are equipped with every convenience, including hairdryers and trouser presses. **Restaurant:** A super-value, five course table d'hôte menu is presented in the inn's dining room, which affords breath-taking views of the valley. The dishes are all freshly prepared, accompanied by a variety of creative sauces and garnishes. The menu is supported by a well-chosen wine list. Light lunches can be taken in the bar, which has a warm, inviting atmosphere. The hotel is closed from mid-November to mid-February. **Nearby:** The area is a paradise for country lovers, with fells and mountains to explore. Wastwater, overlooked by Scafell and Great Gable, is a short drive away. Guests have complimentary use of a nearby leisure complex, while sailing and pony-trekking facilities are available close by. **Directions: Take the A592 Windemere–Ullswater road. From the roundabout drive for 2½ miles, then turn left to Troutbeck and right at the T-junction. The hotel is on the right.**

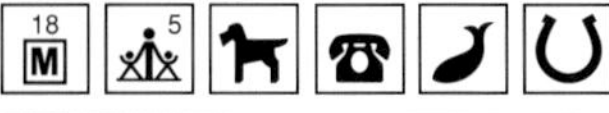

For hotel location, see maps on pages 180–186

THE ROYAL WELLS INN

MOUNT EPHRAIM, TUNBRIDGE WELLS, KENT TN4 8BE
TEL: 01892 511188 FAX: 01892 511908

OWNERS: David and Robert Sloan
CHEF: Robert Sloan

19 rms | 19 ens

S: £55–£60
D: £65–£100

Inn: With a commanding position overlooking Tunbridge Wells Common, just a short walk from the town centre, the Royal Wells is a small, traditional family-run hotel. The inn owes its regal name to Queen Victoria, who visited it frequently as a young princess, and it still carries the royal coat of arms today. There are 19 comfortable en suite bedrooms, all centrally heated and with period furniture and four-poster beds. Guests may enjoy afternoon tea or a pre-dinner drink in the main bar, or a bar meal in the Wells Brasserie surrounded by motoring memorabilia – the hotel owns a 1909 Commer bus once owned by Lord Lonsdale, founder of the Automobile Association. **Restaurant:** A meal in the conservatory restaurant, with its intimate lounge bar, is sure to be one of the highlights of a stay at the Royal Wells. The double attraction of fine food served in delightful surroundings makes it a popular eating place. The three-course menu, based on fresh produce, costs £17.50 and there is also a daily fish speciality. An extensive wine list accompanies the menu. **Nearby:** The inn is an ideal base from which to explore the spa town of Tunbridge Wells, as well as the surrounding countryside of Kent, Surrey and Sussex. Chartwell, Hever Castle and the Bluebell Railway are within easy reach. **Directions: The Royal Wells Inn is situated opposite Tunbidge Wells Common on the section of Mount Ephraim that bypasses the junction of the A26 and the A264.**

For hotel location, see maps on pages 180–186

THE BIRD IN HAND

BATH ROAD, KNOWL HILL, TWYFORD, BERKSHIRE RG10 9UP
TEL: 01628 826622/822781 FAX: 01628 826748

OWNER: Caroline Shone
MANAGERS: Peter and Helen Bland
CHEF: Matthew Green

S: £55–£70
D: £70–£90

Inn: This lovely inn has benefited from being in the same family for three generations. Originally built in the 14th century, it became a famous hostelry when George III, grateful for hospitality following a riding accident, granted it a Royal Charter. Many thoughtful changes have taken place since then, without loss of character, so that today's guests will also wish to give it an accolade. Inside, the oak panelling adds to the warmth generated by the welcoming staff. Big log fires blaze in the winter. The bedrooms face the courtyard and one has been specially designed for guests with mobility problems. Rooms are light and airy, and equipped for today's travellers. There is hand-pumped ale in the spacious Oak Lounge Bar, and the Main Bar offers buffet food for informal eating. **Restaurant:** The elegant restaurant, with an imaginative à la carte menu, has a strong local clientele. It overlooks the courtyard with its fountain – a peaceful spot to enjoy drinks in the summer. There is also the Ashley Room for private celebrations. A wide range of wines is available both in the bars and the restaurant. **Nearby:** Oxford, Windsor and Henley are very accessible, offering historic and riverside attractions. **Directions: The Bird in Hand is just off the A4 between Maidenhead and Reading, leaving the M4 at junction 8/9 or the M40 at junction 4.**

For hotel location, see maps on pages 180–186

THE WHITE LION HOTEL

HIGH STREET, UPTON-UPON-SEVERN, NR MALVERN, WORCESTERSHIRE WR8 0HJ
TEL: 01684 592551 FAX: 01684 592551

OWNERS: Robert and Bridget Withey

10 rms | 10 ens

S: £54.50
D: £74.50

Inn: The Tudor origins of this old coaching inn – once a cockfighting venue – lie behind its Georgian façade. In 1749, Henry Fielding set part of his novel *Tom Jones* here; it has also hosted performances by Sarah Siddons, the famous tragedienne. Much of the inn's former character has been retained in the comfortable, cosy surroundings of the public rooms. The bedrooms, dating from varying periods, are individually designed and furnished to a high standard. Special 2-day breaks are available throughout the year. Closed Christmas and Boxing days. **Restaurant:** The dining room is particularly attractive, providing an intimate setting with candle-lit tables and fine oak-beams. Fresh local produce and home-grown herbs are combined with flair and innovation to produce interesting à la carte and table d'hote menus. The cooking is complemented by a well-balanced and extensive wine list. A wide range of bar meals is also served. **Nearby:** Much of Britain's best-loved countryside, such as the Malvern Hills, the Cotswolds and the Black Mountains, are within easy drive of the inn. Historic towns such as Stratford-upon-Avon, the spa town of Cheltenham and the cathedral city of Gloucester are close by. The inn can supply details of local attractions, including the many National Trust properties in the area. **Directions: From M5 junction 8 follow the M50, then A38 junction 1 travel north. After three miles turn left on to the A4104. Go over the bridge, turn left, then right. The car park is at the rear of the hotel.**

For hotel location, see maps on pages 180–186

The Anchor

WALBERSWICK, SUFFOLK IP18 6UA
TEL: 01502 722112 FAX: 01502 722283

OWNERS: Adnams Hotels Ltd
MANAGER: Kenny Child

S: £40
D: £62–£72

Inn: The original Anchor, a small timber-framed building, was replaced by the present hotel in 1926. Additions, including a cluster of garden rooms, were made in the 1960s creating a somewhat haphazard, but charming, mixture of styles. The five bedrooms within the main hotel vary in size and there are eight more spacious rooms in the garden annexe. The newly refurbished public rooms are simply but comfortably furnished and very welcoming. In the garden of the inn guests are welcome to play croquet or badminton or take tea in the Pavilion. The Anchor is a haven of peace and simplicity, ideal for families, writers and birdwatchers. **Restaurant:** The light and airy dining room, decorated with modern paintings, is a pleasant place to enjoy a restful meal and good wines. Adjacent to it there is a sheltered lawn for eating and drinking out of doors. Excellent snacks and meals are served in the bar, which is hung with paintings of the locality. In chillier months it is warmed by open fires and offers a cosy setting in which to relax. **Nearby:** The village of Walberswick was an ancient settlement and port, with the ruins of a fine 15th century church testifying to its former prosperity. There is a sandy beach nearby, providing safe bathing in shallow water. Places of interest within easy reach include Framlingham Castle, Orford Castle, built by Henry II, and Snape Maltings. **Directions: Take the B1387 off the A12 Ipswich to Lowestoft road.**

Ye Olde Salutation Inn

MARKET PITCH, WEOBLEY, HEREFORDSHIRE HR4 8SJ
TEL: 01544 318443 FAX: 01544 318216

OWNERS: Chris and Frances Anthony
CHEFS: Mark Green and Frances Anthony

5 rms 5 ens

S: £33
D: £56–£62.50

Inn: This black and white timbered inn, an inspired conversion of an ale and cider house and a cottage, over 500 years old, is in the centre of Weobley village. The spire of the 900 year old church is a landmark in the green Herefordshire countryside, as yet undiscovered by tourists. The bedrooms are so individual, with delightful chinzes or patchwork quilts, that returning guests demand their favourite, perhaps one with traditional brass bedsteads or a four-poster. Smoking is not allowed in the bedrooms, but is forgiven in the elegant resident's lounge, with its antiques and big, comfortable furniture. Guests may enjoy the well-equipped fitness room. A self-catering cottage opposite the inn is alternative accommodation.

Restaurant: A non-smoking room, the Oak Room restaurant plays an important role in the inn. Talented chefs prepare sophisticated and aromatic dishes to order, ensuring they arrive fresh at the table. English with a continental accent describes the menu, which refers to puddings as 'the finishing touch'. There is a very well stocked cellar from which to select fine wines. Informal meals are served in the traditonal bar. **Nearby:** Hereford Cathedral, Hay-on-Wye with its antique books, open air Shakespeare at Ludlow Castle, pony-trekking in the Black Mountains and golf. **Directions: Leave Hereford on the A4110, taking the B4320 signed Weobley.**

For hotel location, see maps on pages 180–186

THE WENSLEYDALE HEIFER INN

WEST WITTON, WENSLEYDALE, NORTH YORKSHIRE DL8 4LS
TEL: 01969 622322 FAX: 01969 624183

OWNERS: John and Anne Sharp and Nigel Holdsworth
CHEF: Adrian Craig

S: £44–£49
D: £60–£70
Suites: £85

Inn: Few inns can claim such a beautiful setting as that of The Wensleydale Heifer. This typical Dales inn, dating from 1631, is situated in the tranquil village of West Witton, in the heart of Wensleydale and set against the backdrop of the Yorkshire Dales National Park. The oak-beamed rooms are furnished in chintz, with antiques and log fires to retain the ancient charm of the building. The quaint bedrooms are located in the inn itself and across the road in The Old Reading Room – they are cheerfully decorated, each with its own character. There are two with four-poster beds, as well as a four-poster suite. A private room can be hired for small meetings of up to 10 people. **Restaurant:** Both the informal bistro and the beamed restaurant offer rustic country cooking. Menus are extensive with fresh fish, from sea, river and lake, and shellfish a speciality. All meals are prepared to a high standard. Local produce appears frequently, including trout, Yorkshire pies and sausages and, of course, Wensleydale cheese. There is a good selection of wines to accompany your meal. **Nearby:** Wensleydale is in the heart of James Herriot's famous Dales and offers plenty of opportunities for walking, pony-trekking and other country pursuits. Bolton Castle and the racing stables at Middleham are close by. **Directions: The Wensleydale Heifer is on the A684 trans-Pennine road between Leyburn and Hawes.**

For hotel location, see maps on pages 180–186

THE INN AT WHITEWELL

FOREST OF BOWLAND, CLITHEROE, LANCASHIRE BB7 3AT
TEL: 01200 448222 FAX: 01200 448298

OWNER: Richard Bowman
CHEF: Charles Mumford

S: £49–£55
D: £65–£75
Suite: £95

Inn: An art gallery, wine merchant and shirt maker all share the premises of this friendly, welcoming inn, the earliest parts of which date back to the 14th century. It was at one time inhabited by the Keeper of the 'Forêt' – the Royal hunting ground, and nowadays it is not uncommon for distinguished shooting parties to drop in for lunch. Set within grounds of 3 acres, the inn has a spendid outlook across the dramatically undulating Trough of Bowland. Each bedroom has been attractively furnished with antiques and quality fabrics. All rooms have videos and hi-tech stereo systems. **Restaurant:** The cooking is of a consistently high quality. The à la carte menu features predominately English country recipes such as seasonal roast game with traditional accompaniments: grilled red snapper on a savoury confit, home-made puddings and farmhouse cheeses. Good bar meals and garden lunches are also offered. **Nearby:** 8 miles of water is available to residents only from the banks of the River Hodder, where brown trout, sea trout, salmon and grayling can be caught. Other country sports can be arranged locally. Browsholme Hall and Clitheroe Castle are close by and just across the river there are neolithic cave dwellings. **Directions: From the M6 take junction 32; follow A6 towards Garstang for 1/4 mile. Turn right at first traffic lights towards Longridge, then left at roundabout, then follow signs to Whitewell and Trough of Bowland.**

For hotel location, see maps on pages 180–186

WESLEY HOUSE

THE HIGH STREET, WINCHCOMBE, GLOUSTERSHIRE GL54 5LJ
TEL: 01242 602366 FAX: 01242 602405

OWNERS: Matthew Brown and Jonathan Lewis

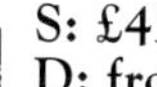

S: £45
D: from £55

Inn: This superb timbered house, in the Saxon town of Winchcombe and dating back to 1435, having been lovingly restored, has many modern amenities without losing its medieval charm. Its name came later, when John Wesley stayed there in 1779. While not spacious the en-suite bedrooms are well designed and characterful. Reserving the Terrace Bedroom will ensure spectacular views across the Cotswolds. The lounge, with its comfortable furnishings and logfire, has a restful feeling. **Restaurant:** Benefiting from the international culinary skills of the Chef/Patron, the restaurant of today attracts guests from a wide area, both for lunch and dinner. Menus are reasonably priced and include some light dishes and salads for those not wanting a full mid-day meal. Special occasions listed are a monthly cookery demonstration and dinner dances. Private celebrations are also possible. **Nearby:** Winchcombe is less than an hour's drive from Oxford and Stratford-upon-Avon. Cheltenham, with its many festivals and race meetings, is 6 miles away. Sudeley Castle is nearby, Golf and riding can be arranged, and help with theatre tickets given. **Directions: Winchcombe is close to the Cheltenham exit of the M5, signposted from the A40 Oxford Road. Wesley House is in the main street, opposite the information centre.**

THE WYKEHAM ARMS

75 KINGSGATE STREET, WINCHESTER, HAMPSHIRE SO23 9PE
TEL: 01962 853834 FAX: 01962 854411

OWNERS: Graeme and Anne Jameson
MANAGER: Doreen Richards
CHEF: Vanessa Booth

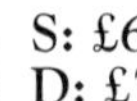

Inn: This inn, in the oldest part of the city between the College and Cathedral, plays an important role in Winchester. It is essentially a local 'pub' while, since the days of Anthony Trollope, it has been a haven for travellers. 150 years later residents are delighted with their charming bedrooms, all available for single occupancy, and equipped with modern facilities. They overlook the peaceful courtyard, in which guests enjoy summer drinks. The ambience downstairs is log fires, candles, real ale and superb food. **Restaurant:** The talented team of chefs changes the menus daily, introducing imagination to traditional English dishes – a rack of Hampshire lamb is served on a bed of apple dauphinoise with a port wine and rosemary jus! Wines and liqueurs are the house speciality, with every wine listed available by the glass – leading to the Wine Pub of the Year Award in 1991. There is a non-smoking area in the restaurant, and a separate breakfast room. **Nearby:** For years the capital of England, this is King Alfred's city, and there is so much history in Winchester to explore. The Cathedral is beautiful. Southampton, with its theatre, is easily reached, as is the New Forest. Sportsmen can enjoy the river and excellent golf courses. **Directions: M3 to Winchester, leaving the City Centre on Southgate Street towards St Cross and watching carefully on the left for narrow Cannon Street, which gives access to the car park.**

For hotel location, see maps on pages 180–186

The Royal Oak Inn

WITHYPOOL, EXMOOR NATIONAL PARK, SOMERSET TA24 7QP
TEL: 01643 831236 FAX: 01643 831659

OWNERS: The Bradley and Lucas families
MANAGER: Mike Bradley
CHEF: Peter Norris

S: £33–£48
D: £56–£80

Inn: The Royal Oak Inn has a reputation for good food and hospitality spanning 300 years. Set in the pretty village of Withypool, it is ideal for exploring Exmoor with its sparkling rivers and fertile valleys. R.D. Blackmore, the author of *Lorna Doone*, was so taken with Withypool that he stayed at the inn while writing his novel in 1866. Today's visitors are offered comfortable accommodation in individually furnished bedrooms. The Residents' and Rod Room Bars, with their beamed ceilings and crackling log fires, epitomise the character of an old country inn. **Restaurant:** The restaurant, open in the evenings, offers guests table d'hôte and à la carte menus. Dishes of the highest calibre are cooked to order with particular emphasis on preparation and presentation. To complement the meal, choose from a list of over 70 carefully selected wines. Extensive lunch and supper menus are available in the Rod Room Bar. **Nearby:** The inn specialises in organising country sports for either groups or individuals. Arrangements can be made for riding, hunting, stabling, game shooting, fly-fishing, sea-fishing and Exmoor Safaris. **Directions: Withypool is seven miles north of Dulverton – just off the B3223 Dulverton–Exford road, or 10 miles off North Devon Link road A361 via North Molton.**

THE OLD TOLLGATE RESTAURANT AND HOTEL

THE STREET, BRAMBER, STEYNING, WEST SUSSEX BN44 3WE
TEL: 01903 879494 FAX: 01903 813399

OWNER: The Old Tollgate Restaurant Ltd
MANAGING DIRECTOR: Peter Sargent
RESTAURANT DIRECTOR: Andrew McNie CHEF DIRECTOR: Peter Arthur

31 rms | 31 ens

D: £55
Suite: £95

Inn: An original tollgate centuries ago, travellers now look forward to stopping here and paying their dues for wonderful hospitality. Part of the old building is still in evidence with newer additions attractively blending. There are some splendid suites, even a four-poster, which are excellent value and delightful bedrooms, some of which are reached across the courtyard. The bar is a popular meeting place for visitors and locals alike, with friendly staff adding to the welcoming ambience. **Restaurant:** The restaurant has built up a fine reputation, extending far beyond Sussex, having a magnificent carvery and sumptuous cold table. Breakfast, lunch and dinner are all catered for at various price structures according to the number of courses devoured! Soups and broths, fresh and smoked fish, roasts and casseroles, pies and puddings, and vegetarian dishes are in abundance. **Nearby:** Bramber is famous for its Norman Castle and spectacular views over the South Downs. Brighton, with its shops, beach and Pavilion is an easy drive away, as is Worthing. Sporting activities nearby include riding, golf and fishing. **Directions: Bramber is off the A283 between Brighton and Worthing, easily accessed from the A24 or A27.**

For hotel location, see maps on pages 180–186

THE BARTON ANGLER COUNTRY INN

IRSTEAD ROAD, NEATISHEAD, NR WROXHAM, NORFOLK NR12 8XP
TEL: 01692 630740

OWNER: King County Hotels Ltd
MANAGER: John King
CHEF: Jenwyn King MHCIMA

7 rms | 5 ens

S: £30
D: £60–£86

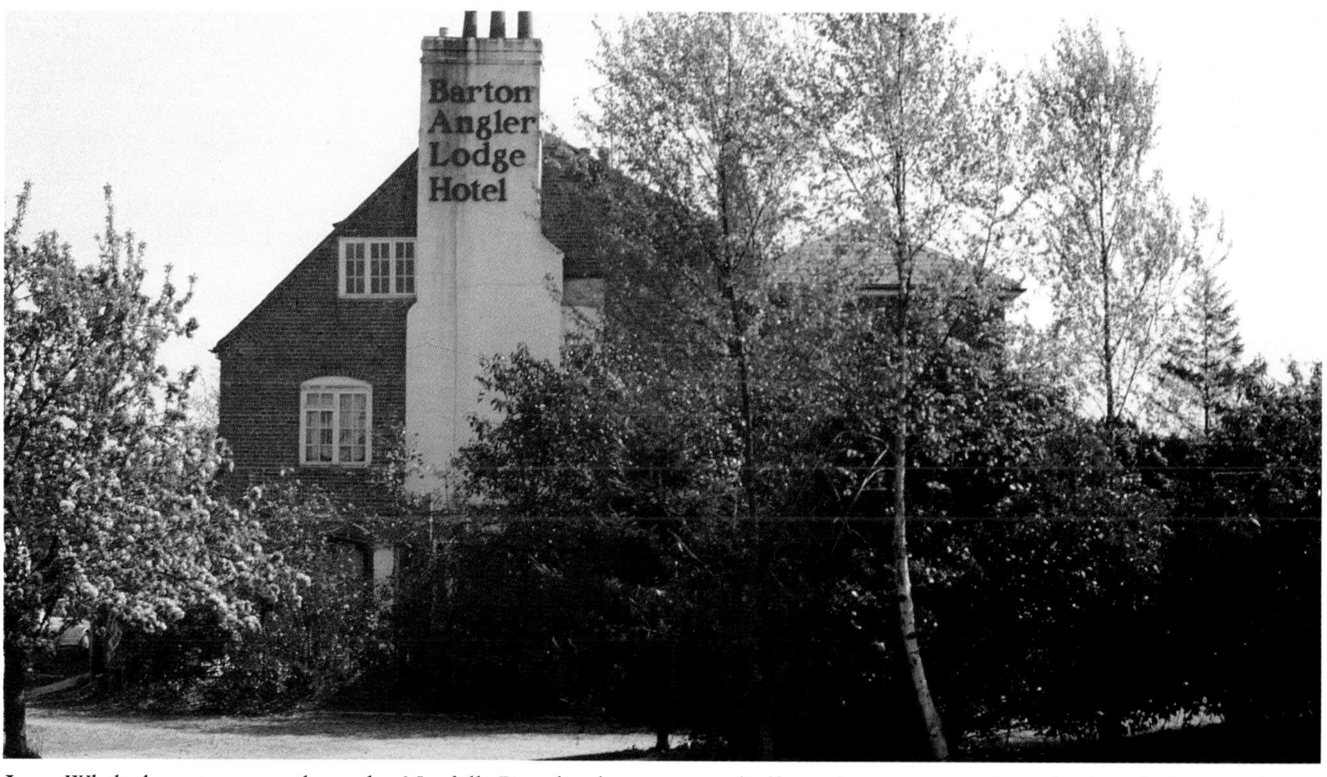

Inn: While learning to sail on the Norfolk Broads, the young Lord Nelson stayed at this unspoiled hostelry that dates back some 450 years. Set in 4-acre gardens, it originally catered exclusively for fishing clubs; it now provides excellent accommodation for anyone wishing to explore North Norfolk. The individually styled bedrooms are pleasantly furnished and some have fine. locally crafted four-poster beds. Open fires, exposed beams and antiques feature in the reception rooms all add to the interesting character of this attractive building. Special week or weekend breaks are available. **Restaurant:** The kitchens are under the supervision of our chef, Jenwyn, and all meals are prepared in the hotel. Bar meals are provided on a first come first served basis. Tables in the restaurant are bookable – which is advised. Barbecues are a regular summer event. **Nearby:** Owned by the English Heritage, Barton Broads, which is now within Broadlands National Park, offers plenty of opportunities for birdwatching, fishing, sailing and cruising. Boats can be hired for guests. The coast and many historic churches and houses are nearby. **Directions: A1151 north from Norwich, turn right one mile beyond Wroxham. The inn lies midway between the villages of Neatishead and Irstead.**

The Royal Oak Hotel

YATTENDON, NEWBURY, BERKSHIRE RG18 0UG
TEL: 01635 201325 FAX: 01635 201926

OWNER: Regal Hotels PLC
MANAGER: Paul Marshall
CHEF: Robbie Macrae

S: from £70
D: from £85

Inn: The Royal Oak's team of friendly, courteous staff make sure guests at this lovely old inn are warmly welcomed. Imbued with history, the inn played host to Cromwell and his generals. There are five pretty bedrooms overlooking the tranquil walled garden or the historic village square. A delightful lounge offers country house comfort, while ale is still pulled from the wood in the bar, with all the character of a traditional country pub. A sunny private room is available for meetings and lunch or dinner parties. On warm days, guests can dine in the garden. **Restaurant:** Chef Robbie Macrae prepares menus based on quality produce. All dishes are cooked to order and might include confit of duck with foie gras and lentil du page or turbot with wild mushrooms and brioche crust. Delicious puddings are followed by farmhouse cheeses. Two courses cost from £19.50. **Nearby:** Reading, racing at Newbury and boat trips on the River Thames. **Directions: From the west: leave M4 at junction 13 and follow signs to Hermitage. At T-junction, turn towards Streatley, then follow signs for Yattendon. From the east: leave M4 at junction 12 and head for Theale. Continue towards Pangbourne taking first left, signed Bradfield/Yattendon. Follow road into Yattendon village square where hotel is situated.**

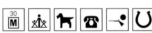

For hotel location, see maps on pages 180–186

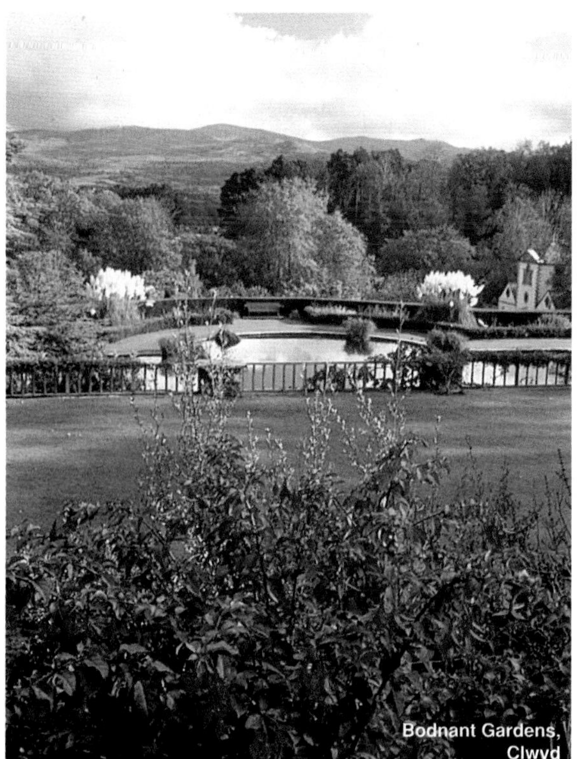

Johansens Recommended Inns with Restaurants in

Wales

Magnificent scenery, a rich variety of natural, cultural and modern leisure attractions, and the very best accommodation awaits the Johansens visitor to Wales.

Each year, millions of visitors head for Wales to discover or rediscover all that the country has to offer. An exceptionally high proportion come back year after year – a sure sign of satisfaction.

Wales has some of the most fabulous scenery imaginable, with much to see and do, and boasts three national parks covering nearly 1,600 square miles, as well as five areas designated as being of Outstanding Natural Beauty.

There are numerous large country parks, nature reserves, sites of special scientific interest and more than 700 miles of breathtakingly beautiful coastline to discover, plus delightful off shore islands, home to colonies of seals and rare birds.

But quite apart from the country's unspoilt natural beauty and endless scenic variety, the principality has a wealth of interesting and unusual attractions to enjoy.

There are a whole host of fascinating places to visit, many of them unique like the Centre for Alternative Technology, the green village of the future at Machynlleth in Mid Wales or Portmeirion, the dreamlike Italianate village in North Wales.

Visitors can take a ride on a narrow gauge steam railway, take a trip on a horse drawn canal boat, go to the summit of the Great Orme in the only cable hauled tramway in Britain, travel across Aberaeron harbour by the Aeron Express Aerial ferry or journey to the summit of Aberystwyth's Constitution Hill by cliff railway, one of the most spectacular in Britain.

In Wales there are working farms open to the public with rare breeds, and also fascinating factory workshops where visitors can watch glass being blown, carpets woven, candles being made and at several potteries visitors can enjoy a real hands-on experience by throwing a pot on a wheel.

The Industrial heritage of the past now provides fascinating visitor attractions like Big Pit in Blaenafon where ex-miners act as underground guides or the ever expanding Rhondda Heritage Park. In North Wales there are vast slate caverns and copper mines to explore, several narrow gauge steam railways to enjoy while in Mid Wales, visitors can tour a real goldmine, try their hand at panning and mining for gold – and keep anything they find!

Apart from these unique attractions, there are old working mills, art and craft centres, mountain and sea zoos, a hawking centre, sea aquariums, bird gardens, butterfly houses and wildlife parks.

There are exceptional museums like the 100 acre Welsh Folk Museum near Cardiff where buildings from all over Wales have been carefully reerected, and museums covering the maritime, motoring, industrial and aviation history of Wales, as well as those dedicated to the memory of famous personalities like Lloyd George and Dylan Thomas.

Wales also has her share of magnificent stately homes with priceless art treasures and antiques, world class gardens like Bodnant or Dyffryn, exciting new attractions like the haunted Llancaiach Fawr Manor in Rhymney Valley – a living history museum with guides dressed in costume, as well as vast medieval fortresses, castles and cromlechs.

There are also excellent leisure centres and sporting facilities throughout the country, in fact, Wales could have been tailormade for activity holidays and visitors can undertake virtually all types of outdoor activities and go abseiling or angling, ballooning or gliding, rafting or riding, climbing, canoeing or caving – to mention a few!

With family fun parks like Oakwood Park in West Wales, Starcoast World on the Llyn peninsula and Ocean Beach Amusement Park in Rhyl, famed for its whiteknuckle rides, Wales truly has something for everyone.

Centre for Alternative Technology
Machynlleth
Powys SY20 9AZ
Tel: 01654 702400

Great Little Trains of Wales
c/o The Station
Llanfair Caereinion
Powys SY21 OSF
Tel: 01938 810441

Big Pit
Blaenafon
Gwent NP4 9XP
Tel: 01495 790311

Rhondda Heritage Park
Lewis Merthyr
Coed Cae Road
Trehafod
Mid Glamorgan CF37 7NP
Tel: 01443 682036

Welsh Folk Museum
St Fagans
Cardiff CF5 6XB
Tel: 01222 569441

Bodnant Gardens
Tal y Cafn
Colwyn Bay
Clwyd LL28 5RE
Tel: 01492 650460

Dyffryn Gardens
St Nicholas
Nr Cardiff
South Glamorgan CF5 6SU
Tel: 01222 593328

Llancaiach Fawr Manor
Gelligaer Road
Nelson
Mid Glamorgan CF46 6ER
Tel: 01443 412248

For more information about Wales, please contact:-

Wales Tourist Board
Brunel House
2 Fitzalan Road
Cardiff CF2 1UY
Tel: 01222 499909

THE CASTLE VIEW HOTEL

16 BRIDGE STREET, CHEPSTOW, GWENT NP6 5EZ
TEL: 01291 620349 FAX: 01291 627397

OWNERS: Martin and Vicky Cardale

12 rms | 11 ens

S: £39.95–£44.50
D: £59.50–£69.50

Inn: This historic 17th century, ivy-clad hotel is set in a prime location opposite Britain's oldest stone castle. It is a friendly, family-owned hostelry, which offers good value accommodation, with Sky T.V. and all the usual modern comforts, in rooms which still have many original features. There is a beautiful hand-turned oak staircase leading to comfortable, well-appointed bedrooms. Some of these have 200-year-old wall paintings and many have views of the castle. There is also a secluded garden which is ablaze with colour during the summer. **Restaurant:** The Kitchen is Egon Ronay and Les Routiers Commended and serves imaginative home-cooked meals. Wye salmon and Welsh lamb often appear on the seasonally changing menu, which always offers fresh vegetables, plus many delicious home-made puddings. There is also an interesting range of bar snacks, real ales, a varied wine list and a few good malts. **Nearby:** Chepstow is on the edge of the Wye Valley and Forest of Dean. It is well situated for international rugby in Cardiff, racing at Chepstow, golf at St Pierre and visits to Tintern Abbey. **Directions: Leave M4 at junction 22, signed to Chepstow, then follow signs to the castle.**

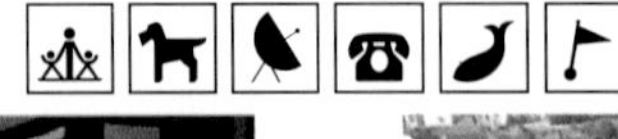

For hotel location, see maps on pages 180–186

GEORGE III HOTEL

PENMAENPOOL, DOLGELLAU, GWYNEDD LL40 1YD
TEL: 01341 422525 FAX: 01341 423565

OWNERS: John and Julia Cartwright

S: £37.50–£45
D: £70–£88

Inn: Superbly situated at the head of the Mawddach Estuary, The George III Hotel is set in the charming hamlet of Penmaenpool. The main hotel was built in the mid 17th century. Once two separate buildings, it was joined in 1890 to make what is now the hotel. There are 12 comfortable bedrooms, ten of which overlook the Estuary and Diffwys range of mountains. Half of the rooms are in the main hotel building, while the other half are situated in the Lodge some 50 yards away. All are equipped with a colour television, tea/coffee making facilities, trouser press, hair dryer and direct-dial telephone. **Restaurant:** The George enjoys an excellent reputation for its food, in particular the specialities within the non-smoking, estuary view restaurant which include local salmon, sea trout, turbot, pheasant, wild duck and venison. The refurbished Cellar Bar, which serves homemade hot and cold bar food and a tempting selection of real ales, has a childrens license which makes it an ideal family venue. **Nearby:** The hotel is within easy reach of most places of interest in North and mid Wales. Possible leisure activities include pony trekking, game and course fishing (free fishing permits are available for hotel residents), golf and cycling (mountain bikes can be hired from the hotel). The RSPB Centre is adjacent to the hotel. **Directions: On the A493 Dolgellau to Tywyn road.**

For hotel location, see maps on pages 180–186

THE WEST ARMS HOTEL

LLANARMON DC, NR LLANGOLLEN, CLWYD LL20 7LD
TEL: 0169600 665 FAX: 0169600 622

OWNER: Mavis Price

S: £55–£75
D: £100–£140

Inn: Originally a 16th century farmhouse, this charming old inn offers good value for money and unpretentious, warm-hearted hospitality. The old character of the building is evident throughout, with log fires, inglenooks, beams and stone floors. The cosy lounges are furnished with chintz-covered sofas and armchairs. All of the bedrooms are furnished to a high standard to provide the utmost comfort. With formal rose gardens and lawns running down to the river, this really is an idyllic setting for a relaxing break. Dogs can be accommodated by prior arrangement. **Restaurant:** The cooking here is of high quality: all of the Welsh, English and continental dishes are carefully prepared with the emphasis on taste and presentation. Specialities include Ceiriog trout and salmon and the menu presents a choice of delicious puddings. To complement your meal, which is served in the beamed dining room, there is a well chosen list of palatable wines. **Nearby:** The inn can offer its residents free private fishing. The unspoiled hills and valleys of the surrounding countryside give plenty of opportunities for walking and pony-trekking. Among the many local attractions are Chirk Castle, the house of the 'Ladies of Llangollen', Erddig Hall and the Roman city of Chester. **Directions: Tale the A5 to Chirk. From Chirk take the B4500 for 11 miles to Llanarmon DC. Once over the bridge, the inn is situated on the right.**

For hotel location, see maps on pages 180–186

THE PLOUGH INN

RHOSMAEN, LLANDEILO, CARMARTHENSHIRE SA19 6NP
TEL: 01558 823431 FAX: 01558 823969

OWNERS: Giulio and Diane Rocca

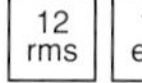

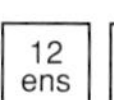

S: £45
D: £60

Inn: Originally a farmhouse, The Plough Inn has been elegantly converted and extended to provide good food and accommodation in the rural market town of Llandeilo. In the older part of the building guests will find a public bar, adjoining which is the cosy and intimate Towy Lounge. The 12 en suite bedrooms enjoy glorious views over surrounding countryside and are all well appointed for your comfort. A gym and sauna provide an added dimension to your stay – why not start the day with an invigorating work-out in the gym or unwind in the sauna before a comfortable night's sleep? A conference suite can cater for business meetings: a comprehensive range of audio-visual aids is available for hire. Closed Christmas.

Restaurant: Guests may dine in style and comfort in the à la carte restaurant. Local salmon and sewin, venison, Welsh lamb and beef, cooked simply or in continental recipes, all feature on the menus. An extensive choice of hot and cold bar meals can be enjoyed in the Towy Lounge. One of the inn's specialities is its tradition for Welsh afternoon teas. These are served in the elegant, chandeliered Penlan Lounge. **Nearby:** The Plough Inn is an ideal point of departure for touring the beautiful Towy Valley and surrounding Dinefwr countryside, including the Brecon Beacons National Park. **Directions: A mile from Llandeilo on the A40, towards Llandovery. The inn is 14 miles from exit 49 at the end of the M4.**

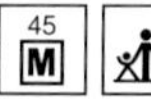

For hotel location, see maps on pages 180–186

The Dragon Hotel

MONTGOMERY, POWYS SY15 6PA
TEL: 01686 668359 FAX: 01686 668359

OWNERS: Mark and Sue Michaels

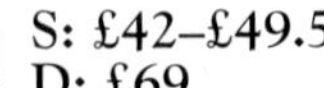

S: £42–£49.50
D: £69

Inn: Parts of this historic hotel date back to the mid 1600s when it was a coaching inn. The bar and lounge feature beams and masonry reputed to have been taken from Montgomery Castle after its destruction by Oliver Cromwell. An enclosed patio, created from the old coaching entrance, leads out to a large car park. Pleasant bedrooms offer a full range of modern amenities, including central heating, colour television, direct-dial telephone and tea making facilities. A ground floor lounge offers residents the opportunity to relax away from the hotel's well appointed bar. An indoor heated swimming pool is open to guests throughout the year. **Restaurant:** Owner Sue Michaels personally supervises the kitchen where fresh fish, local steaks, Welsh lamb and a wide range of fresh local produce are prepared to the highest standards. An extensive wine list is available to complement the menu. **Nearby:** Montgomery provides an ideal base for touring, fishing on the Wye and Severn and playing golf. Situated on Offa's Dyke, it also provides a for the serious walker. Powys Castle and other historic sites are nearby. **Directions: The hotel is in the market square of this village sized town, in the triangle formed by A483, A489 and A490.**

For hotel location, see maps on pages 180–186

THE LION HOTEL AND RESTAURANT

BERRIEW, NR WELSHPOOL, MONTGOMERYSHIRE SY21 8PQ
TEL: 01686 640452 FAX: 01686 640604

OWNERS: Brian and Jean Thomas
CHEF: Lance Thomas

S: £45–£50
D: £80–£90

Inn: Standing next to the church in one of mid-Wales' prettiest villages, The Lion Hotel is a striking 17th century inn, situated on the Shropshire border. A more genuinely friendly welcome than that extended to guests by the Thomas family would be hard to find. The bedrooms, with dark beams, contrasting white walls and lovely views, are all decorated in an attractive cottage style. Real ales and delicious bar meals are served in the two cosy bars. Welsh Tourist Board 4 Crowns Highly Commended. **Restaurant:** Recommended by Taste of Wales, the restaurant has a graceful and intimate atmosphere with a menu that offers a good choice of Welsh dishes as well as a selection of English and continental meals. Choices might include Welsh lamb with a sauce of redcurrants, cranberries, red wine and cream, or local venison fillet. **Nearby:** With the Cambrian Mountains, the River Severn and Shropshire so close, guests can enjoy a variety of beautiful landscapes. The Welshpool Museum contains interesting treasures and historical memorabilia. Powys Castle, just a few miles away, is just one of the many castles to visit in the area. There are three golf courses within 10 miles and pony-trekking nearby too. **Directions: Welshpool is 18 miles west of Shrewsbury on A458. Berriew is signposted off A483 five miles south of Welshpool. Welshpool Airport is 4½ miles to the north.**

For hotel location, see maps on pages 180–186

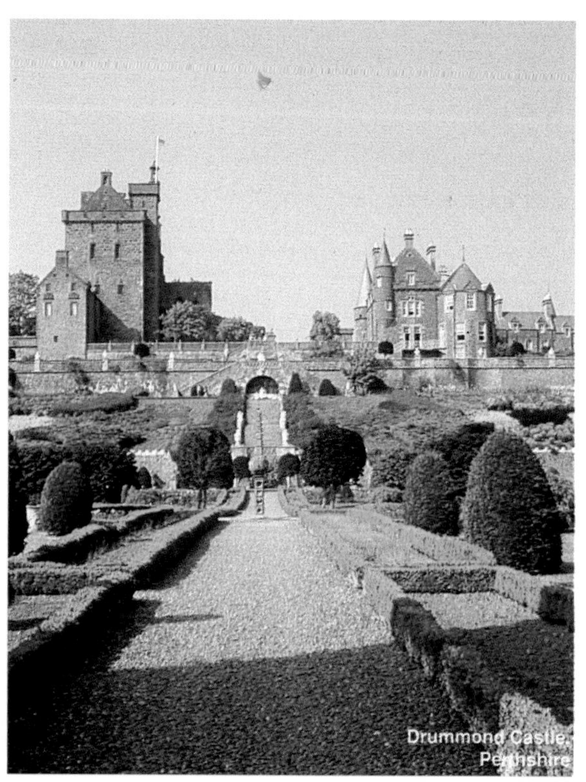

Johansens Recommended Inns with Restaurants in Scotland

*S**cotland** offers the Johansens visitor a fine choice of recommendations amid breathtaking scenery. An abundance of outdoor pursuits will challenge the adventurous, blended with the warmth and charm of traditional hospitality.*

The Scottish Borders is one of the finest introductions to the nature and character of a country. The open space of green hills and rich farming plains with their network of well established fishing rivers indicate a land blessed with good agriculture and unpolluted water.

The picturesque ruins of several abbeys bear witness to the turbulence of centuries of Border wars and religious strife focusing attention on a tapestry of history, heritage, culture and recreation.

Small towns like Kelso and Peebles unspoiled in their rural setting unveil to the visitor the timeless appeal of Scotland - breathing space, charming locations, and people friendly, spirited and generous. All this is evident at the colourful festivals of the Border Ridings hosted in many towns.

Turn north to Scotland's capital, Edinburgh, a stunningly beautiful city. Here nature's gift of volcanic rock as a site for a castle and medieval town enhanced by enlightened municipal planning of magnificent gardens and Georgian architecture has created visual splendour which has escaped the ravages of time. There is no finer stage for the world's biggest festival of arts and music. Take time for a walk in the Royal Botanic Garden renowned for its plant collection, rock garden and with a Chinese garden in the making. There are gardens of all varieties throughout Scotland.

Edinburgh is beside the River Forth close to small towns and villages which hug the coastline to the North Sea. Seaside means golf courses, all challenging and most open to visitors at reasonable cost.

St Andrews, across the Forth, has several courses to test the enthusiast. The Home of Golf it is attractive and is home also to Scotland's oldest medieval university. The Fife coast has a ribbon of former fishing villages (the East Neuk) which are delightful and charming places to relax.

The pastoral landscape is marked in the neighbouring Perthshire which gives a first glimpse of the Highlands. Through Angus to the north east and Royal Deeside and the private home of the Queen and the Royal Family at Balmoral Castle with the gardens open to the public in summer. Nearby, at the eastern end of the Cairngorm Mountains, the village of Braemar, venue for the Braemar Gathering, the best known of the Highland Games.

Sixty miles along Deeside to Aberdeen, award winning Britain in Bloom city endowed with public gardens and parks, granite architecture and wedding its ancient culture of fishing and farming to the modern oil industry. From the overnight trip to the Shetland Isles is an ideal introduction to Scotland's network of passenger and vehicle ferries, most of which operate on the west coast. They reveal a unique world of mystical, timeless experience in the Western Isles. Lewis, Harris, Uist, Skye and Mull are but a few of these magical islands.

Aberdeen is also a base to embark on the adventure of the Malt Whisky Trail in the glens of the Livet and the Spey and their many famous distilleries where a dram awaits. Excellent fishing country, too.

Leave Speyside for Aviemore, premier winter sport resort, one of five in Scotland, and then to Inverness, the Highland capital. To the north the moors and hills of Ross-shire and Sutherland, to the west, Loch Ness with its famous inhabitant. Continue down the Caledonian Canal to Fort William and Britain's highest mountain, Ben Nevis.

The tour circle includes the Pass of Glencoe en route to Glasgow. Glencoe is a climbing and ski centre and notorious in clan history for the massacre of the Macdonalds.

Glasgow has impressive art galleries and museums and a vibrant music and theatre lifestyle. Fashion is a major keynote in its extensive shopping facilities.

Head for the Borders again through Ayrshire, home of the national poet Robert Burns who died in 1796. Many will respect his Immortal Memory on the bicentenary commemoration at his mausoleum in St Michael's Kirkyard, Dumfries.

Palace of Holyroodhouse
Canongate
Edinburgh EH8 8DX
Tel: 0131 556 7371

Inveraray Jail Visitor Centre
Church Square
Inveraray PA32 8TX
Tel: 01499 302 381

Balnain House Heritage Centre
40 Hunty Street
Inverness IV3 5HR
Tel: 01463 715 757

Drummond Castle Gardens
Muthill
Crieff PH7 4HZ
Tel: 01764 681 321

New Lanark Visitor Centre
New Lanark Mills
Lanark ML11 9DB
Tel: 01555 661 345

Discovery Point
Discovery Quay
Dundee DD1 4XA
Tel: 01382 201 245

Burns House
Burns Street
Dumfries DG1 2PS
Tel: 01387 255 297

Malt Whisky Trail
Grampian Highlands and Aberdeen
Migvie House
North Silver Street
Aberdeen AB1 1RJ
Tel: 01224 632727

For more information about Scotland, please contact:-

Scottish Tourist Board
23 Ravelston Terrace
Edinburgh EH4 3EU
Tel: 0131 332 2433

POTARCH HOTEL

BY BANCHORY, ROYAL DEESIDE, KINCARDINESHIRE AB31 4BD
TEL: 013398 84339

OWNERS: Michael, Linda and Maureen Boyle
CHEF: Warren Grooby

S: £40
D: £60

Inn: True Scottish hospitality can be enjoyed at this welcoming, friendly inn, which offers attractive accommodation and excellent value for money. A hostelry has stood at Potarch since 1740, when the nearest crossing of the River Dee was half a mile south at Inchbrae. The area is steeped in history, making it popular with sight-seers and sports enthusiasts who come to enjoy the superb fishing and skiing. The bar also draws locals and visitors, as it serves a wide range of whiskies – many of which are quite rare. **Restaurant:** Charmingly furnished, the dining room provides a very pleasant setting in which to enjoy the inn's traditional Scottish cuisine. The Scottish Chef of the Year 1992/93 makes good use of local fare, including the salmon, game and beef for which Deeside is renowned. **Nearby:** The Potarch is surrounded by spectacular scenery, offering plenty of opportunities for all manner of country pursuits. Riding can be arranged at an equestrian centre just 200 yards away. There are also numerous castles in the area. Aberdeen is 25 miles away, and nearby Aboyne hosts the August Highland Games. **Directions: 25 miles from Aberdeen. The hotel is near Potarch Bridge on the A93 between Banchory and Aboyne.**

For hotel location, see maps on pages 180–186

Comrie Hotel

COMRIE, PERTHSHIRE PH6 2DY
TEL: 01764 670239 FAX: 01764 670330

OWNERS: John and Rowena Herron

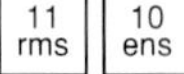

S: £27–£32
D: £54–£64

Inn: The Comrie Hotel is a 100 year old property built of traditional Scottish sandstone. In stands at the foot of the Highlands in the main street of the village of Comrie, famous for being the place where all the world's earthquakes are recorded. Recently almost entirely refurbished in the hands of its new owners, The Comrie offers lovely, spacious bedrooms which are beautifully decorated and furnished. All the rooms have private bathroom or shower, colour television, direct-dial telephone, tea making facilities, hair driers and electric blankets. **Restaurant:** The dining room serves traditional Scottish fare, including venison and smoked salmon. Well presented meals are complemented by a good selection of reasonably priced wines, also sample the extensive collection of malt whiskies and beers in the Lounge Bar. Morning coffee, bar lunches, afternoon teas and light suppers are also available. **Nearby:** Drummond Castle and the Falls of Turret. The hotel is adjacent to Comrie Golf Club and there are another four courses in the locality. This is an excellent spot for keen walkers, while other leisure pursuits include water sports on Loch Earn and visiting the towns and cities in the near vicinity. Edinburgh and Glasgow are both just one hour's drive away. **Directions: The hotel is in the main street of Comrie, which is on the A85 main route seven miles west of Crieff, 20 miles north of Stirling.**

The Winnock Hotel

THE SQUARE, DRYMEN, STIRLINGSHIRE G63 OBL
TEL: 01360 660245 FAX: 01360 660267

OWNERS: David and Frances Warnes
CHEF: Eldon Dunley

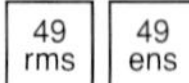

S: £45
D: £69–£89

Inn: Although fully modernised and comfortable, The Winnock Hotel retains all of its 17th century charm. The beautiful beamed ceilings and original log fires recall bygone days, but are combined with simple and pleasant modern day décor and furnishings. The inn overlooks the picturesque village green. **Restaurant:** The inn's Highlander Restaurant is acclaimed for its traditional Scottish Fare. Why not start a meal with West Coast langoustines, whole scampi flamed in cognac and served with garlic butter? Follow this with The Highland Sword of the Hills, fillet of beef and venison grilled on a skewer and served with a pink peppercorn sauce, and finish your meal with a selection of some rare and wonderful Scottish cheeses! **Nearby:** The Winnock Hotel is an excellent base from which to visit the many beautiful landmarks of the Western Highlands. These include Inveraray and its well known castle and Oban, the stepping stone to the Hebridean Islands. Edinburgh is an hour's drive away, while Glasgow can be reached in 30 minutes. Loch Lomond is also very close. **Directions: From Glasgow M8 follow A81 then A809 to Drymen. From Edinburgh follow M9 to Stirling then A811 to Drymen.**

For hotel location, see maps on pages 180–186

THE GLENISLA HOTEL

KIRKTON OF GLENISLA, BY ALYTH, PERTHSHIRE PH11 8PH
TEL: 01575 582223 FAX: 01575 582223

OWNERS: Simon and Lyndy Blake

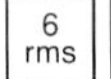  

 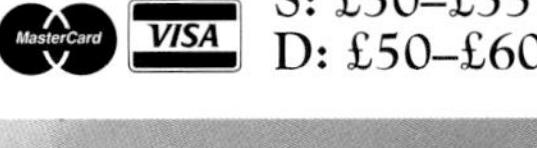

S: £30–£35
D: £50–£60

Inn: A coaching inn in the 17th century, hospitality has long been a tradition at this attractive hotel in the middle of the tiny village of The Kirkton of Glenisla, close to the River Isla. The Drawing Room is filled with flowers, inviting sofas and chairs, and the six bedrooms are charming. Some have a bath, others showers and there is masses of hot water! Locals and guests frequent the big, friendly bar with its log fire, wooden tables, cask ales and malt whiskies and enjoy substantial bar lunches and suppers served at wooden tables. The Games Room in the stable block opens on to the Function Hall where Highland Dances are held. **Restaurant:** The elegant dining room serves the best of Scottish fare, winning several accolades including a recommendation from the Taste of Scotalnd. Orkney herrings, local venison, Aberdeen Angus beef, wild salmon and hill-reared lamb all feature on the menu. There are interesting starters and wicked puddings too! The short wine list is impressive. **Nearby:** The glen is an ideal touring centre for Glamis, Scone, Braemar and Royal Deeside, while immediate activities include trout fishing, skiing, stalking, shooting, salmon fishing and golf. Hill walking, bird-watching and pony trekking are also on the doorstep. **Directions: From the Motorway to Perth take the A93 to Blairgowrie, then A926 by-passing Alyth to next roundabout. Then follow signs to Glenisla for 12 miles, hotel is on the right.**

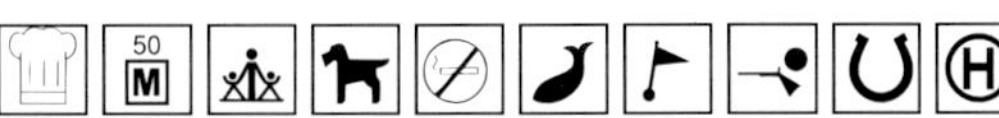

HOTEL EILEAN IARMAIN OR ISLE ORNSAY HOTEL

EILEAN IARMAIN, SLEAT, ISLE OF SKYE IV43 8QR
TEL: 01471 833332 FAX: 01471 833275

OWNERS: Sir Ian and Lady Noble of Eilean Iarmain
MANAGER: Effie Kennedy
CHEFS: Patricia Gudgeon and Morag MacInnes

S: £60
D: £84–£95

Inn: For generations Isle of Ornsay (Eilean Iarmain to Skye people) has been a landmark for travellers by land or sea. The white building standing above the private harbour has always meant *'failte is furan'*, a warmth of welcome unique to Gaelic Scotland. The hotel prides itself on its log fires, inventive cooking and friendly Gaelic-speaking staff. 1995 accolades included the RAC Restaurant of the Year and Merit Award for Hospitality, to AA Courtesy and Care Award and an AA Restaurant Rosette. There are 12 bedrooms, all different – six of them in the pretty Garden House – with special views of sea and hills. Original features, period furniture, pretty fabrics and well chosen pictures create a cosy atmosphere. The hotel reflects Skye's ancient culture with its love of traditional music. **Restaurant:** Every evening the table d'hôte menu features game in season. Frequently, guests can enjoy fish and seafood landed at the pier that day, along with a ready supply of oysters. There is an extensive wine list, including premier cru clarets. A large selection of malt whiskies includes local Poit Dhubh and Talisker – highly regarded by connoisseurs. The bar offers meals at lunchtime and in the evening is a haunt of yachtsmen, the scene of ceilidhs from time to time. **Nearby:** Clan MacDonald Centre, Armadale Castle and Talisker Distillery. Sea-fishing, stalking, shooting and walking. **Directions: The hotel is in Sleat, between Broadford and Armadale on the A851.**

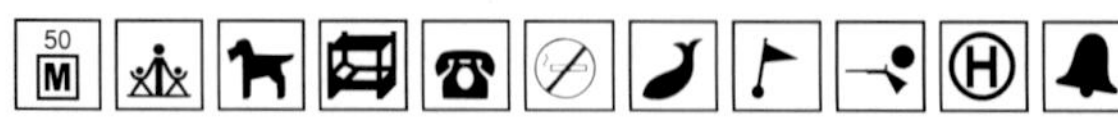

For hotel location, see maps on pages 180–186

KYLESKU HOTEL

KYLESKU, BY LAIRG, SUTHERLAND IV27 4HW
TEL: 01971 502231/502200 FAX: 01971 502313

OWNERS: Marcel and Janice Klein
CHEF: Marcel Klein

 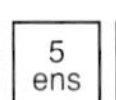 

7 rms 5 ens

  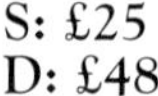

S: £25
D: £48

Inn: This delightful small early 19th century hotel, until recently only reached by ferry, is right on the water's edge, with a backdrop of Quinag. It has seven homely bedrooms, five of which are en suite, with colour T.V. **Restaurant:** Both the bar and restaurant menus feature locally caught seafood, the specialities being lobster, crab, langoustine, scallops, mussels, monkfish and salmon. Fresh mackerel and trout from the previous days fishing excursions can be enjoyed at breakfast. Appropriate wines are available. The restaurant view is often described as the most magnificent in Scotland. Porpoises and seals provide the cabaret.

Nearby: The hotel's boat takes visitors to Eas Coul Aulin, Britain's highest waterfall and also to the Seal Islands. Handa Island, famous for its puffins, is just 15 minutes drive. There is spectacular landscape to explore all around: Cape Wrath, Ardvreek Castle and Inchnadamph Caves are nearby. Fly-fishing tuition is available on the hotel lochs. Sea angling can be arranged. **Directions: From Ullapool take the A835 to Ledmore junction joining A837 from Oykel Bridge. Continue north past Inchnadamph joining A894 at Skiag Bridge just past the ruins of Ardvreek Castle. The hotel is five miles further north.**

CAIRNBANN HOTEL

BY LOCHGILPHEAD, ARGYLL PA31 8SJ
TEL: 01546 603668

OWNER: Sam Ferguson
CHEF: Alexander Tubton-Kier

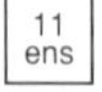

11 ens

Inn: Just two hours from Glasgow Airport, Cairnbaan Hotel is a former coaching inn which was built in the latter part of the 18th century. It has recently been reopened following complete modernisation and refurbishment. The bedrooms have been individually designed and decorated and offer all modern facilities. Guests are invited to relax in the quiet comfort of the elegant lounge, or enjoy a famous malt whiskey in the bar. Sporting guests can enjoy golf at nearby Lochgilphead Golf Club, trail riding, pony trekking and excellent loch fishing and sea angling. Sailing boats and yachts are available for charter. **Restaurant:** An à la carte meal is served in the beautifully decorated restaurant, which offers a range of traditional and special dishes. Appetites are bound to be tempted by dishes such as poached roulade of sole, stuffed with smoked salmon and scampi tails and served with a tarragon butter sauce. Breakfast is served in the Coffee Shop, which also provides a range of snacks throughout the day, in addition to an extensive lunchtime and evening bar meal menu. **Nearby:** The Cairnbaan Hotel is situated at Lock 5, approximately halfway along the Crinan Canal, and forms an ideal base from which to tour Argyll and the Islands. Within easy reach are Inveraray Castle and Dunadd Fort. **Directions: Two hours from Glasgow Airport, via A82 and A83.**

For hotel location, see maps on pages 180–186

MINI LISTINGS: JOHANSENS COUNTRY HOUSES AND SMALL HOTELS

Here in brief are the entries that appear in full in Johansens 1996 Guide to Country Houses and Small Hotels.
To order any of these guides see pages 193–200.

Ambleside
Laurel Villa
Lake Road
Ambleside
Cumbria LA22 0DB
015394 33240

Ambleside (Clappersgate)
Nanny Brow Hotel
Clappersgate
Ambleside
Cumbria LA22 9NF
015394 32036

Appleton-le-Moors
Appleton Hall Hotel
Appleton-le-Moors
North Yorkshire YO6 6TF
01751 417227

Arundel (Burpham)
Burpham Country Hotel
Old Down
Burpham
Nr Arundel
West Sussex BN18 9RV
01903 882160

Ashbourne
Beeches Farmhouse
Waldley
Doveridge
Ashbourne
Derbyshire DE6 1LS
01889 590288

Ashbourne (Biggin-by-Hulland)
Biggin Mill Farm
Biggin-by-Hulland
Nr Ashbourne
Derbyshire DE6 3FN
01335 370414

Ashwater
Blagdon Manor Country Hotel
Ashwater
Devon EX21 5DF
01409 211224

Atherstone
Chapel House
Friars Gate
Atherstone
Warwickshire CV9 1EY
01827 718949

Badminton
Petty France
Dunkirk
Badminton
Avon GL9 1AF
01454 238361

Bakewell (Rowsley)
East Lodge Country House Hotel
Rowsley
Matlock
Derbyshire DE4 2EF
01629 734474

Bakewell (Rowsley)
The Peacock Hotel at Rowsley
Rowsley
Nr Matlock
Derbyshire DE4 2EB
01629 733518

Bamburgh
Waren House Hotel
Waren Mill
Belford
Northumberland NE70 7EE
01668 214581

Bath
Apsley House Hotel
141 Newbridge Hill Road
Bath
Avon BA1 3PT
01225 336966

Bath (Norton St Philip)
Bath Lodge Hotel
Norton St Philip
Bath
Avon BA3 6NH
01225 723040

Bath
Bloomfield House
146 Bloomfield Road
Bath
Avon BA2 2AS
01225 420105

Bath (Box)
Box House
Box
Nr Bath
Wiltshire SN14 9NR
01225 744447

Bath
Eagle House
Church Street
Bathford
Bath
Avon BA1 7RS
01225 859946

Bath (Rode)
Irondale House
67 High Street
Rode
Bath
Avon BA3 6PB
01373 830730

Bath (Monkton Combe)
Monkshill
Shaft Road
Monkton Court
Avon BA2 7HL
01225 833028

Bath
Newbridge House Hotel
35 Kelston Road
Bath
Avon BA1 3QH
01225 446676

Bath
Paradise House
Holloway
Bath
Avon BA2 4PX
01225 317723

Bath (Bradford-on-Avon)
Widbrook Grange
Trowbridge Road
Bradford-on-Avon
Wiltshire BA15 1UH
01225 864750/863173

Beaminster
The Lodge
Beaminster
Dorset DT8 3BL
01308 863468

Beccles
St Peter's House
Old Market
Beccles
Suffolk NR34 9AP
01502 713203

Beer
Bovey House
Beer
Seaton
Devon EX12 3AD
01297 680241

Belper (Shottle)
Dannah Farm Country Guest House
Bowmans Lane
Shottle
Nr Belper
Derbyshire DE5 2DR
01773 550273/630

Bibury
Bibury Court
Bibury
Gloucestershire GL7 5NT
01285 740337

Biggin-by-Hartington
Biggin Hall
Biggin-by-Hartington
Buxton
Derbyshire SK17 0DH
01298 84451

Blockley (Chipping Campden)
Lower Brook House
Blockley
Moreton-in-Marsh
Gloucestershire GL56 9DS
01386 700286

Bolton-by-Bowland
Harrop Fold
Bolton By Bowland
Clitheroe
Lancashire BBY 4PY
01200 447600

Bournemouth
Langtry Manor
Derby Road
East Cliff
Bournemouth
Dorset BH1 3QB
01202 553887

Bourton-on-the-Water
Dial House Hotel
The Chesnuts
High Street
Bourton-on-the-Water
Gloucestershire GL54 2AN
01451 822244

Bridgnorth
Cross Lane House Hotel
Astley Abbots
Bridgnorth
Shropshire WV16 4SJ
01746 764887

Bristol (Chelwood)
Chelwood House
Achelwood
Nr Bristol
Avon BS18 4NH
01761 490730

Broadway
Collin House Hotel
Collin Lane
Broadway
Worcestershire WR12 7PB
01386 858354/852544

Broadway
Leasow House
Laverton Meadows
Broadway
Worcestershire WR12 7NA
01386 584526

Broadway (Willersey)
The Old Rectory
Church Street
Willersey
Nr Broadway
Worcestershire WR12 7PN
01386 853729

Brockenhurst
The Thatched Cottage
16 Brookley Road
Brockenhurst
New Forest
Hampshire SO42 7RR
01590 623090

Brockenhurst
Whitley Ridge and Country House Hotel
Beaulieu Road
Brockenhurst
New Forest
Hampshire SO42 7QL
01590 622354

Bury St Edmunds
Bradfield House
Bradfield Combust
Bury St Edmunds
Suffolk IP30 OL3
01284 386301

Buttermere (Lorton)
New House Farm
Loreton
Cockermouth
Cumbria CA13 9UU
01900 85404

Cambridge (Duxford)
Duxford Lodge Hotel
Ickleton Road
Duxford
Cambridgeshire CB2 4RU
01223 836444

Cambridge (Melbourn)
Melbourn Bury
Melbourn
Nr Royston
Hertfordshire SG3 6DE
01763 261151

Carlisle (Crosby-on-Eden)
Crosby Lodge Country House Hotel
High Crosby
Crosby-on-Eden
Carisle
Cumbria CA6 4QZ
01228 573618

Cartmel
Aynsome Manor Hotel
Cartmel
Nr Grange-over-Sands
Cumbria LA11 6HH
015395 36653

Castleton (Hope)
Underleigh House
Off Edale Road
Hope
Derbyshire S30 2RF
01433 621372

Castleton (Hope)
Twitchill Farm Cottages
Edale Road
Hope
Derbyshire S30 2RF
01433 621426

Chagford
Easton Court Hotel
Easton Cross
Chagford
Devon TQ13 8JL
01647 433469

Cheltenham (Charlton Kings)
Charlton Kings Hotel
Charlton Kings
Cheltenham
Gloucestershire GL52 6UU
01242 231061

Cheltenham (Withington)
Halewell
Halewell Close
Withington
Nr Cheltenham
Gloucestershire GL54 4BN
01242 890238

Chester (Broxton)
Frogg Manor
Nantwich Road
Fullers Moor
Broxton
Chester
Cheshire CH3 9JH
01829 782629

Chester (Huxley)
Higher Huxley Hall
Huxley
Chester CH3 9BZ
01829 781484

Chipping Campden (Broad Campden)
Malt House
Broad Campden
Chipping Campden
Gloucestershire GL55 6UU
01386 840295

Cirencester (Woodmancote)
Cotswold Park
Woodmancote
Cirencester
Gloucestershire GL7 7EL
01285 831414

Cirencester (Ablington)
Hinton House
Ablington
Cirencester
Gloucestershire GL7 5NY
01285 740233

Clovelly (Horn's Cross)
Foxdown Manor
Horn's Cross
Nr Clovelly
Devon EX39 5PJ
01237 451325

Colchester (Higham)
The Bauble
Higham
Colchester
Essex CO7 6LA
01206 337254

Colchester (Frating)
Hockley Place
Frating
Colchester
Essex CO7 7HF
01206 251703

Combe Martin (Berrynarbor)
Bessemer Thatch
Berrynarbor
Nr Combe Martin
North Devon EX34 9SE
01271 882296

Corbridge (Stocksbridge)
Glenview
6 Meadowfield Road
Stocksfield
Northumberland NE43 7QX
01661 843674

Cornhill-on-Tweed
Wark Farm House
Wark
Cornhill-on-Tweed
Northumberland TD12 4RE
01890 883570

Dartmoor (Leusdon)
Leusdon Lodge Hotel
Leusdon
Poundsgate
Nr Ashburton
Devon TQ13 7PE
01364 631304

Dartmoor (Lydford)
Moor View Hotel
Vale Down
Lydford
Devon EX20 4BB
01822 282220

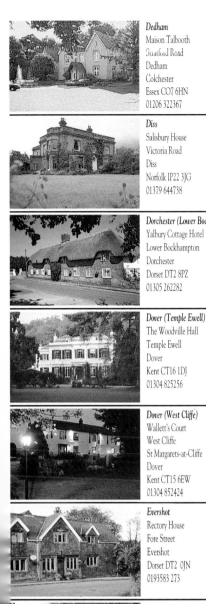

Dedham
Maison Talbooth
Stratford Road
Dedham
Colchester
Essex CO7 6HN
01206 322367

Diss
Salisbury House
Victoria Road
Diss
Norfolk IP22 3JG
01379 644738

Dorchester (Lower Bockhampton)
Yalbury Cottage Hotel
Lower Bockhampton
Dorchester
Dorset DT2 8PZ
01305 262282

Dover (Temple Ewell)
The Woodville Hall
Temple Ewell
Dover
Kent CT16 1DJ
01304 825256

Dover (West Cliffe)
Wallett's Court
West Cliffe
St Margarets-at-Cliffe
Dover
Kent CT15 6EW
01304 852424

Evershot
Rectory House
Fore Street
Evershot
Dorset DT2 0JN
0193583 273

Evesham (Harvington)
The Mill at Harvington
Anchor Lane
Harvington
Evesham
Worcestershire WR11 5NR
01386 870688

Exeter (Dunchideock)
The Lord Haldon Hotel
Dunchideock
Nr Exeter
Devon EX6 7YF
01392 832483

Exford (Exmoor)
The Crown Hotel
Exford
Exmoor National Park
Somerset TA24 7PP
01643 831554/5

Fenny Drayton (Leicestershire)
White Wings
Quaker Close
Fenny Drayton
Nr Nuneaton
Leicestershire Cv13 6BS
01827 716100

Fordingbridge
Lions Court Restaurant and Hotel
Fordingbridge
New Forest
Hampshire SP6 1AS
01425 652006

Fressingfield (Diss)
Chippenhall Hall
Fressingfield
Eye
Suffolk IP21 5TD
01379 588180

Gatwick (Charlwood)
Stanhill Court Hotel
Stanhill Road
Charlwood
Nr Horley
Surrey RH6 0EP
01293 862166

Gissing (Diss)
The Old Rectory
Gissing
Diss
Norfolk IP22 3XB
01379 677575

Glossop
The Wind in the Willows
Level
Glossop
Derbyshire SK13 9PT
01457 868001

Grasmere (Rydal Water)
White Moss House
Rydal Water
Grasmere
Cunbria LA22 9SE
015394 35295

Great Snoring
The Old Rectory
Great Snoring
Fakenham
Norfolk NR21 0HP
01328 820597

Greenhill (Coalville)
Abbots Oak
Greenhill
Coalville
Leicester LE67 4UY
01530 832328

Guildford (Newlands Corner)
The Manor
Newlands Corner
Guidford
Surrey GU4 8SE
01483 222624

Hampton Court
Chase Lodge
10 Park Road
Hampton Wick
Kingston-upon-Thames
Surrey KT1 4AS
0181 943 1862

Harrogate
The White House
10 Park Parade
Harrogate
North Yorkshire HG1 5AH
01423 501388

Hawes
Rookhurst Georgian Country
House Hotel
West End
Gayle
Hawes
North Yorkshire DL6 3RT
01969 667454

Helford
Tregildry Hotel
Gillan Manaccan
Helston
Cornwall TR12 6HG
01326 231378

Helston
Nanslow Manor
Meneage Road
Helston
Cornwall TR13 0SB
01326 574691

Hereford (Ullingswick)
The Steppes
Ullingswick
Nr Hereford
Herefordshire NR1 3JG
01432 820424

Keswick (Lake Thirlmere)
Dale Head Hall
Thirlmere
Keswick
Cumbria CA12 4TN
017687 72478

Keswick (Newlands)
Swinside Lodge Hotel
Grange Road
Newlands
Keswick
Cumbria CA12 8UE
017687 72948

Keswick-On-Derwent-Water
The Grange Country House Hotel
Manor Brow
Keswick-On-Derwent-Water
Cumbria CA12 4BA
017687 72500

Kirkby Lonsdale
Hipping Hall
Cowan Bridge
Kirkby Lonsdale
Cumbria LA6 2JJ
015242 71187

Lavenham
The Great House Restaurant
Market Place
Lavenham
Suffolk CO10 9QZ
01787 247431

Leominster
Lower Bache
Kimbolton
Nr Leominster
Herefordshire HR6 0ER
01568 750304

Lifton (Sprytown)
The Thatched Cottage
Country Hotel
Sprytown
Lifton
Devon PL16 0AY
01566 784224

Lincoln (Washingborough)
Washingborough Hall
Church Hill
Washingborough
Lincolnshire LN4 1BE
01522 790340

Looe (Talland Bay)
Allhays Country House
Talland Bay
Looe
Cornwall PL13 2JB
01503 272434

Looe (Widegates)
Coombe Farm
Widegates
Nr Looe
Cornwall PL13 1QN
01503 240223

Ludlow (Downton)
The Brakes
Downton
Nr Ludlow
Shropshire SY8 2LF
01584 856485

Ludlow (Diddlebury)
Delbury Hall
Diddlebury
Craven Arms
Shropshire SY7 9DH
01584 841267

Luton (Little Offley)
Little Offley
Hitchin
Hertfordshire SG5 3BU
01462 768243

Lymington (Hordle)
The Gordleton Mill Hotel
Silver Street
Hordle
Nr Lymington
Hampshire SO41 6DJ
01590 682219

Maidstone (Boughton Monchelsea)
Tanyard
Wierton Hill
Boughton Monchelsea
Nr Maidstone
Kent ME17 4JT
01622 744705

Malton
Newstead Grange
Norton
Malton
North Yorkshire YO17 9PJ
01653 692502

Middlecombe (Minehead)
Periton Park Hotel
Middlecombe
Nr Minehead
Somerset TA24 8SW
01643 706885

Middleham (Wensleydale)
The Millers House Hotel
Market Place
Middleham
Wensleydale
North Yorkshire DL8 4NR
01969 622630

Minchinhampton
Burleigh Court
Burleigh
Minchinhampton
Gloucestershire GL5 2PF
01453 883804

Morchard Bishop
Wigham
Morchard Bishop
Nr Crediton
Devon EX17 6RJ
01363 877350

Moretonhampstead (Lustleigh)
Eastbrey Barton Hotel
Lustleigh
Newton Abbott
Devon TQ13 9SN
01647 277338

New Romney (Littlestone)
Romney Bay House
Coast Road
Littlestone
New Romney
Kent TN28 8QY
01797 364747

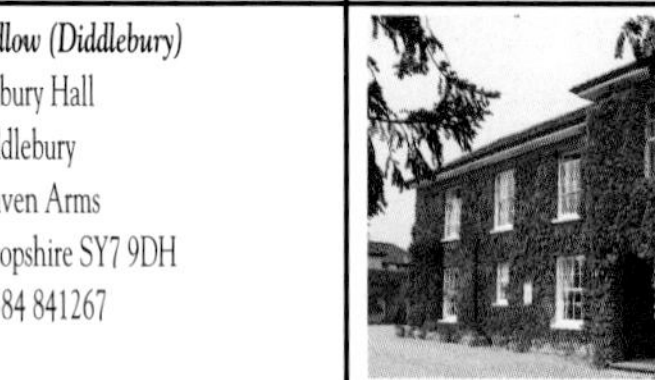

North Walsham
Beechwood Hotel
Cromer Road
North Walsham
Norfolk NR28 0HD
01692 403231

Norwich
The Beeches Hotel & Victorian Gardens
4-6 Earlham Road
Norwich
Norfolk NR2 3DB
01603 621167

Norwich (Old Catton)
Catton Old Hall
Lodge Lane
Catton
Norwich
Norfolk NR6 7HG
01603 419379

Norwich (Drayton)
The Stower Grange
School Road
Drayton
Norwich
Norfolk NR8 6EF
01603 860210

Nutley
Down House
Down Street
Nutley
East Sussex TN22 3LE
01825 712328

Oswestry
Pen-Y-Dwffryn Hall
Rhydycroesau
Nr Oswestry
Shropshire SY10 7DT
01691 653700

Oxford (Kingston Bagpuize)
Fallowfields
Southmoor
Kingston Bagpuize
Oxford OX13 5BH
01865 820416

Porthleven, nr Helston
Tye Rock Hotel
Loe Bar Road
Porthleven
Cornwall TR13 9EW
01326 572695

Pulborough
Chequers Hotel
Church Place
Pulborough
West Sussex RH20 1AD
01798 872486

Redditch
The Old Rectory
Ipsley Lane
Redditch
Hereford & Worcester B98 0AP
01527 523000

Ross-on-Wye (Glewstone)
Glewstone Court
Nr Ross-on-Wye
Herefordshire HR9 6AW
01989 770367

Ross-on-Wye (Kilcot)
Orchard House
Astoningham Road
Kilcot
Gloucestershire GL18 1NP
01989 720417

Ross-on-Wye
Peterstow Country House
Peterstow
Ross-on-Wye
Herefordshire HR9 6LB
01989 562826

Ross-on-Wye (Yatton)
Rock's Place
Yatton
Ross-on-Wye
Hertfordshire HR9 7RD
01531 660218

Seavington St Mary (Nr Ilminster)
The Pheasant Hotel
Seavington St Mary
Nr Ilminster
Somerset TA19 0HQ
01460 240502

Sherborne
The Eastbury Hotel
Long Street
Sherborne
Dorset DT9 3BY
01935 813131

Simonsbath (Exmoor)
Simonsbath House Hotel
Simonsbath
Exmoor
Somerset TA24 7SH
01643 831259

South Molton
Marsh Hall Country House Hotel
South Molton
Devon EX36 3HQ
01769 572666

St Ives (Trink)
The Countryman At Trink
Old Coach Road
St Ives
Cornwall TR26 3JQ
01736 797571

Stamford (Ketton)
The Priory
Church Road
Ketton
Stamford
Lincolnshire PE9 3RD
01780 720215

Staverton, Nr Totnes
Kingston House
Staverton
Totnes
Devon TQ9 6AR
01803 762235

Stroud (Middle Lypiatt)
Middle Lypiatt House
Middle Lypiatt
Stroud
Gloucestershire GL6 7LW
01453 882151

Taunton (Hatch Beauchamp)
Farthings Hotel and Restaurant
Hatch Beauchamp
Taunton
Somerset TA3 6SG
01823 480664

Tewkesbury
Upper Court
Kemerton
Nr Tewkesbury
Gloucestershire GL20 7HY
01386 725351

Thetford
Broom Hall
Richmond Road
Sahamtoney
Thetford
Norfolk IP25 7EX
01953 882125

Tintagel (Trenale)
Trebrea Lodge
Trenale
Tintagel
Cornwall PL34 0HR
01840 770410

Uckfield
Hooke Hall
High Street
Uckfield
East Sussex TN22 1EN
01825 761578

Wareham (East Stoke)
Kemps Country House Hotel & Restaurant
East Stoke
Wareham
Dorset BH20 6AL
01929 462563

Wells
Beryl
Wells
Somerset
Avon BA5 3JP
01749 678738

Wells (Wookey Hole)
Glencot House
Glencot Lane
Wookey Hole
Wells
Somerset BA5 1BH
01749 677160

Whitby (Dunsley)
Dunsley Hall
Dunsley
Whitby
North Yorkshire YO21 3TL
01947 893437

Wimborne Minster
Beechleas
17 Poole Road
Wimborne Minster
Dorset BH21 1QA
01202 841684

Winchelsea
The Country House at Winchelsea
Hastings Road
Winchelsea
East Sussex TN36 4AD
01797 226669

Windermere (Bowness)
Fayrer Garden House Hotel
Upper Stores Road
Bowness-on-Windermere
Cumbria LA23 3JP
015394 88195

Witherslack
The Old Vicarage Country House Hotel
Church Road
Witherslack
Grange-over-Sands
Cumbria LA11 6RS
015395 52381

Woodbridge (Otley)
Otley House
Helmingham Road
Otley
Suffolk IP6 9NR
01473 890253

York
4 South Parade
York
North Yorkshire YO2 2BA
01904 628229

York (Escrick)
The Parsonage Country House Hotel
Escrick
York
North Yorkshire YO4 6LF
01904 728111

Abergavenny (Glancrwyney)
Glancrwyney Court
Glancrwyney
Nr Abergavenny
Powys
01873 811288

Abergavenny
Llanwenarth House
Govilon
Abergavenny
Gwent NP7 9SF
01873 830289

Abergavenny (Llanfihangel Crucorney)
Penyclawdd Court
Llanfihangel Crucorney
Nr Abergavenny
Gwent
01873 890719

Barmouth (Glandwr)
Plasbach
Glandwr
Nr Barmouth
Gwyndd LL42 1TG
01341 281234

Betws-Y-Coed
Tan-Y-Foel
Capel Garmon
Nr Betws-Y-Coed
Gwynedd LL26 0RE
01690 710507

Brecon (Three Cocks)
Old Gwernyfed Country Manor
Felindre
Three Cocks
Brecon
Powys LD3 0SU
01497 847376

Caernarfon
Ty'n Rhos
Llanddeiniolen
Caernarfon
Gwynedd
01248 670489

Conwy
Berthlwyd Hall Hotel
Llechwedd
Nr Conwy
Gwynedd LL32 8DQ
01492 592409

Conwy
The Old Rectory
Conwy
Llanwrst Road
Llansanffraid Glan Conwy
Gwynedd LL28 5LF
01492 580611

Corwen (Llandrillo)
Tyddyn Llan Country House Hotel
Llandrillo
Nr Corwen
Clwyd LL21 0ST
01490 440264

Criccieth
Myndd Ednyfed Country House Hotel
Caernafon Road
Criccieth
Gwynedd LL52 0PH
01766 523269

Dolgellau (Ganllwyd)
Dolmelynllyn Hall Hotel
Ganllwyd
Dolgellau
Gwynedd LL40 2HP
01341 440273

Fishguard
Plas Glyn-Y-Mel
Lower Town
Fishguard
Dyfed SA65 9LY
01348 872296

Fishguard (Welsh Hook)
Stone Hall
Welsh Hook
Haverford
WestPembrokeshire
Dyfed SA62 5NS
01348 840212

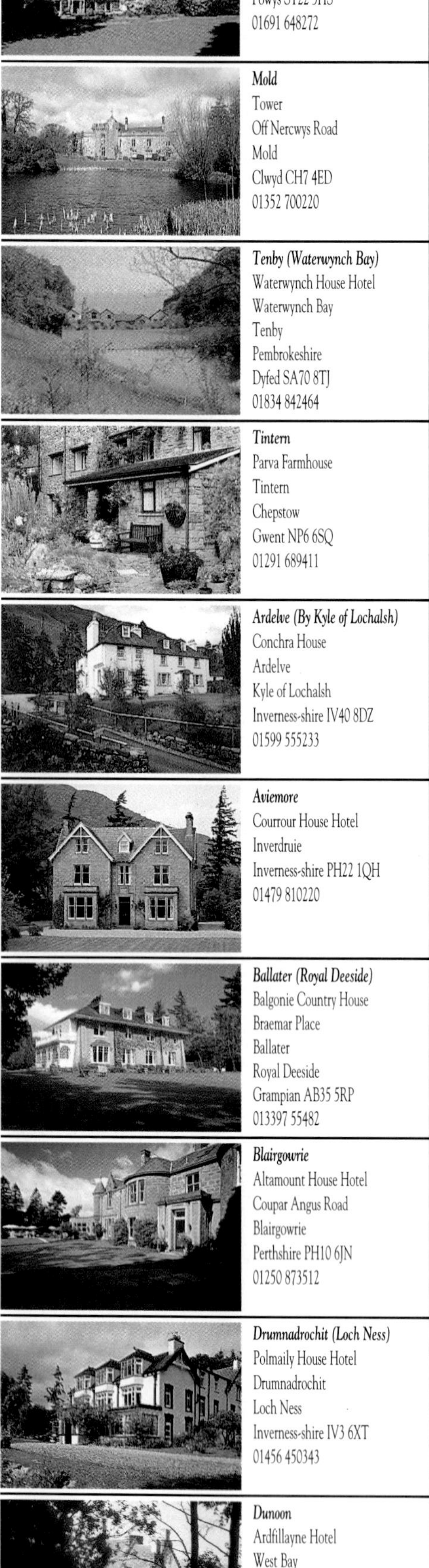

Llanfyllin
Bodfach Hall Country House Hotel
Llanfyllin
Powys SY22 5HS
01691 648272

Mold
Tower
Off Nercwys Road
Mold
Clwyd CH7 4ED
01352 700220

Tenby (Waterwynch Bay)
Waterwynch House Hotel
Waterwynch Bay
Tenby
Pembrokeshire
Dyfed SA70 8TJ
01834 842464

Tintern
Parva Farmhouse
Tintern
Chepstow
Gwent NP6 6SQ
01291 689411

Ardelve (By Kyle of Lochalsh)
Conchra House
Ardelve
Kyle of Lochalsh
Inverness-shire IV40 8DZ
01599 555233

Aviemore
Courrour House Hotel
Inverdruie
Inverness-shire PH22 1QH
01479 810220

Ballater (Royal Deeside)
Balgonie Country House
Braemar Place
Ballater
Royal Deeside
Grampian AB35 5RP
013397 55482

Blairgowrie
Altamount House Hotel
Coupar Angus Road
Blairgowrie
Perthshire PH10 6JN
01250 873512

Drumnadrochit (Loch Ness)
Polmaily House Hotel
Drumnadrochit
Loch Ness
Inverness-shire IV3 6XT
01456 450343

Dunoon
Ardfillayne Hotel
West Bay
Dunoon
Argyll
Argyllshire PA23 7QJ
01369 702267

Fintry (Stirlingshire)
Culcreuch Castle Hotel
Fintry
Loch Lomond
Stirling & Trossachs
Stirlingshire
01360 860228

Forres
Knockomie Hotel
Grantown Road
Forres
Morray IV36 0SG
01309 673146

Grantown-on-Spey
Culdearn House
Woodlands Terrace
Grantown-on-Spey
Moray
Morayshire PH26 3JU
01479 872106

Inverness
Culduthel Lodge
14 Culduthel Road
Inverness
Inverness-shire IV2 4AG
01463 240089

Isle Of Harris
Ardvourlie Castle
Aird A Mhulaidh
Isle Of Harris
Western Isles HS3 3AB
01859 502307

Isle Of Mull
Killiechronan
Killiechronan
Isle of Mull
Argyll PA72 6JU
01680 300403

Isle Of Skye (By Dunvegan)
Harlosh House
By Dunvegan
Isle of Skye
Inverness-shire IV55 8ZG
01470 521367

Killiecrankie, By Pitlochry
The Killiecrankie Hotel
Killiecrankie
By Pitlochry
Perthshire PH16 5LG
01796 473220

Moffat
Well View Hotel
Ballplay Road
Moffat
Dumfriesshire DG10 9JU
01683 220184

Oban
The Manor House
Gallanach Road
Oban
Scotland PA34 4LS
01631 562087

Perth
Dupplin Castle
Dupplin Estate
By Perth
Perthshire PH2 0PY
01738 623224

Pitlochry
Craigmhor Lodge
27 West Moulin Road
Pitlochry PH16 5EF
01796 472123

Pitlochry
Dunfallandy House
Logierait Road
Pitlochry
Perthshire PH16 5NA
01796 472648

Port Of Menteith
The Lake Hotel
Port Of Menteith
Perthshire FK8 3RA
01877 385258

Strath Brora
Sciberscross Lodge
Strath Brora
Rogart
Sutherland IV28 3YQ
01408 641246

Birr, Co Offaly
Kinnitty Castle
Kinnitty
Birr
Co Offaly
353 509 37318

Craigantlet, Newtownards
Beech Hill
23 Ballymoney Road
Craigantlet
Newtownards
Co Down
Northern Ireland BT23 4TG
01232 425892

Letterkenny, Co Donegal
Castlegrove Country House
Ramelton Road
Letterkenny
Co Donegal
353 745 1118

Malahide, Co Dublin
Belcamp Hutchinson
Balgriffin
Dublin
353 846 0843

Nenagh, Co Tipperary
St David's Country House and Restaurant
Ballycommon
Nenagh
Co Tipperary
353 672 4145

Newtownards (Co Down, Northern Ireland)
Edenvale House
130 Portaferry Road
Newtownards
Co Down BT22 2AH
01247 814881

Portaferry (Co Down, Northern Ireland)
Portaferry Hotel
The Strand
Portaferry
Co Down BT22 1PE
012477 28231

Riverstown, Co Sligo
Coopershill House
Riverstown
Co Sligo
353 716 5108

Skibbereen, Co Cork
Liss Ard Lake Lodge
Skibbereen
Co Cork
353 282 2365

Wicklow, Co Wicklow
The Old Rectory
Wicklow Town
Co Wicklow
343 404 67048

Guernsey (Fermain Bay)
La Favorita Hotel
Fermain Bay
Guernsey GY4 6SD
01481 35666

Sligo, Co Sligo
Markree Castle
Collooney
Co Sligo
353 716 7800

Guernsey (Castel)
Les Embruns Hotel
Route De La Margion
Vazon Bay
Castel
Guernsey
01481 64834

Jersey (St Helier)
Almorah Hotel
One Almorah Crescent
Lower Kings Cliff
La Pouque Lay
St Helier, Jersey JE2 3GU
01534 21648

Straffan, Co Kildare
Barberstown Castle
Straffan
Co Kildare
353 628 8157

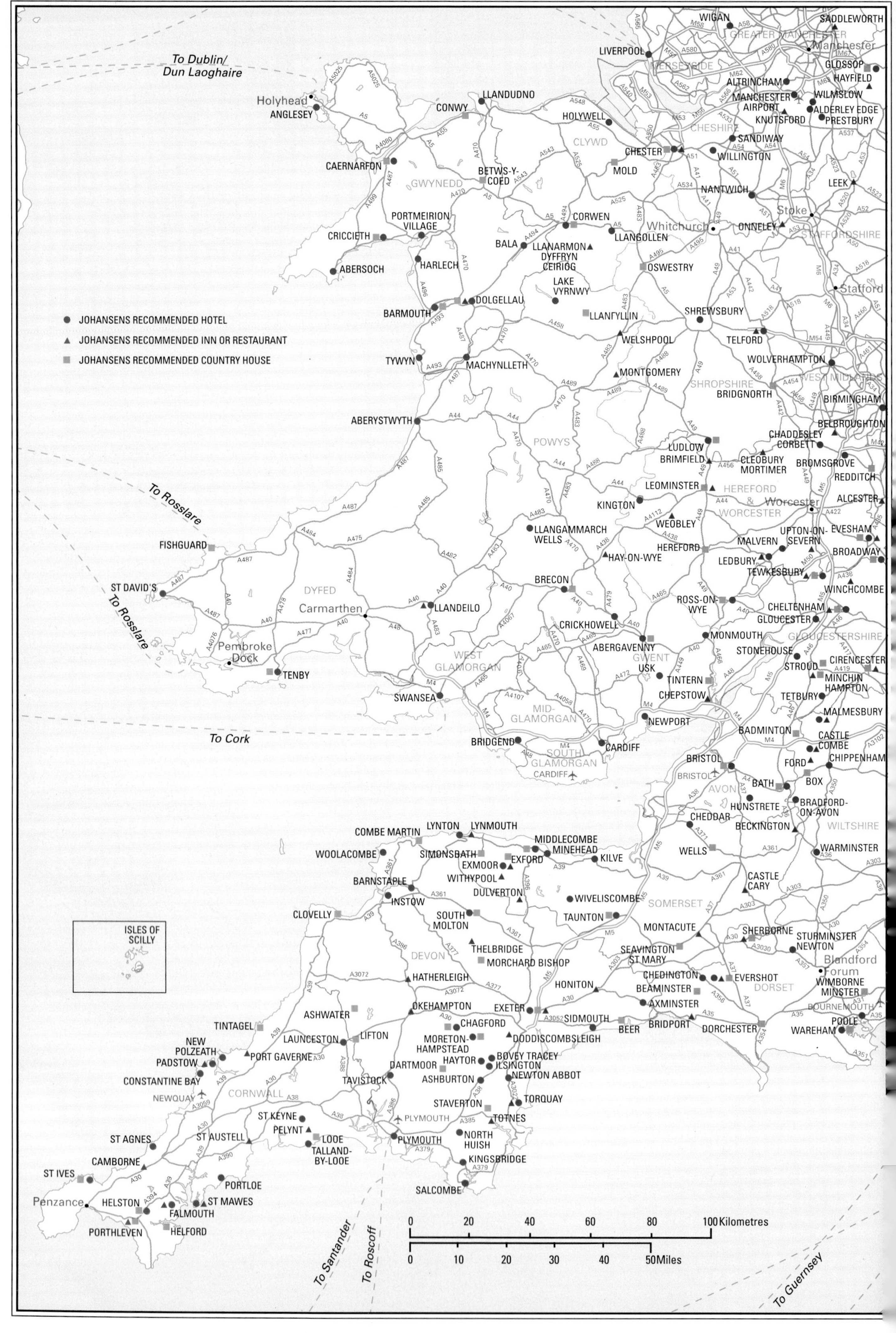

● JOHANSENS RECOMMENDED HOTEL
▲ JOHANSENS RECOMMENDED INN OR RESTAURANT
■ JOHANSENS RECOMMENDED COUNTRY HOUSE
To Dublin/
Dun Laoghaire
To Rosslare
To Rosslare
To Cork
To Santander
To Roscoff
To Guernsey
ISLES OF
SCILLY
0 20 40 60 80 100 Kilometres
0 10 20 30 40 50 Miles
Holyhead
ANGLESEY
CONWY
LLANDUDNO
HOLYWELL
CLYWD
CAERNARFON
GWYNEDD
BETWS-Y-
COED
MOLD
CHESTER
PORTMEIRION
VILLAGE
CRICCIETH
ABERSOCH
HARLECH
BALA
CORWEN
LLANGOLLEN
LLANARMON
DYFFRYN
CEIRIOG
OSWESTRY
LAKE
VYRNWY
BARMOUTH
DOLGELLAU
LLANFYLLIN
WELSHPOOL
TYWYN
MACHYNLLETH
MONTGOMERY
ABERYSTWYTH
POWYS
FISHGUARD
ST DAVID'S
DYFED
Carmarthen
LLANDEILO
Pembroke
Dock
TENBY
LLANGAMMARCH
WELLS
HAY-ON-WYE
BRECON
CRICKHOWELL
ABERGAVENNY
GWENT
USK
WEST
GLAMORGAN
SWANSEA
MID-
GLAMORGAN
BRIDGEND
CARDIFF
SOUTH
GLAMORGAN
CARDIFF
NEWPORT
CHEPSTOW
TINTERN
MONMOUTH
KINGTON
WIGAN
SADDLEWORTH
LIVERPOOL
GREATER MANCHESTER
MERSEYSIDE
Manchester
GLOSSOP
HAYFIELD
ALTRINCHAM
MANCHESTER
AIRPORT
WILMSLOW
ALDERLEY EDGE
KNUTSFORD
PRESTBURY
CHESHIRE
SANDIWAY
WILLINGTON
NANTWICH
LEEK
Stoke
Whitchurch
ONNELEY
STAFFORDSHIRE
Stafford
SHREWSBURY
TELFORD
WOLVERHAMPTON
SHROPSHIRE
BRIDGNORTH
WEST MIDLANDS
BIRMINGHAM
BELBROUGHTON
CHADDESLEY
CORBETT
LUDLOW
BRIMFIELD
CLEOBURY
MORTIMER
BROMSGROVE
REDDITCH
LEOMINSTER
HEREFORD
&
WORCESTER
Worcester
ALCESTER
WEOBLEY
HEREFORD
MALVERN
UPTON-ON-
SEVERN
EVESHAM
BROADWAY
LEDBURY
TEWKESBURY
WINCHCOMBE
ROSS-ON-
WYE
CHELTENHAM
GLOUCESTER
GLOUCESTERSHIRE
STONEHOUSE
STROUD
CIRENCESTER
MINCHIN
HAMPTON
TETBURY
MALMESBURY
BADMINTON
CASTLE
COMBE
CHIPPENHAM
BRISTOL
BRISTOL
FORD
AVON
BATH
BOX
HUNSTRETE
BRADFORD-
ON-AVON
CHEDDAR
BECKINGTON
WILTSHIRE
WELLS
WARMINSTER
COMBE MARTIN
LYNTON
LYNMOUTH
WOOLACOMBE
SIMONSBATH
MIDDLECOMBE
MINEHEAD
EXFORD
EXMOOR
KILVE
WITHYPOOL
BARNSTAPLE
DULVERTON
INSTOW
WIVELISCOMBE
SOMERSET
CLOVELLY
SOUTH
MOLTON
TAUNTON
CASTLE
CARY
MONTACUTE
SHERBORNE
STURMINSTER
NEWTON
THELBRIDGE
DEVON
MORCHARD BISHOP
SEAVINGTON
ST MARY
Blandford
Forum
CHEDINGTON
EVERSHOT
WIMBORNE
MINSTER
HATHERLEIGH
HONITON
BEAMINSTER
DORSET
AXMINSTER
BOURNEMOUTH
OKEHAMPTON
EXETER
SIDMOUTH
BEER
BRIDPORT
DORCHESTER
POOLE
WAREHAM
ASHWATER
CHAGFORD
TINTAGEL
LAUNCESTON
LIFTON
MORETON-
HAMPSTEAD
DODDISCOMBSLEIGH
NEW
POLZEATH
PORT GAVERNE
BOVEY TRACEY
PADSTOW
DARTMOOR
HAYTOR
ILSINGTON
CONSTANTINE BAY
TAVISTOCK
ASHBURTON
NEWTON ABBOT
NEWQUAY
CORNWALL
TORQUAY
STAVERTON
ST KEYNE
PLYMOUTH
TOTNES
PELYNT
LOOE
ST AGNES
ST AUSTELL
PLYMOUTH
NORTH
HUISH
TALLAND-
BY-LOOE
CAMBORNE
KINGSBRIDGE
ST IVES
PORTLOE
SALCOMBE
Penzance
HELSTON
ST MAWES
FALMOUTH
PORTHLEVEN
HELFORD

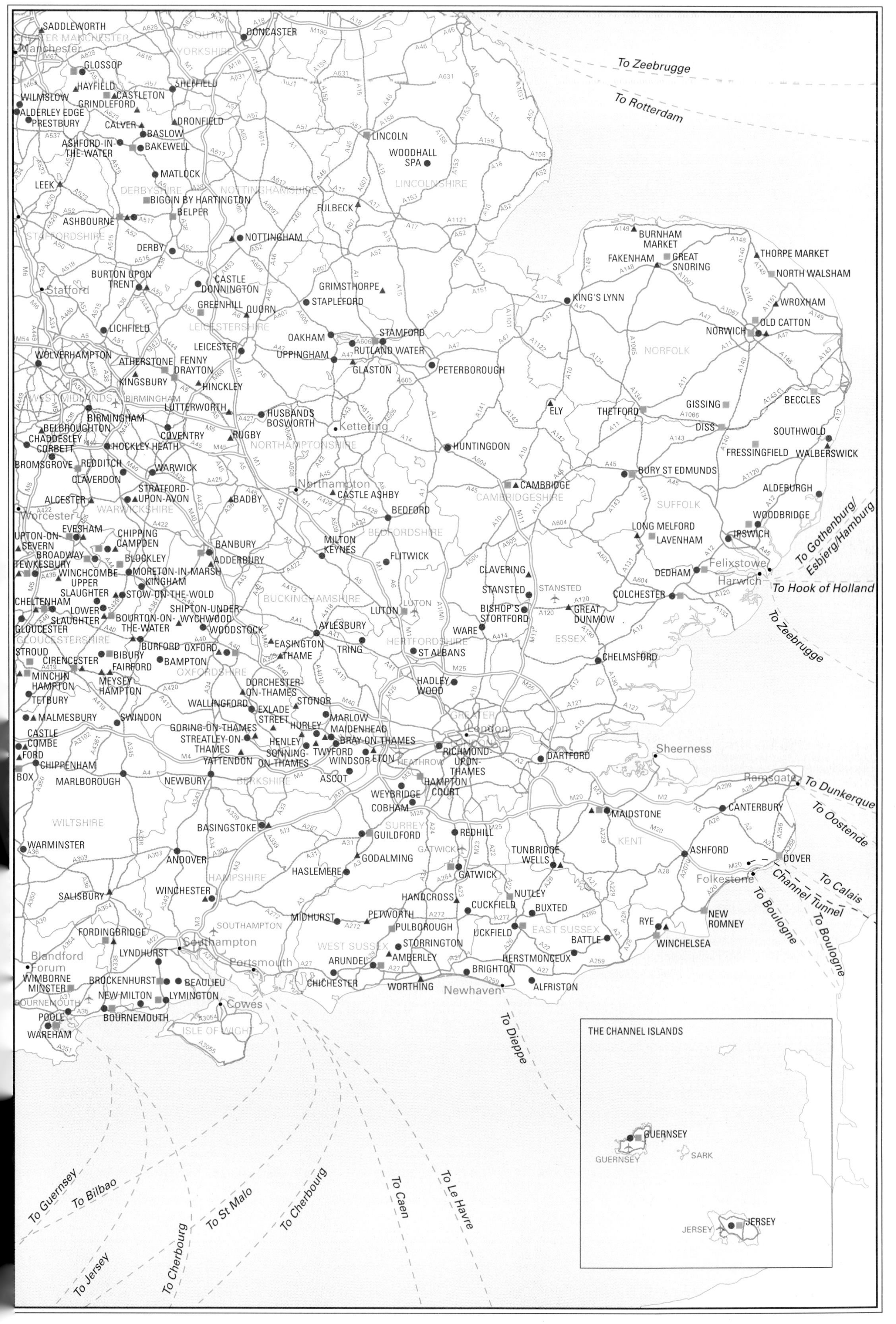
SADDLEWORTH
GREATER MANCHESTER
Manchester
DONCASTER
SOUTH YORKSHIRE
GLOSSOP
HAYFIELD
CASTLETON
SHEFFIELD
WILMSLOW
GRINDLEFORD
ALDERLEY EDGE
PRESTBURY
DRONFIELD
CALVER
BASLOW
ASHFORD-IN-THE-WATER
BAKEWELL
LINCOLN
WOODHALL SPA
MATLOCK
LEEK
DERBYSHIRE
NOTTINGHAMSHIRE
LINCOLNSHIRE
BIGGIN BY HARTINGTON
FULBECK
ASHBOURNE
BELPER
STAFFORDSHIRE
NOTTINGHAM
DERBY
BURTON UPON TRENT
CASTLE DONNINGTON
GRIMSTHORPE
Stafford
GREENHILL
QUORN
STAPLEFORD
LICHFIELD
LEICESTERSHIRE
OAKHAM
STAMFORD
LEICESTER
RUTLAND WATER
UPPINGHAM
WOLVERHAMPTON
ATHERSTONE
FENNY DRAYTON
GLASTON
PETERBOROUGH
KINGSBURY
HINCKLEY
WEST MIDLANDS
BIRMINGHAM
LUTTERWORTH
HUSBANDS BOSWORTH
Kettering
BELBROUGHTON
COVENTRY
RUGBY
CHADDESLEY CORBETT
HOCKLEY HEATH
NORTHAMPTONSHIRE
HUNTINGDON
BROMSGROVE
REDDITCH
WARWICK
CLAVERDON
Northampton
STRATFORD-UPON-AVON
CASTLE ASHBY
ALCESTER
BADBY
WARWICKSHIRE
Worcester
BEDFORD
EVESHAM
CHIPPING CAMPDEN
BEDFORDSHIRE
UPTON-ON-SEVERN
BANBURY
MILTON KEYNES
BROADWAY
BLOCKLEY
ADDERBURY
FLITWICK
TEWKESBURY
WINCHCOMBE
MORETON-IN-MARSH
UPPER SLAUGHTER
KINGHAM
STOW-ON-THE-WOLD
BUCKINGHAMSHIRE
LUTON
CHELTENHAM
SHIPTON-UNDER-WYCHWOOD
LOWER SLAUGHTER
BOURTON-ON-THE-WATER
GLOUCESTER
WOODSTOCK
AYLESBURY
GLOUCESTERSHIRE
BURFORD
OXFORD
EASINGTON
STROUD
BIBURY
THAME
TRING
HERTFORDSHIRE
ST ALBANS
CIRENCESTER
BAMPTON
FAIRFORD
OXFORDSHIRE
MINCHIN HAMPTON
MEYSEY HAMPTON
DORCHESTER-ON-THAMES
HADLEY WOOD
TETBURY
WALLINGFORD
STONOR
EXLADE STREET
MALMESBURY
SWINDON
MARLOW
HURLEY
MAIDENHEAD
GREATER London
CASTLE COMBE
GORING-ON-THAMES
STREATLEY-ON-THAMES
HENLEY
BRAY-ON-THAMES
FORD
SONNING-ON-THAMES
TWYFORD
YATTENDON
WINDSOR
ETON
RICHMOND-UPON-THAMES
HEATHROW
CHIPPENHAM
BOX
MARLBOROUGH
NEWBURY
BERKSHIRE
ASCOT
HAMPTON COURT
WEYBRIDGE
COBHAM
WILTSHIRE
BASINGSTOKE
GUILDFORD
REDHILL
WARMINSTER
GATWICK
GODALMING
ANDOVER
SURREY
HASLEMERE
HAMPSHIRE
WINCHESTER
SALISBURY
HANDCROSS
PETWORTH
MIDHURST
FORDINGBRIDGE
SOUTHAMPTON
PULBOROUGH
Southampton
LYNDHURST
WEST SUSSEX
STORRINGTON
Blandford Forum
Portsmouth
ARUNDEL
AMBERLEY
WIMBORNE MINSTER
BROCKENHURST
BEAULIEU
CHICHESTER
WORTHING
BOURNEMOUTH
NEW MILTON
LYMINGTON
Cowes
POOLE
WAREHAM
ISLE OF WIGHT
To Zeebrugge
To Rotterdam
BURNHAM MARKET
THORPE MARKET
FAKENHAM
GREAT SNORING
NORTH WALSHAM
KING'S LYNN
WROXHAM
OLD CATTON
NORWICH
NORFOLK
ELY
THETFORD
GISSING
BECCLES
DISS
SOUTHWOLD
FRESSINGFIELD
WALBERSWICK
BURY ST EDMUNDS
CAMBRIDGE
CAMBRIDGESHIRE
SUFFOLK
ALDEBURGH
WOODBRIDGE
LONG MELFORD
LAVENHAM
IPSWICH
To Gothenburg/Esbjerg/Hamburg
CLAVERING
DEDHAM
Felixstowe
Harwich
STANSTED
To Hook of Holland
COLCHESTER
BISHOP'S STORTFORD
GREAT DUNMOW
WARE
ESSEX
To Zeebrugge
CHELMSFORD
Sheerness
DARTFORD
Ramsgate
To Dunkerque
CANTERBURY
To Oostende
MAIDSTONE
KENT
ASHFORD
TUNBRIDGE WELLS
DOVER
To Calais
Folkestone
Channel Tunnel
NUTLEY
CUCKFIELD
BUXTED
NEW ROMNEY
To Boulogne
To Boulogne
UCKFIELD
EAST SUSSEX
RYE
BATTLE
WINCHELSEA
HERSTMONCEUX
BRIGHTON
ALFRISTON
Newhaven
To Dieppe
THE CHANNEL ISLANDS
GUERNSEY
SARK
JERSEY
To Guernsey
To Bilbao
To Jersey
To Cherbourg
To St Malo
To Cherbourg
To Caen
To Le Havre

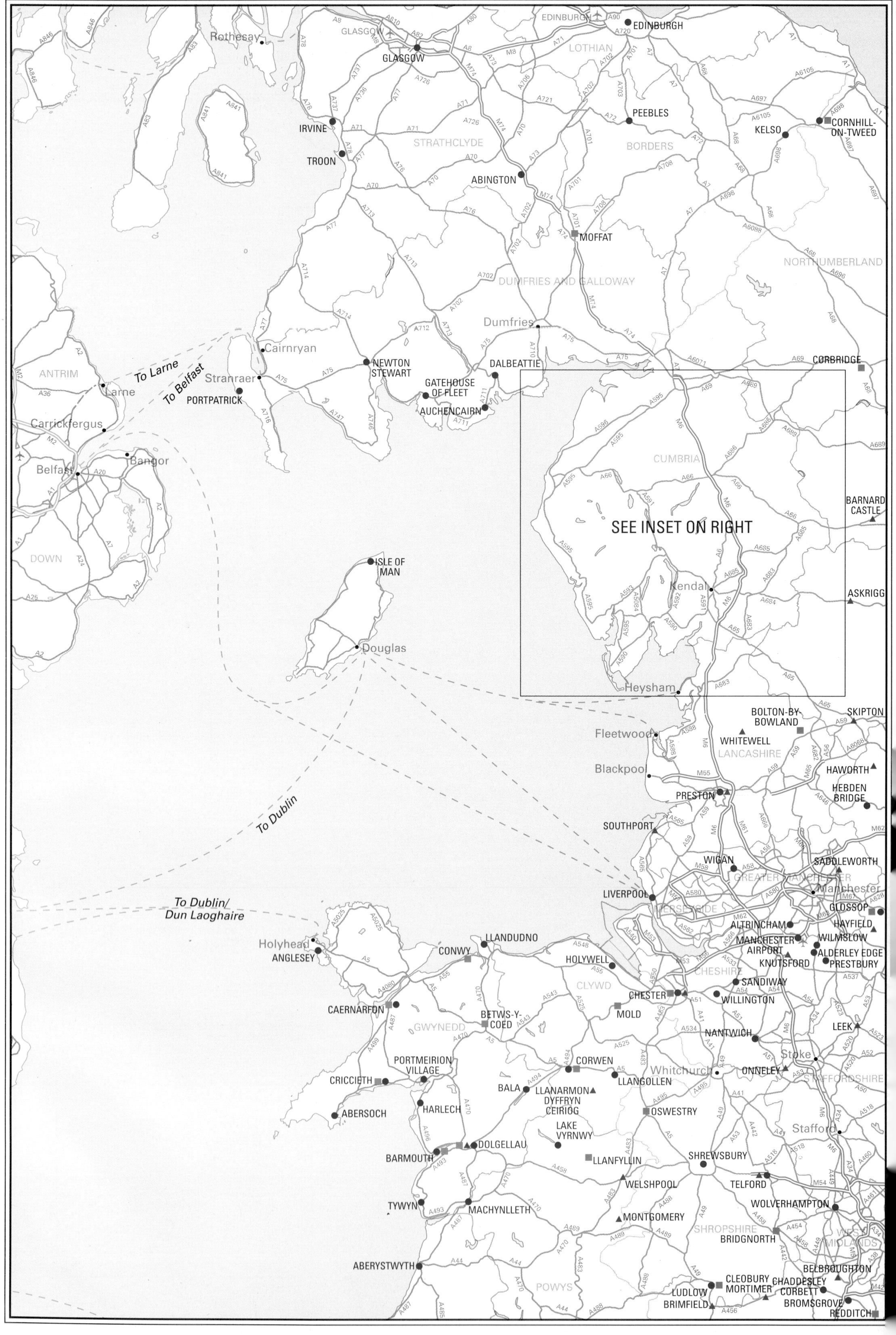
EDINBURGH
GLASGOW
Rothesay
LOTHIAN
IRVINE
TROON
PEEBLES
KELSO
CORNHILL-ON-TWEED
STRATHCLYDE
BORDERS
ABINGTON
MOFFAT
NORTHUMBERLAND
DUMFRIES AND GALLOWAY
Dumfries
Cairnryan
NEWTON STEWART
DALBEATTIE
CORBRIDGE
To Larne
To Belfast
Stranraer
PORTPATRICK
GATEHOUSE OF FLEET
AUCHENCAIRN
ANTRIM
Larne
Carrickfergus
Belfast
Bangor
CUMBRIA
BARNARD CASTLE
SEE INSET ON RIGHT
DOWN
ISLE OF MAN
Kendal
ASKRIGG
Douglas
Heysham
BOLTON-BY-BOWLAND
SKIPTON
WHITEWELL
Fleetwood
LANCASHIRE
Blackpool
HAWORTH
PRESTON
HEBDEN BRIDGE
To Dublin
SOUTHPORT
WIGAN
SADDLEWORTH
GREATER MANCHESTER
LIVERPOOL
Manchester
MERSEYSIDE
GLOSSOP
To Dublin/
Dun Laoghaire
ALTRINCHAM
HAYFIELD
Holyhead
ANGLESEY
LLANDUDNO
CONWY
HOLYWELL
MANCHESTER AIRPORT
WILMSLOW
ALDERLEY EDGE
KNUTSFORD
PRESTBURY
CHESHIRE
SANDIWAY
CLYWD
CHESTER
WILLINGTON
MOLD
CAERNARFON
BETWS-Y-COED
GWYNEDD
LEEK
NANTWICH
PORTMEIRION VILLAGE
CORWEN
Stoke
CRICCIETH
Whitchurch
ONNELEY
STAFFORDSHIRE
LLANGOLLEN
BALA
LLANARMON DYFFRYN CEIRIOG
OSWESTRY
ABERSOCH
HARLECH
Stafford
LAKE VYRNWY
DOLGELLAU
BARMOUTH
SHREWSBURY
LLANFYLLIN
TELFORD
WELSHPOOL
TYWYN
MACHYNLLETH
WOLVERHAMPTON
MONTGOMERY
SHROPSHIRE
BRIDGNORTH
WEST MIDLANDS
ABERYSTWYTH
BELBROUGHTON
CLEOBURY MORTIMER
CHADDESLEY CORBETT
POWYS
LUDLOW
BRIMFIELD
BROMSGROVE
REDDITCH

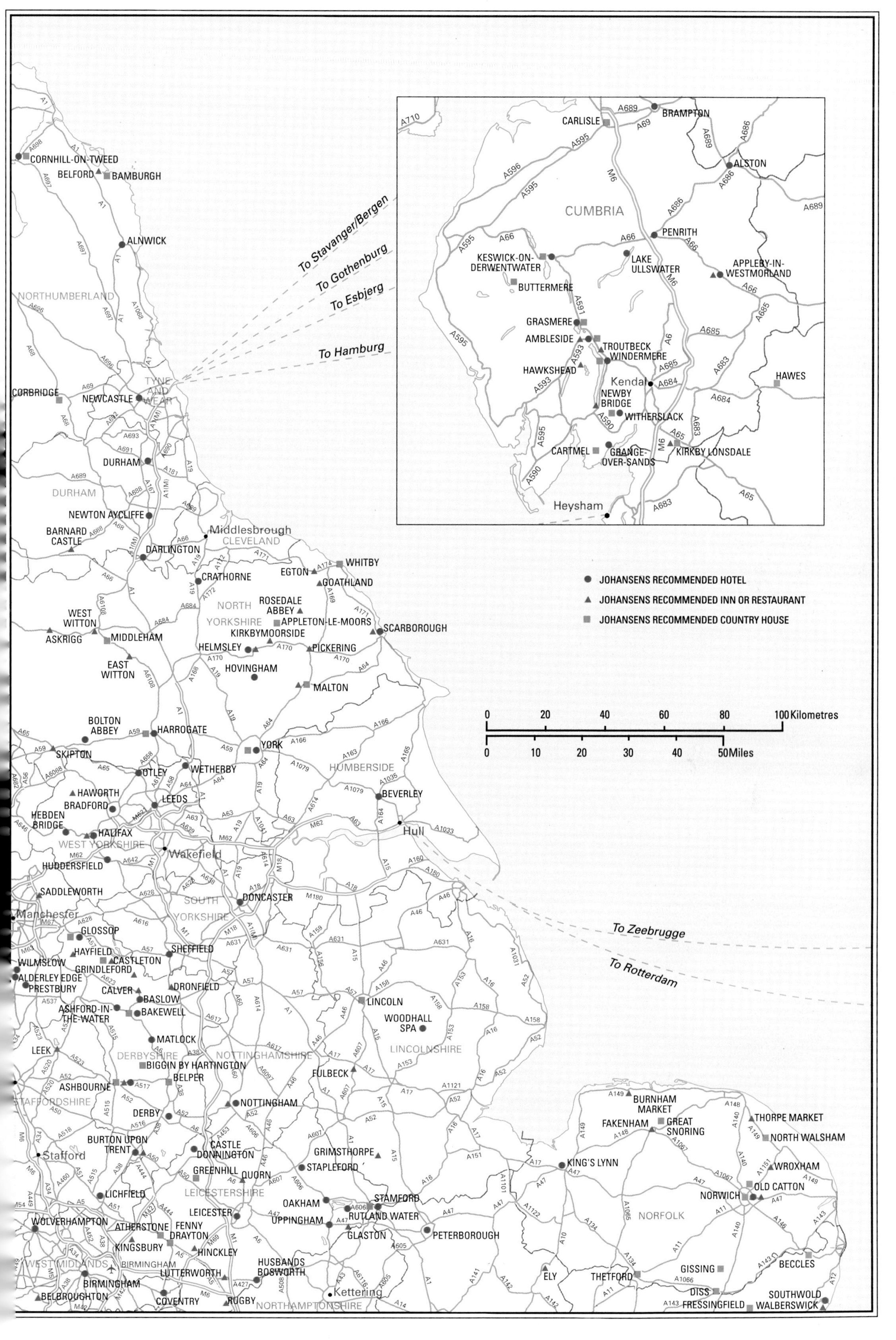
CARLISLE
BRAMPTON
ALSTON
CUMBRIA
PENRITH
KESWICK-ON-DERWENTWATER
LAKE ULLSWATER
APPLEBY-IN-WESTMORLAND
BUTTERMERE
GRASMERE
AMBLESIDE
TROUTBECK
WINDERMERE
HAWKSHEAD
Kendal
HAWES
NEWBY BRIDGE
WITHERSLACK
CARTMEL
GRANGE-OVER-SANDS
KIRKBY LONSDALE
Heysham
To Stavanger/Bergen
To Gothenburg
To Esbjerg
To Hamburg
CORNHILL-ON-TWEED
BELFORD
BAMBURGH
ALNWICK
NORTHUMBERLAND
CORBRIDGE
NEWCASTLE
TYNE AND WEAR
DURHAM
NEWTON AYCLIFFE
BARNARD CASTLE
Middlesbrough
CLEVELAND
DARLINGTON
CRATHORNE
EGTON
WHITBY
GOATHLAND
NORTH YORKSHIRE
ROSEDALE ABBEY
APPLETON-LE-MOORS
KIRKBYMOORSIDE
SCARBOROUGH
WEST WITTON
ASKRIGG
MIDDLEHAM
HELMSLEY
PICKERING
HOVINGHAM
EAST WITTON
MALTON
● JOHANSENS RECOMMENDED HOTEL
▲ JOHANSENS RECOMMENDED INN OR RESTAURANT
■ JOHANSENS RECOMMENDED COUNTRY HOUSE
0 20 40 60 80 100 Kilometres
0 10 20 30 40 50 Miles
BOLTON ABBEY
HARROGATE
YORK
SKIPTON
OTLEY
WETHERBY
HUMBERSIDE
HAWORTH
BRADFORD
LEEDS
BEVERLEY
HEBDEN BRIDGE
HALIFAX
Hull
WEST YORKSHIRE
Wakefield
HUDDERSFIELD
SADDLEWORTH
SOUTH YORKSHIRE
DONCASTER
Manchester
GLOSSOP
HAYFIELD
SHEFFIELD
To Zeebrugge
To Rotterdam
WILMSLOW
CASTLETON
GRINDLEFORD
ALDERLEY EDGE
PRESTBURY
CALVER
DRONFIELD
BASLOW
ASHFORD-IN-THE-WATER
BAKEWELL
LINCOLN
WOODHALL SPA
MATLOCK
LEEK
LINCOLNSHIRE
DERBYSHIRE
NOTTINGHAMSHIRE
BIGGIN BY HARTINGTON
ASHBOURNE
BELPER
FULBECK
STAFFORDSHIRE
NOTTINGHAM
BURNHAM MARKET
DERBY
THORPE MARKET
FAKENHAM
GREAT SNORING
NORTH WALSHAM
BURTON UPON TRENT
CASTLE DONNINGTON
Stafford
GRIMSTHORPE
STAPLEFORD
KING'S LYNN
WROXHAM
GREENHILL
QUORN
LICHFIELD
LEICESTERSHIRE
OAKHAM
STAMFORD
OLD CATTON
NORWICH
LEICESTER
RUTLAND WATER
WOLVERHAMPTON
ATHERSTONE
FENNY DRAYTON
UPPINGHAM
NORFOLK
GLASTON
PETERBOROUGH
KINGSBURY
HINCKLEY
WEST MIDLANDS
BIRMINGHAM
HUSBANDS BOSWORTH
LUTTERWORTH
GISSING
BECCLES
ELY
THETFORD
Kettering
COVENTRY
DISS
SOUTHWOLD
BELBROUGHTON
RUGBY
NORTHAMPTONSHIRE
FRESSINGFIELD
WALBERSWICK

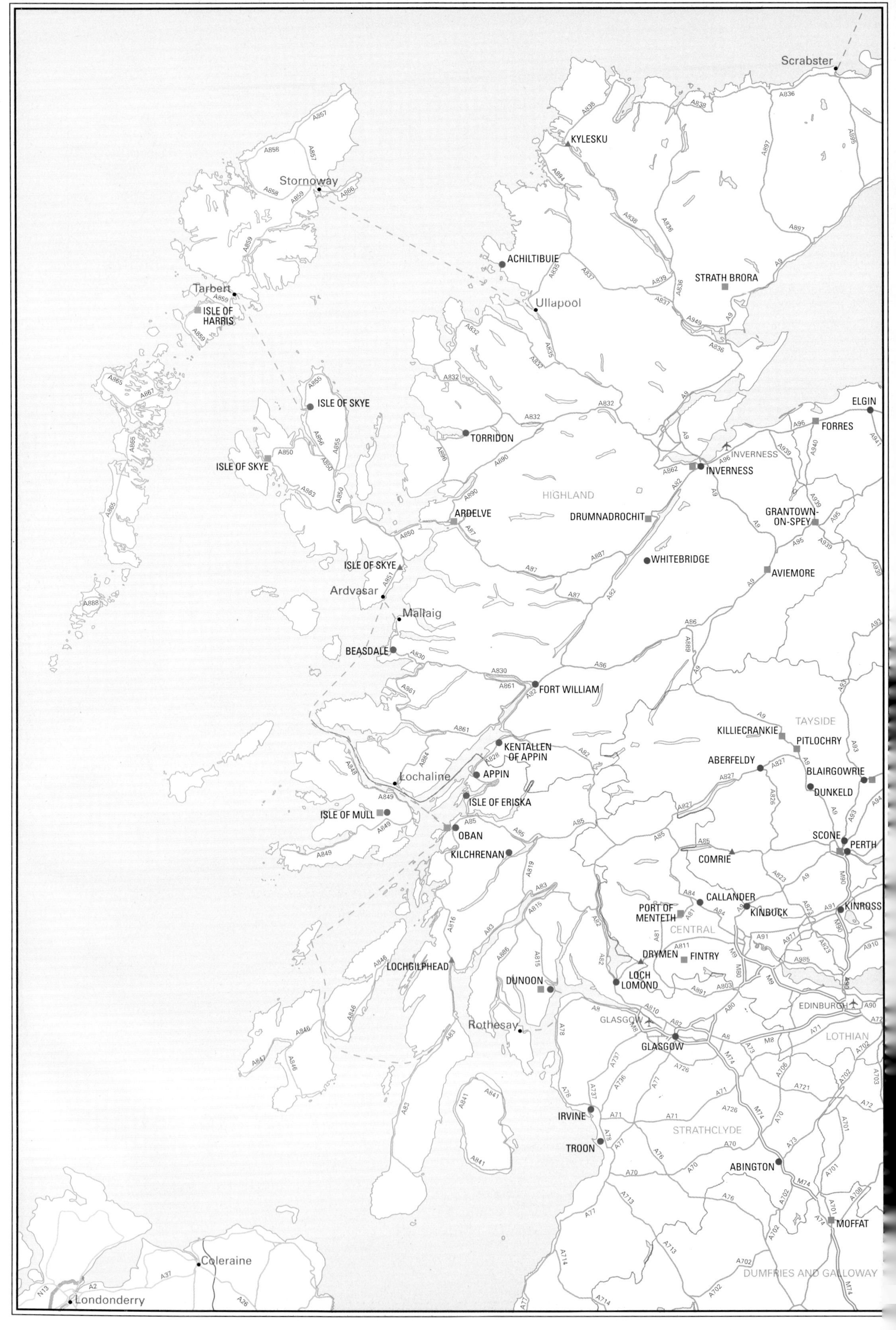
Scrabster
KYLESKU
Stornoway
ACHILTIBUIE
Ullapool
STRATH BRORA
Tarbert
ISLE OF HARRIS
ISLE OF SKYE
ISLE OF SKYE
TORRIDON
ELGIN
FORRES
INVERNESS
INVERNESS
HIGHLAND
DRUMNADROCHIT
ARDELVE
GRANTOWN-ON-SPEY
ISLE OF SKYE
WHITEBRIDGE
AVIEMORE
Ardvasar
Mallaig
BEASDALE
FORT WILLIAM
TAYSIDE
KILLIECRANKIE
PITLOCHRY
KENTALLEN OF APPIN
ABERFELDY
BLAIRGOWRIE
APPIN
Lochaline
DUNKELD
ISLE OF ERISKA
ISLE OF MULL
OBAN
SCONE
PERTH
KILCHRENAN
COMRIE
CALLANDER
PORT OF MENTETH
KINBUCK
KINROSS
CENTRAL
DRYMEN
FINTRY
LOCHGILPHEAD
DUNOON
LOCH LOMOND
EDINBURGH
GLASGOW
Rothesay
GLASGOW
LOTHIAN
IRVINE
STRATHCLYDE
TROON
ABINGTON
MOFFAT
Coleraine
DUMFRIES AND GALLOWAY
Londonderry

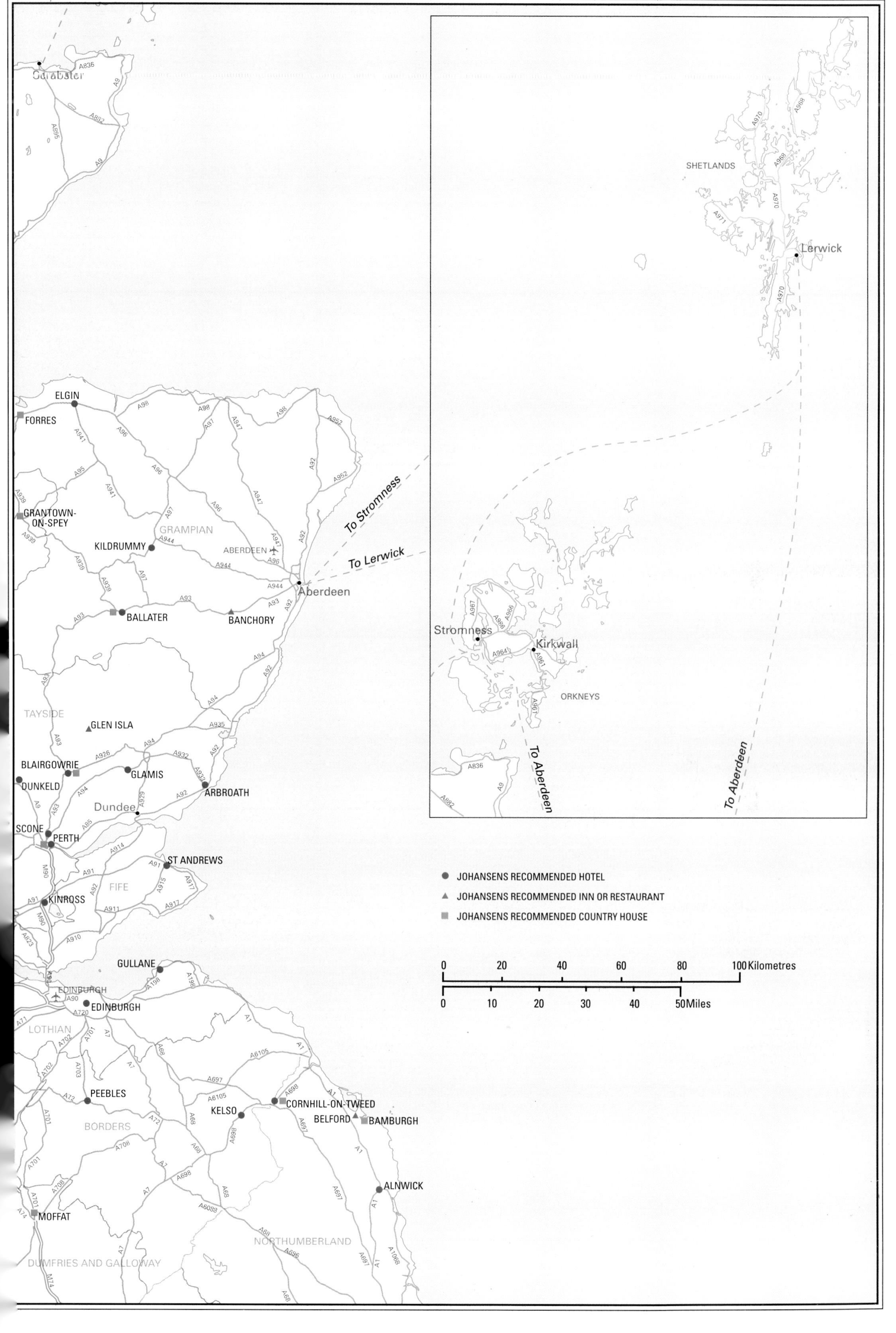

Scrabster
SHETLANDS
Lerwick
ELGIN
FORRES
GRANTOWN-ON-SPEY
GRAMPIAN
KILDRUMMY
ABERDEEN
Aberdeen
To Stromness
To Lerwick
BALLATER
BANCHORY
Stromness
Kirkwall
ORKNEYS
To Aberdeen
To Aberdeen
TAYSIDE
GLEN ISLA
BLAIRGOWRIE
DUNKELD
GLAMIS
ARBROATH
Dundee
SCONE
PERTH
ST ANDREWS
FIFE
KINROSS
JOHANSENS RECOMMENDED HOTEL
JOHANSENS RECOMMENDED INN OR RESTAURANT
JOHANSENS RECOMMENDED COUNTRY HOUSE
0 20 40 60 80 100 Kilometres
0 10 20 30 40 50 Miles
GULLANE
EDINBURGH
EDINBURGH
LOTHIAN
PEEBLES
KELSO
CORNHILL-ON-TWEED
BELFORD
BAMBURGH
BORDERS
ALNWICK
MOFFAT
NORTHUMBERLAND
DUMFRIES AND GALLOWAY

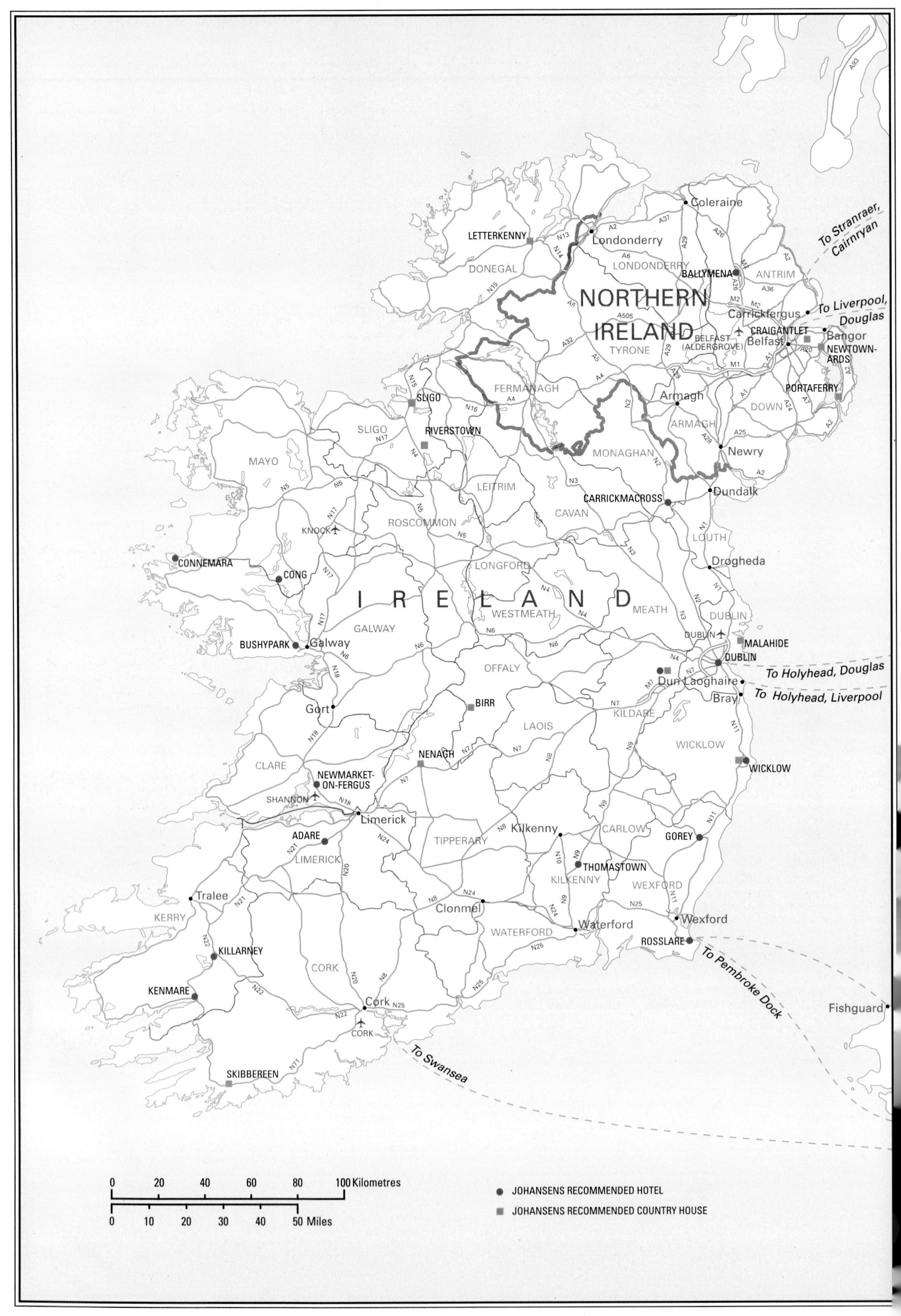

NORTHERN
IRELAND
IRELAND
To Stranraer, Cairnryan
To Liverpool, Douglas
To Holyhead, Douglas
To Holyhead, Liverpool
To Pembroke Dock
To Swansea
Fishguard
Coleraine
LETTERKENNY
Londonderry
DONEGAL
LONDONDERRY
BALLYMENA
ANTRIM
Carrickfergus
CRAIGANTLET
Bangor
Belfast
BELFAST (ALDERGROVE)
NEWTOWN-ARDS
TYRONE
PORTAFERRY
FERMANAGH
Armagh
ARMAGH
DOWN
SLIGO
RIVERSTOWN
Newry
MONAGHAN
MAYO
LEITRIM
CARRICKMACROSS
Dundalk
CAVAN
KNOCK
ROSCOMMON
LOUTH
CONNEMARA
CONG
LONGFORD
Drogheda
WESTMEATH
MEATH
GALWAY
DUBLIN
BUSHYPARK
Galway
MALAHIDE
OFFALY
Dun Laoghaire
Bray
Gort
BIRR
KILDARE
LAOIS
WICKLOW
CLARE
NENAGH
NEWMARKET-ON-FERGUS
SHANNON
Limerick
Kilkenny
CARLOW
ADARE
TIPPERARY
GOREY
LIMERICK
THOMASTOWN
KILKENNY
WEXFORD
Tralee
KERRY
Clonmel
Wexford
Waterford
WATERFORD
ROSSLARE
KILLARNEY
CORK
KENMARE
Cork
SKIBBEREEN
0 20 40 60 80 100 Kilometres
0 10 20 30 40 50 Miles
JOHANSENS RECOMMENDED HOTEL
JOHANSENS RECOMMENDED COUNTRY HOUSE

To enable you to use your 1996 Johansens Recommended Inns with Restaurants Guide more effectively, the following four pages of indexes contain a wealth of useful information about the establishments featured in the Guide. As well as listing the hotels alphabetically, by region and by county, the indexes also show at a glance which Inns with Restaurants offer certain specialised facilities.

The indexes are listed as follows:

- Alphabetically by region
- By county
- With a swimming pool
- With fishing nearby
- With shooting locally
- With conference facilities for 100 delegates or more
- Double rooms for £50 or under
- Single rooms for £30 or under
- Index of advertisers

1996 Johansens Recommended Inns with Restaurants listed alphabetically by region

ENGLAND

The Acorn Inn Hotel ... Evershot ... 53
The Anchor Inn ... Dulverton ... 47
The Anchor Inn ... Ely ... 51
The Anchor ... Walberswick ... 147
Arrow Mill ... Alcester ... 9
Baraset Barn Restaurant ... Stratford-upon-Avon ... 134
The Barn Owl Inn ... Torquay ... 141
The Barnacles Restaurant ... Hinkley ... 79
The Barton Angler Country Inn ... Wroxham ... 155
The Bell Hotel ... Tewkesbury ... 137
The Bird in Hand ... Twyford ... 145
The Black Horse Inn ... Grimsthorpe ... 68
The Blue Bell Hotel ... Belford ... 20
The Blue Boar Inn ... Stratford-upon-Avon ... 135
The Blue Lion ... East Witton ... 49
Boars Head Hotel ... Burton-upon-Trent ... 27
The Boathouse Brasserie ... Amberley ... 10
Boulters Lock Hotel ... Maidenhead ... 93
The Castle Inn ... Castle Combe ... 35
The Chequers at Slaugham ... Handcross ... 71
The Chequers Inn ... Calver ... 29
The Christopher Hotel ... Eton/Windsor ... 52
Cotswold Gateway Hotel ... Burford ... 24
The Countrymen ... Long Melford ... 90
The Cricketers ... Clavering ... 41
The Cridford Inn ... Exeter ... 55
The Crown at Hopton ... Cleobury Mortimer ... 42
East Ayton Lodge Country Hotel ... Scarborough ... 125
The Falcon Hotel and Restaurant ... Castle Ashby ... 33
The Feathers Hotel ... Ledbury ... 87
The Feversham Arms Hotel ... Helmsley ... 77
The Fox Country Hotel ... Ibstone ... 78
Freshmans Restaurant ... Belbroughton ... 19
The Garden House Hotel ... Norwich ... 102
The George and Dragon Hotel ... Kirkbymoorside ... 85
The George Hotel ... Basingstoke ... 17
The George Hotel ... Castle Carey ... 34
The George Hotel ... Dorchester-on-Thames ... 45
The George Hotel ... Hatherleigh ... 72
The Golden Lion Inn of Easenhall ... Rugby ... 119
Green Farm Restaurant and Hotel ... Thorpe Market ... 140
The Green Man ... Malton ... 97
The Greyhound ... Lutterworth ... 91
The Harbour Inn ... Porthleven ... 115
Hare & Hounds ... Fulbeck ... 62
The Harrow at Warren Street ... Maidstone ... 94
The Highwayman ... Exlade Street ... 56
Holcombe Hotel ... Oxford ... 106
Home Farm Hotel ... Honiton ... 80
The Horse and Groom Inn ... Malmesbury ... 96
The Hoste Arms Hotel ... Burnham Market ... 26
Hotel des Clos ... Nottingham ... 103
The Hundred House Hotel ... Telford ... 136
The Inn at Whitewell ... Whitewell ... 150
The Inn on the Lake ... Godalming ... 65
The Jersey Arms ... Oxford ... 107
Jubilee Inn ... Pelynt ... 111
The Kings Arms Hotel and Restaurant ... Askrigg ... 14
The Kings Arms Inn Hotel and Restaurant ... Montacute ... 100
The Kings Head Inn and Restaurant ... Stow-on-the-Wold ... 132
Kingshead House Restaurant ... Cheltenham ... 37
The Lamb Inn ... Burford ... 25
The Lamb Inn ... Shipton-under-Wychwood ... 127
Leatherne Bottel Riverside Inn ... Goring-on-Thames ... 66
Longview Hotel and Restaurant ... Knutsford ... 86
Mallyan Spout Hotel ... Goathland ... 64
The Manor Hotel ... Bridport ... 22
Manor House Hotel and Restaurant ... Dronfield ... 46
Marston Farm Hotel ... Kingsbury ... 81
The Masons Arms ... Meysey Hampton ... 98
The Maynard Arms ... Grindleford ... 69
The Mermaid Inn ... Rye ... 120
The Milburn Arms ... Rosedale Abbey ... 118
Milford Hall Hotel and Restaurant ... Salisbury ... 124
The Mill and Old Swan ... Oxford ... 108
The Mole and Chicken ... Easington ... 48
The Monckton Arms Hotel ... Glaston ... 63
The Morritt Arms Hotel ... Barnard Castle ... 16
The Mortal Man Hotel ... Troutbeck ... 143
The New Dungeon Ghyll Hotel ... Ambleside ... 11
The New Inn ... Cirencester ... 40
The Nobody Inn ... Doddiscombeleigh ... 44
The Noel Arms ... Chipping Campden ... 39
The Old Beams Restaurant ... Ashbourne ... 13
The Old Bell Inn Hotel ... Saddleworth ... 123
The Old Custom House Inn ... Padstow ... 110
The Old Manse ... Bourton-on-the Water ... 21
The Old Tollgate Restaurant and Hotel ... Worthing ... 154
The Old Vicarage ... Burton-upon-Trent ... 28
The Old White Lion Hotel ... Howarth ... 74
The Oxenham Arms ... Okehampton ... 104
Panos Hotel and Restaurant ... Cambridge ... 31
The Pheasant Inn ... Chester ... 38
The Pheasant Inn ... Kirkby Lonsdale ... 82
Poppies at the Roebuck ... Brimfield ... 23
Port Gaverne Hotel ... Port Gaverne ... 114
Quorn Grange ... Quorn ... 117
Quy Mill Hotel ... Cambridge ... 32
The Ragged Cot ... Minchinhampton ... 99
The Red Lion Inn ... Adderbury ... 8
The Red Lion Inn ... Hawkshead ... 73
The Redfern Hotel ... Cleobury Mortimer ... 43
Rhydspence Inn ... Hay-on-Wye ... 75
Ringlestone Inn ... Maidstone ... 95
The Rising Sun Hotel ... Lynmouth ... 92
The Rising Sun ... St Mawes ... 122
Riverside Restaurant and Hotel ... Evesham ... 54
The Rock Inn Hotel ... Halifax ... 70
The Royal Oak Hotel ... Yattendon ... 156
The Royal Oak Inn ... Appleby-in-Westmorland ... 12
The Royal Oak Inn ... Exmoor ... 57
The Royal Oak Inn ... Withypool ... 153
Royal Wells Inn ... Tunbridge Wells ... 144
The Royalist ... Stow-on-the-Wold ... 133
Sculthorpe Mill ... Fakenham ... 58
The Sea Trout Inn ... Totnes ... 142
Shaven Crown Hotel ... Shipton-under-Wychwood ... 128
The Snooty Fox ... Kirkby Lonsdale ... 83
The Starr Restaurant with Rooms ... Great Dunmow ... 67
The Stonor Arms ... Stonor ... 131
The Swan Hotel ... Newby Bridge ... 101
The Talkhouse ... Oxford ... 109
The Tempest Arms ... Skipton ... 129
Thatchers Hotel and Restaurant ... Thame ... 138
Thelbridge Cross Inn ... Thelbridge ... 139
The Three Horseshoes Inn ... Leek ... 88
Tree Tops Country House Restaurant ... Southport ... 130
Trengilly Wartha Country Inn ... Falmouth ... 59
Tyacks Hotel ... Camborne ... 30
Walnut Tree ... Sherborne ... 126
The Waltzing Weasel ... Hayfield ... 76
The Wensleydale Heifer ... West Witton ... 149
Wesley House ... Winchcombe ... 151
The Wheatsheaf Inn ... Egton ... 50
The Wheatsheaf Inn at Onneley ... Onneley ... 105
Wheelbarrow Castle ... Leominster ... 89
The White Hart ... Ford ... 60
The White Hart Hotel ... St Austell ... 121
The White Horse Inn ... Petworth ... 112
White Lion Hotel ... Upton-upon-Severn ... 146
The White Swan ... Pickering ... 113
Whoop Hall Inn ... Kirkby Lonsdale ... 84
The Windmill Inn Hotel ... Badby ... 15
The Woodfalls Inn ... Fordingbridge ... 61
The Woolpack Inn ... Beckington ... 18
The Wyckham Arms ... Winchester ... 152
Ye Horn's Inn ... Preston ... 116
Ye Olde Salutation Inn ... Weobley ... 148

WALES

Castle View Hotel ... Chepstow ... 158
The Dragon Hotel ... Montgomery ... 162
George III Hotel ... Dolgellau ... 159
The Lion Hotel and Restaurant ... Welshpool ... 163
The Plough Inn ... Llandeilo ... 161
The West Arms Hotel ... Llanarmon DC ... 160

SCOTLAND

Cairnbaan Hotel ... Loch Gilphead ... 172
Comrie Hotel ... Comrie ... 167
The Glenisla Hotel ... Glenisla ... 169
Hotel Eilean Iarmain ... Isle of Skye ... 170
Kylesku Hotel ... Kylesku ... 171
Potarch Hotel ... Banchory ... 166
The Winnock Hotel ... Drymen ... 168

1996 Johansens Recommended Inns and Restaurants by county

ENGLAND

Avon

The Woolpack Inn ... Beckington ... 18

Berkshire

The Bird in Hand ... Twyford ... 145
Boulters Lock Hotel ... Maidenhead ... 93
The Christopher Hotel ... Eton/Windsor ... 52
The Highwayman ... Exlade Street ... 56
Leatherne Bottel Riverside Inn ... Goring-on-Thames ... 66
The Royal Oak Hotel ... Yattendon ... 156

Buckinghamshire

Fox Country Hotel ... Henley ... 78
The Mole and Chicken ... Easington ... 48

Cambridgeshire

The Anchor Inn ... Ely ... 51
Panos Hotel and Restaurant ... Cambridge ... 31
Quy Mill Hotel ... Cambridge ... 32

Cheshire

Longview Hotel and Restaurant ... Knutsford ... 86
The Pheasant Inn ... Chester ... 38

Cornwall

The Harbour Inn ... Porthleven ... 115
Jubilee Inn ... Pelynt ... 111
The Old Custom House Inn ... Padstow ... 110
Port Gaverne Hotel ... Port Gaverne ... 114
The Rising Sun ... St Mawes ... 122
Trengilly Wartha Country Inn ... Falmouth ... 59
Tyacks Hotel ... Camborne ... 30
The White Hart Hotel ... St Austell ... 121

Cumbria

The Mortal Man Hotel ... Troutbeck ... 143
The New Dungeon Ghyll Hotel ... Ambleside ... 11
The Pheasant Inn ... Kirkby Lonsdale ... 82
The Red Lion Inn ... Hawkshead ... 73
The Royal Oak Inn ... Appleby-in-Westmorland ... 12
The Snooty Fox ... Kirkby Lonsdale ... 83
The Swan Hotel ... Newby Bridge ... 101
Whoop Hall Inn ... Kirkby Lonsdale ... 84

Derbyshire

Boars Head Hotel ... Burton-upon-Trent ... 27
The Chequers Inn ... Calver ... 29
Manor House Hotel and Restaurant ... Dronfield ... 46
The Maynard Arms ... Grindleford ... 69
The Waltzing Weasel ... Hayfield ... 76
Ye Olde Nag's Head ... Castleton ... 36

Devon

The Barn Owl Inn ... Torquay ... 141
The Cridford Inn ... Exeter ... 55
The George Hotel ... Hatherleigh ... 72
Home Farm Hotel ... Honiton ... 80
The Nobody Inn ... Doddiscombeleigh ... 44
The Oxenham Arms ... Okehampton ... 104
The Rising Sun Hotel ... Lynmouth ... 92
The Sea Trout Inn ... Totnes ... 142
Thelbridge Cross Inn ... Thelbridge ... 139

Dorset

The Acorn Inn Hotel ... Evershot ... 53
Manor Hotel ... Bridport ... 22

Durham

The Morritt Arms Hotel ... Barnard Castle ... 16

East Sussex

The Mermaid Inn ... Rye ... 120

Essex

The Cricketers ... Clavering ... 41
The Starr Restaurant with Rooms ... Great Dunmow ... 67

Gloucestershire

The Bell Hotel ... Tewkesbury ... 137
Kingshead House Restaurant ... Cheltenham ... 37
The Masons Arms ... Meysey Hampton ... 98
The New Inn ... Cirencester ... 40
The Noel Arms ... Chipping Campden ... 39
The Old Manse ... Bourton-on-the-Water ... 21
The Ragged Cot ... Minchinhampton ... 99
The Royalist ... Stow-on-the-Wold ... 133
Wesley House ... Winchcombe ... 151

Hampshire

The George Hotel ... Basingstoke ... 17
The Woodfalls Inn ... Fordingbridge ... 61
The Wyckham Arms ... Winchester ... 152

Hereford and Worcester

The Crown at Hopton ... Cleobury Mortimer ... 42
The Feathers Hotel ... Ledbury ... 87
Freshmans Restaurant ... Belbroughton ... 19
Rhydspence Inn ... Hay-on-Wye ... 75
Riverside Restaurant and Hotel ... Evesham ... 54
Wheelbarrow Castle ... Leominster ... 89
The White Lion Hotel ... Upton-upon-Severn ... 146
Ye Olde Salutation Inn ... Weobley ... 148

Kent

The Harrow at Warren Street ... Maidstone ... 94
Ringlestone Inn ... Maidstone ... 95
Royal Wells Inn ... Tunbridge Wells ... 144

Lancashire

The Inn at Whitewell ... Whitewell ... 150
The Old Bell Inn Hotel ... Saddleworth ... 123
Ye Horn's Inn ... Preston ... 116

Leicestershire

Barnacles Restaurant ... Hinkley ... 79
The Greyhound ... Lutterworth ... 91
The Monckton Arms Hotel ... Glaston ... 63
Quorn Grange ... Quorn ... 117

Lincolnshire

The Black Horse Inn ... Grimsthorpe ... 68
Hare & Hounds ... Fulbeck ... 62

Merseyside

Tree Tops Country House Restaurant ... Southport ... 130

Norfolk

The Barton Angler Country Inn ... Wroxham ... 155
The Garden House Hotel ... Norwich ... 102
Green Farm Restaurant and Hotel ... Thorpe Market ... 140
The Hoste Arms Hotel ... Burnham Market ... 26
Sculthorpe Mill ... Fakenham ... 58

North Yorkshire

The Blue Lion ... East Witton ... 49
East Ayton Lodge Country Hotel ... Scarborough ... 125
The Feversham Arms ... Helmsley ... 77
The George and Dragon ... Kirkbymoorside ... 85
The Green Man ... Malton ... 97
The Kings Arms Hotel and Restaurant ... Askrigg ... 14
Mallyan Spout Hotel ... Goathland ... 64
The Milburn Arms ... Rosedale Abbey ... 118
The Tempest Arms ... Skipton ... 129
The Wensleydale Heifer ... West Witton ... 149
The Wheatsheaf Inn ... Egton ... 50
The White Swan ... Pickering ... 113

Northamptonshire

The Falcon Hotel and Restaurant ... Castle Ashby ... 33
The Windmill Inn Hotel ... Badby ... 15

Northumberland

Blue Bell Hotel ... Belford ... 20

Nottinghamshire

Hotel des Clos ... Nottingham ... 103

Oxfordshire

Cotswold Gateway Hotel ... Burford ... 24
The George Hotel ... Dorchester-on-Thames ... 45
Holcombe Hotel ... Oxford ... 106
The Jersey Arms ... Oxford ... 107
The Kings Head Inn and Restaurant ... Stow-on-the-Wold ... 132
The Lamb Inn ... Burford ... 25
The Lamb Inn ... Shipton-under-Wychwood ... 127
The Mill and Old Swan ... Oxford ... 108
The Red Lion Inn ... Adderbury ... 8
Shaven Crown Hotel ... Shipton-under-Wychwood ... 128
The Stonor Arms ... Stonor ... 131
The Talkhouse ... Oxford ... 109
Thatchers Hotel and Restaurant ... Thame ... 138

Shropshire

The Hundred House Hotel ... Telford ... 136
Poppies at the Roebuck ... Brimfield ... 23
The Redfern Hotel ... Cleobury Mortimer ... 43

Somerset

The Anchor Inn ... Dulverton ... 47
The George Hotel ... Castle Carey ... 34
The Kings Arms Innl ... Montecute ... 100
The Royal Oak Inn ... Exmoor ... 57
The Royal Oak Inn ... Withypool ... 153
Walnut Tree ... Sherbourne ... 126

Staffordshire

The Old Beams Restaurant ... Ashbourne ... 13
The Old Vicarage ... Burton-upon-Trent ... 28
The Three Horseshoes Inn ... Leek ... 88
The Wheatsheaf Inn at Onneley ... Onneley ... 105

Suffolk

The Anchor ... Walberswick ... 147
The Countrymen ... Long Melford ... 90

Surrey

The Inn on the Lake ... Godalming ... 65

Warwickshire

Arrow Mill ... Alcester ... 9
Baraset Barn Restaurant ... Stratford-upon-Avon ... 134
The Blue Boar Inn ... Stratford-upon-Avon ... 135
The Golden Lion Inn of Easenhall ... Rugby ... 119
Marston Farm Hotel ... Kingsbury ... 81

West Sussex

The Boathouse Brasserie ... Amberley ... 10
The Chequers at Slaugham ... Handcross ... 71
The Old Tollgate Restaurant and Hotel ... Worthing ... 154
The White Horse Inn ... Petworth ... 112

West Yorkshire

The Old White Lion Hotel ... Howarth ... 74
The Rock Inn Hotel ... Halifax ... 70

Wiltshire

The Castle Inn ... Castle Combe ... 35
The Horse and Groom Inn ... Malmesbury ... 96
Milford Hall Hotel and Restaurant ... Salisbury ... 124
The White Hart ... Ford ... 60

WALES

Clwyd

The West Arms Hotel ... Llanarmon DC ... 160

Dyfed

The Plough Inn ... Llandeilo ... 161

Gwent

Castle View Hotel ... Chepstow ... 158

Gwynedd

George III Hotel ... Dolgellau ... 159

Powys

The Dragon Hotel ... Montgomery ... 162
The Lion Hotel and Restaurant ... Welshpool ... 163

SCOTLAND

Argyll

Cairnbann Hotel ... Loch Gilphead ... 172

Isle of Skye

Hotel Eilean Iarmain ... Isle of Skye ... 170

Kincardineshire

Potarch Hotel ... Banchory ... 166

Perthshire

Comrie Hotel ... Comrie ... 167
The Glenisla Hotel ... Glenisla ... 169

Stirlingshire

The Winnock Hotel ... Drymen ... 168

Sutherland

Kylesku Hotel ... Kylesku ... 171

Inns with a swimming pool

ENGLAND

The Feversham Arms Hotel ... Helmsley ... 77
The George Hotel ... Hatherleigh ... 72
Tree Tops Country House Restaurant ... Southport ... 130

Wheelbarrow Castle ... Leominster ... 89
The White Hart ... Ford ... 60

WALES

The Dragon Hotel ... Montgomery ... 162

Inns with fishing nearby

ENGLAND

The Acorn Inn Hotel ... Evershot ... 53
The Anchor Inn ... Dulverton ... 47
The Anchor Inn ... Ely ... 51
The Anchor ... Walberswick ... 147
Arrow Mill ... Alcester ... 9
The Barnacles Restaurant ... Hinkley ... 79
The Barton Angler Country Inn ... Wroxham ... 155
The Bell Hotel ... Tewkesbury ... 137
The Black Horse Inn ... Grimsthorpe ... 68
The Blue Bell Hotel ... Belford ... 20
The Blue Lion ... East Witton ... 49
Boulters Lock Hotel ... Maidenhead ... 93
The Castle Inn ... Castle Combe ... 35
The Christopher Hotel ... Eton/Windsor ... 52
The Countrymen ... Long Melford ... 90
The Cricketers ... Clavering ... 41
The Cridford Inn ... Exeter ... 55
East Ayton Lodge Country Hotel ... Scarborough ... 125
The Falcon Hotel and Restaurant ... Castle Ashby ... 33
The Feversham Arms Hotel ... Helmsley ... 77
The Garden House Hotel ... Norwich ... 102
The George and Dragon Hotel ... Kirkbymoorside ... 85
The George Hotel ... Castle Carey ... 34
The George Hotel ... Hatherleigh ... 72
The Golden Lion Inn of Easenhall ... Rugby ... 119
Green Farm Restaurant and Hotel ... Thorpe Market ... 140
The Green Man ... Malton ... 97
The Harbour Inn ... Porthleven ... 115
Hare & Hounds ... Fulbeck ... 62
The Horse and Groom Inn ... Malmesbury ... 96
The Hoste Arms Hotel ... Burnham Market ... 26
The Hundred House Hotel ... Telford ... 136
The Inn at Whitewell ... Whitewell ... 150
The Jersey Arms ... Oxford ... 107
Jubilee Inn ... Pelynt ... 111
The Kings Arms Hotel and Restaurant ... Askrigg ... 14
The Kings Head Inn and Restaurant ... Stow-on-the-Wold ... 132
The Lamb Inn ... Burford ... 25
Mallyan Spout Hotel ... Goathland ... 64
The Manor Hotel ... Bridport ... 22
Manor House Hotel and Restaurant ... Dronfield ... 46
Marston Farm Hotel ... Kingsbury ... 81
The Masons Arms ... Meysey Hampton ... 98
The Maynard Arms ... Grindleford ... 69
Milford Hall Hotel and Restaurant ... Salisbury ... 124
The Mill and Old Swan ... Oxford ... 108
The Mole and Chicken ... Easington ... 48
The Monckton Arms Hotel ... Glaston ... 63
The Morritt Arms Hotel ... Barnard Castle ... 16
The Mortal Man Hotel ... Troutbeck ... 143
The New Dungeon Ghyll Hotel ... Ambleside ... 11
The New Inn ... Cirencester ... 40
The Nobody Inn ... Doddiscombeleigh ... 44
The Noel Arms ... Chipping Campden ... 39
The Old Beams Restaurant ... Ashbourne ... 13
The Old Bell Inn Hotel ... Saddleworth ... 123
The Old Custom House Inn ... Padstow ... 110
The Old Manse ... Bourton-on-the Water ... 21
The Old White Lion Hotel ... Howarth ... 74
The Oxenham Arms ... Okehampton ... 104
The Pheasant Inn ... Chester ... 38
Poppies at the Roebuck ... Brimfield ... 23
Port Gaverne Hotel ... Port Gaverne ... 114
Quorn Grange ... Quorn ... 117
Quy Mill Hotel ... Cambridge ... 32
The Ragged Cot ... Minchinhampton ... 99
The Red Lion Inn ... Adderbury ... 8
The Red Lion Inn ... Hawkshead ... 73
The Redfern Hotel ... Cleobury Mortimer ... 43
Rhydspence Inn ... Hay-on-Wye ... 75
The Rising Sun Hotel ... Lynmouth ... 92
Riverside Restaurant and Hotel ... Evesham ... 54
The Rock Inn Hotel ... Halifax ... 70
The Royal Oak Inn ... Appleby-in-Westmorland ... 12
The Royal Oak Inn ... Exmoor ... 57
The Royal Oak Inn ... Withypool ... 153
Sculthorpe Mill ... Fakenham ... 58
The Sea Trout Inn ... Totnes ... 142
Shaven Crown Hotel ... Shipton-under-Wychwood ... 128
The Snooty Fox ... Kirkby Lonsdale ... 83
The Swan Hotel ... Newby Bridge ... 101
The Talkhouse ... Oxford ... 109
The Tempest Arms ... Skipton ... 129
Thelbridge Cross Inn ... Thelbridge ... 139
Trengilly Wartha Country Inn ... Falmouth ... 59
The Waltzing Weasel ... Hayfield ... 76
The Wensleydale Heifer ... West Witton ... 149
Wesley House ... Winchcombe ... 151
The Wheatsheaf Inn ... Egton ... 50
The White Hart ... Ford ... 60
The White Hart Hotel ... St Austell ... 121
The White Horse Inn ... Petworth ... 112
White Lion Hotel ... Upton-upon-Severn ... 146
The White Swan ... Pickering ... 113
Whoop Hall Inn ... Kirkby Lonsdale ... 84
The Woolpack Inn ... Beckington ... 18
Ye Horn's Inn ... Preston ... 116
Ye Olde Salutation Inn ... Weobley ... 148

WALES

Castle View Hotel ... Chepstow ... 158
The Dragon Hotel ... Montgomery ... 162
George III Hotel ... Dolgellau ... 159
The Lion Hotel and Restaurant ... Welshpool ... 163
The Plough Inn ... Llandeilo ... 161
The West Arms Hotel ... Llanarmon DC ... 160

SCOTLAND

Comrie Hotel ... Comrie ... 167
The Glenisla Hotel ... Glenisla ... 169
Hotel Eilean Iarmain ... Isle of Skye ... 170
Kylesku Hotel ... Kylesku ... 171
Potarch Hotel ... Banchory ... 166
The Winnock Hotel ... Drymen ... 168

Inns with shooting nearby

ENGLAND

The Acorn Inn Hotel ... Evershot ... 53
The Anchor Inn ... Dulverton ... 47
Arrow Mill ... Alcester ... 9
The Black Horse Inn ... Grimsthorpe ... 68
The Blue Bell Hotel ... Belford ... 20
The Blue Lion ... East Witton ... 49
Boars Head Hotel ... Burton-upon-Trent ... 27
Boulters Lock Hotel ... Maidenhead ... 93
The Castle Inn ... Castle Combe ... 35
The Countrymen ... Long Melford ... 90
The Cridford Inn ... Exeter ... 55
East Ayton Lodge Country Hotel ... Scarborough ... 125
The Falcon Hotel and Restaurant ... Castle Ashby ... 33
The Feathers Hotel ... Ledbury ... 87
The Feversham Arms Hotel ... Helmsley ... 77
The George and Dragon Hotel ... Kirkbymoorside ... 85
The George Hotel ... Castle Carey ... 34
The George Hotel ... Hatherleigh ... 72
Green Farm Restaurant and Hotel ... Thorpe Market ... 140
The Green Man ... Malton ... 97
Hare & Hounds ... Fulbeck ... 62
Holcombe Hotel ... Oxford ... 106
The Horse and Groom Inn ... Malmesbury ... 96
The Inn at Whitewell ... Whitewell ... 150
The Jersey Arms ... Oxford ... 107
The Kings Arms Hotel and Restaurant ... Askrigg ... 14
The Kings Head Inn and Restaurant ... Stow-on-the-Wold ... 132
The Lamb Inn ... Burford ... 25
The Manor Hotel ... Bridport ... 22
Marston Farm Hotel ... Kingsbury ... 81
The Maynard Arms ... Grindleford ... 69
Milford Hall Hotel and Restaurant ... Salisbury ... 124
The Mill and Old Swan ... Oxford ... 108
The Mole and Chicken ... Easington ... 48
The Monckton Arms Hotel ... Glaston ... 63
The Morritt Arms Hotel ... Barnard Castle ... 16
The New Dungeon Ghyll Hotel ... Ambleside ... 11
The New Inn ... Cirencester ... 40
The Nobody Inn ... Doddiscombeleigh ... 44
The Noel Arms ... Chipping Campden ... 39
The Old Beams Restaurant ... Ashbourne ... 13
The Old White Lion Hotel ... Howarth ... 74
The Pheasant Inn ... Chester ... 38
Poppies at the Roebuck ... Brimfield ... 23
Quorn Grange ... Quorn ... 117
Quy Mill Hotel ... Cambridge ... 32
The Ragged Cot ... Minchinhampton ... 99
The Red Lion Inn ... Hawkshead ... 73
The Redfern Hotel ... Cleobury Mortimer ... 43
Rhydspence Inn ... Hay-on-Wye ... 75
The Rising Sun Hotel ... Lynmouth ... 92
The Rock Inn Hotel ... Halifax ... 70
The Royal Oak Hotel ... Yattendon ... 156
The Royal Oak Inn ... Appleby-in-Westmoreland ... 12
The Royal Oak Inn ... Exmoor ... 57
The Royal Oak Inn ... Withypool ... 153
The Sea Trout Inn ... Totnes ... 142
Shaven Crown Hotel ... Shipton-under-Wychwood ... 128
The Snooty Fox ... Kikby Lonsdale ... 83
The Swan Hotel ... Newby Bridge ... 101
The Talkhouse ... Oxford ... 109
The Tempest Arms ... Skipton ... 129
Tree Tops Country House Restaurant ... Southport ... 130
The Waltzing Weasel ... Hayfield ... 76
The Wheatsheaf Inn ... Egton ... 50
The Wheatsheaf Inn at Onneley ... Onneley ... 105
The White Hart ... Ford ... 60
The White Horse Inn ... Petworth ... 112
The White Swan ... Pickering ... 113
Whoop Hall Inn ... Kirkby Lonsdale ... 84
The Windmill Inn Hotel ... Badby ... 15
The Woolpack Inn ... Beckington ... 18
Ye Horn's Inn ... Preston ... 116
Ye Olde Salutation Inn ... Weobley ... 148

WALES

The Dragon Hotel ... Montgomery ... 162
George III Hotel ... Dolgellau ... 159
The West Arms Hotel ... Llanarmon DC ... 160

SCOTLAND

The Glenisla Hotel ... Glenisla ... 169
Hotel Eilean Iarmain ... Isle of Skye ... 170
Kylesku Hotel ... Kylesku ... 171
Potarch Hotel ... Banchory ... 166
The Winnock Hotel ... Drymen ... 168

Inns with conference facilities for 100 delegates or more

ENGLAND

The Blue Bell Hotel ... Belford ... 20
East Ayton Lodge Country Hotel ... Scarborough ... 125
The Feathers Hotel ... Ledbury ... 87
The Green Man ... Malton ... 97
The Inn on the Lake ... Godalming ... 65
The Maynard Arms ... Grindleford ... 69
The Morritt Arms Hotel ... Barnard Castle ... 16
The Old White Lion Hotel ... Howarth ... 74
Quorn Grange ... Quorn ... 117
The Rock Inn Hotel ... Halifax ... 70
The Tempest Arms ... Skipton ... 129
Tree Tops Country House Restaurant ... Southport ... 130
The Woodfalls Inn ... Fordingbridge ... 61

SCOTLAND

Cairnbaan Hotel ... Loch Gilphead ... 172

Inns with single rooms for £30 per night or under

ENGLAND

The Barton Angler Country Inn ..... Wroxham 155
Hare & Hounds ..... Fulbeck 62
Home Farm Hotel ..... Honiton 80
The Masons Arms ..... Meysey Hampton 98
The Nobody Inn ..... Doddiscombeleigh 44
Rhydspence Inn ..... Hay-on-Wye 75
Ringlestone Inn ..... Maidstone 95
Sculthorpe Mill ..... Fakenham 58
The Snooty Fox ..... Kirkby Lonsdale 83
The Wheatsheaf Inn at Onneley ..... Onneley 105

SCOTLAND

Comrie Hotel ..... Comrie 167
The Glenisla Hotel ..... Glenisla 169
Kylesku Hotel ..... Kylesku 171

Inns with double rooms for £50 per night or under

ENGLAND

Boars Head Hotel ..... Burton-upon-Trent 27
The Chequers Inn ..... Calver 29
Cotswold Gateway Hotel ..... Burford 24
The Garden House Hotel ..... Norwich 102
The George Hotel ..... Hatherleigh 72
The Golden Lion Inn of Easenhall ..... Rugby 119
Hare & Hounds ..... Fulbeck 62
The Harrow at Warren Street ..... Maidstone 94
The Masons Arms ..... Meysey Hampton 98
The Nobody Inn ..... Doddiscombeleigh 44
The Old White Lion Hotel ..... Howarth 74
The Oxenham Arms ..... Okehampton 104
The Sea Trout Inn ..... Totnes 142
The Snooty Fox ..... Kikby Lonsdale 83
The Three Horseshoes Inn ..... Leek 88
Trengilly Wartha Country Inn ..... Falmouth 59
The Wheatsheaf Inn ..... Egton 50
The Wheatsheaf Inn at Onneley ..... Onneley 105
Wheelbarrow Castle ..... Leominster 89
The Windmill Inn Hotel ..... Badby 15
The Woodfalls Inn ..... Fordingbridge 61

SCOTLAND

The Glenisla Hotel ..... Glenisla 169
Kylesku Hotel ..... Kylesku 171

Advertisers Index

Knight Frank & Rutley ..... IFC
MasterCard 5/IBC
Walkers Shortbread 164

PLAY THE ROLE OF HOTEL INSPECTOR!

At the back of this book you will notice a quantity of Guest Survey Forms. If you have had an enjoyable stay at one of our recommendations, or alternatively you have been in some way disappointed, please complete one of these forms and send it to us FREEPOST.

These reports essentially complement the assessments made by our team of professional inspectors, continually monitoring the standards of hospitality in every establishment in our guides.

Guest Survey reports also have an important influence on the selection of nominations for our annual awards for excellence.

'Diversity and excellence for the discerning traveller'.

GUEST SURVEY REPORT

Name and location of hotel: ______________________ Date of visit: __________

Name and address of guest: ______________________

______________________ Postcode: __________

Please tick one box in each category below:	Excellent	Good	Disappointing	Poor
Bedrooms				
Public Rooms				
Restaurant/Cuisine				
Service				
Welcome/Friendliness				
Value For Money				

PLEASE return your Guest Survey Report form!

Occasionally we may allow other reputable organisations to write with offers which may be of interest.

If you prefer not to here from them, tick this box ☐

To: Johansens, FREEPOST (CB264), 175-179 St John Street, London EC1B 1JQ

Your own Johansens 'inspection' gives reliability to our guides and assists in the selection of Award Nominations

GUEST SURVEY REPORT

Name and location of hotel: ______________________ Date of visit: __________

Name and address of guest: ______________________

______________________ Postcode: __________

Please tick one box in each category below:	Excellent	Good	Disappointing	Poor
Bedrooms				
Public Rooms				
Restaurant/Cuisine				
Service				
Welcome/Friendliness				
Value For Money				

PLEASE return your Guest Survey Report form!

Occasionally we may allow other reputable organisations to write with offers which may be of interest.

If you prefer not to here from them, tick this box ☐

To: Johansens, FREEPOST (CB264), 175-179 St John Street, London EC1B 1JQ

Your own Johansens 'inspection' gives reliability to our guides and assists in the selection of Award Nominations

GUEST SURVEY REPORT

Name and location of hotel: ______________________ Date of visit: __________

Name and address of guest: ______________________

______________________ Postcode: __________

Please tick one box in each category below:	Excellent	Good	Disappointing	Poor
Bedrooms				
Public Rooms				
Restaurant/Cuisine				
Service				
Welcome/Friendliness				
Value For Money				

PLEASE return your Guest Survey Report form!

Occasionally we may allow other reputable organisations to write with offers which may be of interest.

If you prefer not to here from them, tick this box ☐

To: Johansens, FREEPOST (CB264), 175-179 St John Street, London EC1B 1JQ

Your own Johansens 'inspection' gives reliability to our guides and assists in the selection of Award Nominations

Order Coupon

To order Johansens guides, simply indicate which publications you require by putting the quantity(ies) in the boxes provided. Choose you preferred method of payment and return this coupon (NO STAMP REQUIRED). You may also place your order using FREEPHONE 0800 269397 or by fax on 0171 490 2538.

❑ I enclose a cheque for £______________ payable to Biblios PDS Ltd (Johansens book distributor).
❑ I enclose my order on company letterheading, please invoice me. (UK companies only)
❑ Please debit my credit/charge card account (please tick)
❑ MASTERCARD ❑ VISA ❑ DINERS ❑ AMEX

Card Number ______________________________

Signature ______________________ Expiry Date ______________
Name (Mr/Mrs/Miss) ______________________________
Address ______________________________
______________________________ Postcode ______________

(We aim to despatch your order with 10 days, but please allow 28 days for delivery)

Occasionally we may allow reputable organisations to write to you with offers which may interest you. If you prefer not to hear from them, tick this box ❑

CALL THE JOHANSENS CREDIT CARD ORDER SERVICE FREE ☎ **0800 269397**

save £10 WHEN YOU BUY A SET OF ALL THREE 1996 UK JOHANSENS GUIDES	PRICE	QTY	TOTAL
	£35.80		
Boxed presentation set of three 1996 UK Johansens guides with slip case	£39.00		
Johansens Recommended Hotels in Great Britain & Ireland 1996	£21.90		
Johansens Recommended Inns with Restaurants in Great Britain 1996	£11.95		
Johansens Recommended Country Houses and Small Hotels in Great Britain & Ireland 1996	£11.95		
Johansens Recommended Hotels in Europe 1996	£11.95		

ALL PRICES INCLUDE HANDLING AND UK POSTAGE ONLY **37J**

Outside the UK add £3 for each single guide ordered, or £5 for a set or boxed set to cover additional postage. ***PRICES VALID UNTIL 31/12/96***

Post free to:
JOHANSENS, FREEPOST (CB264), HORSHAM, WEST SUSSEX RH13 8ZA

Order Coupon

To order Johansens guides, simply indicate which publications you require by putting the quantity(ies) in the boxes provided. Choose you preferred method of payment and return this coupon (NO STAMP REQUIRED). You may also place your order using FREEPHONE 0800 269397 or by fax on 0171 490 2538.

❑ I enclose a cheque for £______________ payable to Biblios PDS Ltd (Johansens book distributor).
❑ I enclose my order on company letterheading, please invoice me. (UK companies only)
❑ Please debit my credit/charge card account (please tick)
❑ MASTERCARD ❑ VISA ❑ DINERS ❑ AMEX

Card Number ______________________________

Signature ______________________ Expiry Date ______________
Name (Mr/Mrs/Miss) ______________________________
Address ______________________________
______________________________ Postcode ______________

(We aim to despatch your order with 10 days, but please allow 28 days for delivery)

Occasionally we may allow reputable organisations to write to you with offers which may interest you. If you prefer not to hear from them, tick this box ❑

CALL THE JOHANSENS CREDIT CARD ORDER SERVICE FREE ☎ **0800 269397**

save £10 WHEN YOU BUY A SET OF ALL THREE 1996 UK JOHANSENS GUIDES	PRICE	QTY	TOTAL
	£35.80		
Boxed presentation set of three 1996 UK Johansens guides with slip case	£39.00		
Johansens Recommended Hotels in Great Britain & Ireland 1996	£21.90		
Johansens Recommended Inns with Restaurants in Great Britain 1996	£11.95		
Johansens Recommended Country Houses and Small Hotels in Great Britain & Ireland 1996	£11.95		
Johansens Recommended Hotels in Europe 1996	£11.95		

ALL PRICES INCLUDE HANDLING AND UK POSTAGE ONLY **37J**

Outside the UK add £3 for each single guide ordered, or £5 for a set or boxed set to cover additional postage. ***PRICES VALID UNTIL 31/12/96***

Post free to:
JOHANSENS, FREEPOST (CB264), HORSHAM, WEST SUSSEX RH13 8ZA

Order Coupon

To order Johansens guides, simply indicate which publications you require by putting the quantity(ies) in the boxes provided. Choose you preferred method of payment and return this coupon (NO STAMP REQUIRED). You may also place your order using FREEPHONE 0800 269397 or by fax on 0171 490 2538.

❑ I enclose a cheque for £______________ payable to Biblios PDS Ltd (Johansens book distributor).
❑ I enclose my order on company letterheading, please invoice me. (UK companies only)
❑ Please debit my credit/charge card account (please tick)
❑ MASTERCARD ❑ VISA ❑ DINERS ❑ AMEX

Card Number ______________________________

Signature ______________________ Expiry Date ______________
Name (Mr/Mrs/Miss) ______________________________
Address ______________________________
______________________________ Postcode ______________

(We aim to despatch your order with 10 days, but please allow 28 days for delivery)

Occasionally we may allow reputable organisations to write to you with offers which may interest you. If you prefer not to hear from them, tick this box ❑

CALL THE JOHANSENS CREDIT CARD ORDER SERVICE FREE

save £10 WHEN YOU BUY A SET OF ALL THREE 1996 UK JOHANSENS GUIDES	PRICE	QTY	TOTAL
	£35.80		
Boxed presentation set of three 1996 UK Johansens guides with slip case	£39.00		
Johansens Recommended Hotels in Great Britain & Ireland 1996	£21.90		
Johansens Recommended Inns with Restaurants in Great Britain 1996	£11.95		
Johansens Recommended Country Houses and Small Hotels in Great Britain & Ireland 1996	£11.95		
Johansens Recommended Hotels in Europe 1996	£11.95		

ALL PRICES INCLUDE HANDLING AND UK POSTAGE ONLY **37J**

Outside the UK add £3 for each single guide ordered, or £5 for a set or boxed set to cover additional postage. ***PRICES VALID UNTIL 31/12/96***

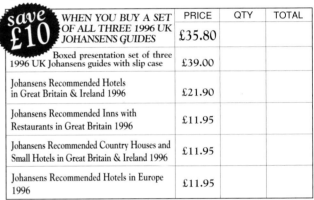

Post free to:
JOHANSENS, FREEPOST (CB264), HORSHAM, WEST SUSSEX RH13 8ZA

GUEST SURVEY REPORT

Name and location of hotel: ______________________ Date of visit: __________

Name and address of guest: ______________________________________

______________________________________ Postcode: __________

Please tick one box in each category below:	Excellent	Good	Disappointing	Poor
Bedrooms				
Public Rooms				
Restaurant/Cuisine				
Service				
Welcome/Friendliness				
Value For Money				

PLEASE return your Guest Survey Report form!

Occasionally we may allow other reputable organisations to write with offers which may be of interest.

If you prefer not to here from them, tick this box ☐

To: Johansens, FREEPOST (CB264), 175-179 St John Street, London EC1B 1JQ

Your own Johansens 'inspection' gives reliability to our guides and assists in the selection of Award Nominations

GUEST SURVEY REPORT

Name and location of hotel: ______________________ Date of visit: __________

Name and address of guest: ______________________________________

______________________________________ Postcode: __________

Please tick one box in each category below:	Excellent	Good	Disappointing	Poor
Bedrooms				
Public Rooms				
Restaurant/Cuisine				
Service				
Welcome/Friendliness				
Value For Money				

PLEASE return your Guest Survey Report form!

Occasionally we may allow other reputable organisations to write with offers which may be of interest.

If you prefer not to here from them, tick this box ☐

To: Johansens, FREEPOST (CB264), 175-179 St John Street, London EC1B 1JQ

Your own Johansens 'inspection' gives reliability to our guides and assists in the selection of Award Nominations

GUEST SURVEY REPORT

Name and location of hotel: ______________________ Date of visit: __________

Name and address of guest: ______________________________________

______________________________________ Postcode: __________

Please tick one box in each category below:	Excellent	Good	Disappointing	Poor
Bedrooms				
Public Rooms				
Restaurant/Cuisine				
Service				
Welcome/Friendliness				
Value For Money				

PLEASE return your Guest Survey Report form!

Occasionally we may allow other reputable organisations to write with offers which may be of interest.

If you prefer not to here from them, tick this box ☐

To: Johansens, FREEPOST (CB264), 175-179 St John Street, London EC1B 1JQ

Your own Johansens 'inspection' gives reliability to our guides and assists in the selection of Award Nominations

Order Coupon

To order Johansens guides, simply indicate which publications you require by putting the quantity(ies) in the boxes provided. Choose you preferred method of payment and return this coupon (NO STAMP REQUIRED). You may also place your order using FREEPHONE 0800 269397 or by fax on 0171 490 2538.

❑ I enclose a cheque for £______________ payable to Biblios PDS Ltd (Johansens book distributor).
❑ I enclose my order on company letterheading, please invoice me. (UK companies only)
❑ Please debit my credit/charge card account (please tick)
❑ MASTERCARD ❑ VISA ❑ DINERS ❑ AMEX

Card Number ______________________________

Signature ______________________ Expiry Date __________

Name (Mr/Mrs/Miss) ______________________________

Address ______________________________

____

______________________ Postcode __________

(We aim to despatch your order with 10 days, but please allow 28 days for delivery)

Occasionally we may allow reputable organisations to write to you with offers which may interest you. If you prefer not to hear from them, tick this box ❑

CALL THE JOHANSENS CREDIT CARD ORDER SERVICE FREE ☎ **0800 269397**

save £10	PRICE	QTY	TOTAL
WHEN YOU BUY A SET OF ALL THREE 1996 UK JOHANSENS GUIDES	£35.80		
Boxed presentation set of three 1996 UK Johansens guides with slip case	£39.00		
Johansens Recommended Hotels in Great Britain & Ireland 1996	£21.90		
Johansens Recommended Inns with Restaurants in Great Britain 1996	£11.95		
Johansens Recommended Country Houses and Small Hotels in Great Britain & Ireland 1996	£11.95		
Johansens Recommended Hotels in Europe 1996	£11.95		

ALL PRICES INCLUDE HANDLING AND UK POSTAGE ONLY **37J**

Outside the UK add £3 for each single guide ordered, or £5 for a set or boxed set to cover additional postage. ***PRICES VALID UNTIL 31/12/96***

Post free to:
JOHANSENS, FREEPOST (CB264), HORSHAM, WEST SUSSEX RH13 8ZA

Order Coupon

To order Johansens guides, simply indicate which publications you require by putting the quantity(ies) in the boxes provided. Choose you preferred method of payment and return this coupon (NO STAMP REQUIRED). You may also place your order using FREEPHONE 0800 269397 or by fax on 0171 490 2538.

❑ I enclose a cheque for £______________ payable to Biblios PDS Ltd (Johansens book distributor).
❑ I enclose my order on company letterheading, please invoice me. (UK companies only)
❑ Please debit my credit/charge card account (please tick)
❑ MASTERCARD ❑ VISA ❑ DINERS ❑ AMEX

Card Number ______________________________

Signature ______________________ Expiry Date __________

Name (Mr/Mrs/Miss) ______________________________

Address ______________________________

____

______________________ Postcode __________

(We aim to despatch your order with 10 days, but please allow 28 days for delivery)

Occasionally we may allow reputable organisations to write to you with offers which may interest you. If you prefer not to hear from them, tick this box ❑

CALL THE JOHANSENS CREDIT CARD ORDER SERVICE FREE ☎ **0800 269397**

save £10	PRICE	QTY	TOTAL
WHEN YOU BUY A SET OF ALL THREE 1996 UK JOHANSENS GUIDES	£35.80		
Boxed presentation set of three 1996 UK Johansens guides with slip case	£39.00		
Johansens Recommended Hotels in Great Britain & Ireland 1996	£21.90		
Johansens Recommended Inns with Restaurants in Great Britain 1996	£11.95		
Johansens Recommended Country Houses and Small Hotels in Great Britain & Ireland 1996	£11.95		
Johansens Recommended Hotels in Europe 1996	£11.95		

ALL PRICES INCLUDE HANDLING AND UK POSTAGE ONLY **37J**

Outside the UK add £3 for each single guide ordered, or £5 for a set or boxed set to cover additional postage. ***PRICES VALID UNTIL 31/12/96***

Post free to:
JOHANSENS, FREEPOST (CB264), HORSHAM, WEST SUSSEX RH13 8ZA

Order Coupon

To order Johansens guides, simply indicate which publications you require by putting the quantity(ies) in the boxes provided. Choose you preferred method of payment and return this coupon (NO STAMP REQUIRED). You may also place your order using FREEPHONE 0800 269397 or by fax on 0171 490 2538.

❑ I enclose a cheque for £______________ payable to Biblios PDS Ltd (Johansens book distributor).
❑ I enclose my order on company letterheading, please invoice me. (UK companies only)
❑ Please debit my credit/charge card account (please tick)
❑ MASTERCARD ❑ VISA ❑ DINERS ❑ AMEX

Card Number ______________________________

Signature ______________________ Expiry Date __________

Name (Mr/Mrs/Miss) ______________________________

Address ______________________________

____

______________________ Postcode __________

(We aim to despatch your order with 10 days, but please allow 28 days for delivery)

Occasionally we may allow reputable organisations to write to you with offers which may interest you. If you prefer not to hear from them, tick this box ❑

CALL THE JOHANSENS CREDIT CARD ORDER SERVICE FREE ☎ **0800 269397**

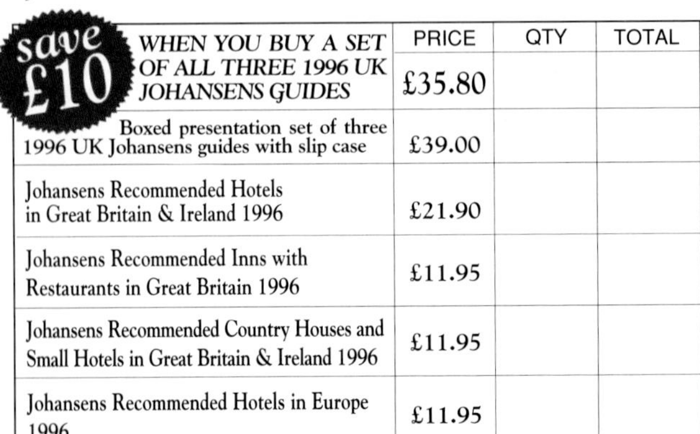

save £10	PRICE	QTY	TOTAL
WHEN YOU BUY A SET OF ALL THREE 1996 UK JOHANSENS GUIDES	£35.80		
Boxed presentation set of three 1996 UK Johansens guides with slip case	£39.00		
Johansens Recommended Hotels in Great Britain & Ireland 1996	£21.90		
Johansens Recommended Inns with Restaurants in Great Britain 1996	£11.95		
Johansens Recommended Country Houses and Small Hotels in Great Britain & Ireland 1996	£11.95		
Johansens Recommended Hotels in Europe 1996	£11.95		

ALL PRICES INCLUDE HANDLING AND UK POSTAGE ONLY **37J**

Outside the UK add £3 for each single guide ordered, or £5 for a set or boxed set to cover additional postage. ***PRICES VALID UNTIL 31/12/96***

Post free to:
JOHANSENS, FREEPOST (CB264), HORSHAM, WEST SUSSEX RH13 8ZA

GUEST SURVEY REPORT

Name and location of hotel: ______________________ Date of visit: ____________

Name and address of guest: ____

____ Postcode: ____________

Please tick one box in each category below:	Excellent	Good	Disappointing	Poor
Bedrooms				
Public Rooms				
Restaurant/Cuisine				
Service				
Welcome/Friendliness				
Value For Money				

PLEASE return your Guest Survey Report form!

Occasionally we may allow other reputable organisations to write with offers which may be of interest.

If you prefer not to here from them, tick this box ☐

To: Johansens, FREEPOST (CB264), 175-179 St John Street, London EC1B 1JQ

Your own Johansens 'inspection' gives reliability to our guides and assists in the selection of Award Nominations

GUEST SURVEY REPORT

Name and location of hotel: ______________________ Date of visit: ____________

Name and address of guest: ____

____ Postcode: ____________

Please tick one box in each category below:	Excellent	Good	Disappointing	Poor
Bedrooms				
Public Rooms				
Restaurant/Cuisine				
Service				
Welcome/Friendliness				
Value For Money				

PLEASE return your Guest Survey Report form!

Occasionally we may allow other reputable organisations to write with offers which may be of interest.

If you prefer not to here from them, tick this box ☐

To: Johansens, FREEPOST (CB264), 175-179 St John Street, London EC1B 1JQ

Your own Johansens 'inspection' gives reliability to our guides and assists in the selection of Award Nominations

GUEST SURVEY REPORT

Name and location of hotel: ______________________ Date of visit: ____________

Name and address of guest: ____

____ Postcode: ____________

Please tick one box in each category below:	Excellent	Good	Disappointing	Poor
Bedrooms				
Public Rooms				
Restaurant/Cuisine				
Service				
Welcome/Friendliness				
Value For Money				

PLEASE return your Guest Survey Report form!

Occasionally we may allow other reputable organisations to write with offers which may be of interest.

If you prefer not to here from them, tick this box ☐

To: Johansens, FREEPOST (CB264), 175-179 St John Street, London EC1B 1JQ

Your own Johansens 'inspection' gives reliability to our guides and assists in the selection of Award Nominations

Order Coupon

To order Johansens guides, simply indicate which publications you require by putting the quantity(ies) in the boxes provided. Choose you preferred method of payment and return this coupon (NO STAMP REQUIRED). You may also place your order using FREEPHONE 0800 269397 or by fax on 0171 490 2538.

❑ I enclose a cheque for £_____________ payable to Biblios PDS Ltd (Johansens book distributor).
❑ I enclose my order on company letterheading, please invoice me. (UK companies only)
❑ Please debit my credit/charge card account (please tick)
❑ MASTERCARD ❑ VISA ❑ DINERS ❑ AMEX

Card Number ______________________________

Signature ______________________ Expiry Date ____________

Name (Mr/Mrs/Miss) ______________________________

Address ______________________________

______________________________ Postcode ____________

(We aim to despatch your order with 10 days, but please allow 28 days for delivery)

Occasionally we may allow reputable organisations to write to you with offers which may interest you. If you prefer not to hear from them, tick this box ❑

CALL THE JOHANSENS CREDIT CARD ORDER SERVICE FREE ☎ **0800 269397**

save £10 WHEN YOU BUY A SET OF ALL THREE 1996 UK JOHANSENS GUIDES	PRICE	QTY	TOTAL
	£35.80		
Boxed presentation set of three 1996 UK Johansens guides with slip case	£39.00		
Johansens Recommended Hotels in Great Britain & Ireland 1996	£21.90		
Johansens Recommended Inns with Restaurants in Great Britain 1996	£11.95		
Johansens Recommended Country Houses and Small Hotels in Great Britain & Ireland 1996	£11.95		
Johansens Recommended Hotels in Europe 1996	£11.95		

ALL PRICES INCLUDE HANDLING AND UK POSTAGE ONLY **37J**

Outside the UK add £3 for each single guide ordered, or £5 for a set or boxed set to cover additional postage. ***PRICES VALID UNTIL 31/12/96***

Post free to:
JOHANSENS, FREEPOST (CB264), HORSHAM, WEST SUSSEX RH13 8ZA

Order Coupon

To order Johansens guides, simply indicate which publications you require by putting the quantity(ies) in the boxes provided. Choose you preferred method of payment and return this coupon (NO STAMP REQUIRED). You may also place your order using FREEPHONE 0800 269397 or by fax on 0171 490 2538.

❑ I enclose a cheque for £_____________ payable to Biblios PDS Ltd (Johansens book distributor).
❑ I enclose my order on company letterheading, please invoice me. (UK companies only)
❑ Please debit my credit/charge card account (please tick)
❑ MASTERCARD ❑ VISA ❑ DINERS ❑ AMEX

Card Number ______________________________

Signature ______________________ Expiry Date ____________

Name (Mr/Mrs/Miss) ______________________________

Address ______________________________

______________________________ Postcode ____________

(We aim to despatch your order with 10 days, but please allow 28 days for delivery)

Occasionally we may allow reputable organisations to write to you with offers which may interest you. If you prefer not to hear from them, tick this box ❑

CALL THE JOHANSENS CREDIT CARD ORDER SERVICE FREE ☎ **0800 269397**

save £10 WHEN YOU BUY A SET OF ALL THREE 1996 UK JOHANSENS GUIDES	PRICE	QTY	TOTAL
	£35.80		
Boxed presentation set of three 1996 UK Johansens guides with slip case	£39.00		
Johansens Recommended Hotels in Great Britain & Ireland 1996	£21.90		
Johansens Recommended Inns with Restaurants in Great Britain 1996	£11.95		
Johansens Recommended Country Houses and Small Hotels in Great Britain & Ireland 1996	£11.95		
Johansens Recommended Hotels in Europe 1996	£11.95		

ALL PRICES INCLUDE HANDLING AND UK POSTAGE ONLY **37J**

Outside the UK add £3 for each single guide ordered, or £5 for a set or boxed set to cover additional postage. ***PRICES VALID UNTIL 31/12/96***

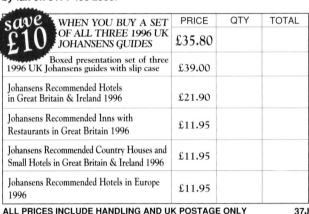

Post free to:
JOHANSENS, FREEPOST (CB264), HORSHAM, WEST SUSSEX RH13 8ZA

GUEST SURVEY REPORT

Name and location of hotel: ______________________ Date of visit: __________

Name and address of guest: ______________________

______________________ Postcode: __________

Please tick one box in each category below:	Excellent	Good	Disappointing	Poor
Bedrooms				
Public Rooms				
Restaurant/Cuisine				
Service				
Welcome/Friendliness				
Value For Money				

PLEASE return your Guest Survey Report form!

Occasionally we may allow other reputable organisations to write with offers which may be of interest.

If you prefer not to here from them, tick this box ☐

To: Johansens, FREEPOST (CB264), 175-179 St John Street, London EC1B 1JQ

Your own Johansens 'inspection' gives reliability to our guides and assists in the selection of Award Nominations

GUEST SURVEY REPORT

Name and location of hotel: ______________________ Date of visit: __________

Name and address of guest: ______________________

______________________ Postcode: __________

Please tick one box in each category below:	Excellent	Good	Disappointing	Poor
Bedrooms				
Public Rooms				
Restaurant/Cuisine				
Service				
Welcome/Friendliness				
Value For Money				

PLEASE return your Guest Survey Report form!

Occasionally we may allow other reputable organisations to write with offers which may be of interest.

If you prefer not to here from them, tick this box ☐

To: Johansens, FREEPOST (CB264), 175-179 St John Street, London EC1B 1JQ

Your own Johansens 'inspection' gives reliability to our guides and assists in the selection of Award Nominations

GUEST SURVEY REPORT

Name and location of hotel: ______________________ Date of visit: __________

Name and address of guest: ______________________

______________________ Postcode: __________

Please tick one box in each category below:	Excellent	Good	Disappointing	Poor
Bedrooms				
Public Rooms				
Restaurant/Cuisine				
Service				
Welcome/Friendliness				
Value For Money				

PLEASE return your Guest Survey Report form!

Occasionally we may allow other reputable organisations to write with offers which may be of interest.

If you prefer not to here from them, tick this box ☐

To: Johansens, FREEPOST (CB264), 175-179 St John Street, London EC1B 1JQ

Your own Johansens 'inspection' gives reliability to our guides and assists in the selection of Award Nominations

Order Coupon

To order Johansens guides, simply indicate which publications you require by putting the quantity(ies) in the boxes provided. Choose you preferred method of payment and return this coupon (NO STAMP REQUIRED). You may also place your order using FREEPHONE 0800 269397 or by fax on 0171 490 2538.

❑ I enclose a cheque for £______________ payable to Biblios PDS Ltd (Johansens book distributor).
❑ I enclose my order on company letterheading, please invoice me. (UK companies only)
❑ Please debit my credit/charge card account (please tick)
❑ MASTERCARD ❑ VISA ❑ DINERS ❑ AMEX

Card Number ______________________________

Signature ______________________ Expiry Date __________

Name (Mr/Mrs/Miss) ______________________________

Address ______________________________

____

______________________ Postcode __________

(We aim to despatch your order with 10 days, but please allow 28 days for delivery)

Occasionally we may allow reputable organisations to write to you with offers which may interest you. If you prefer not to hear from them, tick this box ❑

CALL THE JOHANSENS CREDIT CARD ORDER SERVICE FREE ☎ **0800 269397**

save £10 WHEN YOU BUY A SET OF ALL THREE 1996 UK JOHANSENS GUIDES	PRICE	QTY	TOTAL
	£35.80		
Boxed presentation set of three 1996 UK Johansens guides with slip case	£39.00		
Johansens Recommended Hotels in Great Britain & Ireland 1996	£21.90		
Johansens Recommended Inns with Restaurants in Great Britain 1996	£11.95		
Johansens Recommended Country Houses and Small Hotels in Great Britain & Ireland 1996	£11.95		
Johansens Recommended Hotels in Europe 1996	£11.95		

ALL PRICES INCLUDE HANDLING AND UK POSTAGE ONLY **37J**

Outside the UK add £3 for each single guide ordered, or £5 for a set or boxed set to cover additional postage. ***PRICES VALID UNTIL 31/12/96***

Post free to:
JOHANSENS, FREEPOST (CB264), HORSHAM, WEST SUSSEX RH13 8ZA

To order Johansens guides, simply indicate which publications you require by putting the quantity(ies) in the boxes provided. Choose you preferred method of payment and return this coupon (NO STAMP REQUIRED). You may also place your order using FREEPHONE 0800 269397 or by fax on 0171 490 2538.

❑ I enclose a cheque for £______________ payable to Biblios PDS Ltd (Johansens book distributor).
❑ I enclose my order on company letterheading, please invoice me. (UK companies only)
❑ Please debit my credit/charge card account (please tick)
❑ MASTERCARD ❑ VISA ❑ DINERS ❑ AMEX

Card Number ______________________________

Signature ______________________ Expiry Date __________

Name (Mr/Mrs/Miss) ______________________________

Address ______________________________

____

______________________ Postcode __________

(We aim to despatch your order with 10 days, but please allow 28 days for delivery)

Occasionally we may allow reputable organisations to write to you with offers which may interest you. If you prefer not to hear from them, tick this box ❑

CALL THE JOHANSENS CREDIT CARD ORDER SERVICE FREE ☎ **0800 269397**

save £10 WHEN YOU BUY A SET OF ALL THREE 1996 UK JOHANSENS GUIDES	PRICE	QTY	TOTAL
	£35.80		
Boxed presentation set of three 1996 UK Johansens guides with slip case	£39.00		
Johansens Recommended Hotels in Great Britain & Ireland 1996	£21.90		
Johansens Recommended Inns with Restaurants in Great Britain 1996	£11.95		
Johansens Recommended Country Houses and Small Hotels in Great Britain & Ireland 1996	£11.95		
Johansens Recommended Hotels in Europe 1996	£11.95		

ALL PRICES INCLUDE HANDLING AND UK POSTAGE ONLY **37J**

Outside the UK add £3 for each single guide ordered, or £5 for a set or boxed set to cover additional postage. ***PRICES VALID UNTIL 31/12/96***

Post free to:
JOHANSENS, FREEPOST (CB264), HORSHAM, WEST SUSSEX RH13 8ZA

To order Johansens guides, simply indicate which publications you require by putting the quantity(ies) in the boxes provided. Choose you preferred method of payment and return this coupon (NO STAMP REQUIRED). You may also place your order using FREEPHONE 0800 269397 or by fax on 0171 490 2538.

❑ I enclose a cheque for £______________ payable to Biblios PDS Ltd (Johansens book distributor).
❑ I enclose my order on company letterheading, please invoice me. (UK companies only)
❑ Please debit my credit/charge card account (please tick)
❑ MASTERCARD ❑ VISA ❑ DINERS ❑ AMEX

Card Number ______________________________

Signature ______________________ Expiry Date __________

Name (Mr/Mrs/Miss) ______________________________

Address ______________________________

____

______________________ Postcode __________

(We aim to despatch your order with 10 days, but please allow 28 days for delivery)

Occasionally we may allow reputable organisations to write to you with offers which may interest you. If you prefer not to hear from them, tick this box ❑

CALL THE JOHANSENS CREDIT CARD ORDER SERVICE FREE ☎ **0800 269397**

save £10 WHEN YOU BUY A SET OF ALL THREE 1996 UK JOHANSENS GUIDES	PRICE	QTY	TOTAL
	£35.80		
Boxed presentation set of three 1996 UK Johansens guides with slip case	£39.00		
Johansens Recommended Hotels in Great Britain & Ireland 1996	£21.90		
Johansens Recommended Inns with Restaurants in Great Britain 1996	£11.95		
Johansens Recommended Country Houses and Small Hotels in Great Britain & Ireland 1996	£11.95		
Johansens Recommended Hotels in Europe 1996	£11.95		

ALL PRICES INCLUDE HANDLING AND UK POSTAGE ONLY **37J**

Outside the UK add £3 for each single guide ordered, or £5 for a set or boxed set to cover additional postage. ***PRICES VALID UNTIL 31/12/96***

Post free to:
JOHANSENS, FREEPOST (CB264), HORSHAM, WEST SUSSEX RH13 8ZA

Gift Order Subscription Form

You may use this order form to send a gift subscription to a friend or colleague, or to purchse guides for yourself. Simply indicate which guides you require in the boxes provided. Choose your preferred method of payment and return with the order form (NO STAMP REQUIRED). Remember to include your details and also those of the recipient, if sending a gift subscription.

❏ I enclose a cheque for £______________ payable to Biblios PDS Ltd (Johansens book distributor).
❏ Please debit my credit/charge card account (please tick)
❏ MASTERCARD ❏ VISA ❏ DINERS ❏ AMEX

Card Number ______________________________

Signature ______________________ Expiry Date __________
Name (Mr/Mrs/Miss) ______________________________
Address ______________________________
______________________ Postcode __________
Recipient's name ______________________________
Address ______________________________
____
______________________ Postcode __________
Your message to be included with your order (max 10 words) __________
____
____

(We aim to dispatch your order in 10 days, but please allow 28 days for delivery)

save £10 — WHEN YOU BUY A SET OF ALL THREE 1996 UK JOHANSENS GUIDES	PRICE	QTY	TOTAL
	£35.80		
Boxed presentation set of three 1996 UK Johansens guides with slip case	£39.00		
Johansens Recommended Hotels in Great Britain & Ireland 1996	£21.90		
Johansens Recommended Inns with Restaurants in Great Britain 1996	£11.95		
Johansens Recommended Country Houses and Small Hotels in Great Britain & Ireland 1996	£11.95		
Johansens Recommended Hotels in Europe 1996	£11.95		

ALL PRICES INCLUDE HANDLING AND UK POSTAGE ONLY **15J**

Outside the UK add £3 for each single guide ordered, or £5 for a set or boxed set to cover additional postage. ***PRICES VALID UNTIL 31/12/96***

Post free to:
JOHANSENS, FREEPOST (CB264), HORSHAM, WEST SUSSEX RH13 8ZA

Gift Order Subscription Form

You may use this order form to send a gift subscription to a friend or colleague, or to purchse guides for yourself. Simply indicate which guides you require in the boxes provided. Choose your preferred method of payment and return with the order form (NO STAMP REQUIRED). Remember to include your details and also those of the recipient, if sending a gift subscription.

❏ I enclose a cheque for £______________ payable to Biblios PDS Ltd (Johansens book distributor).
❏ Please debit my credit/charge card account (please tick)
❏ MASTERCARD ❏ VISA ❏ DINERS ❏ AMEX

Card Number ______________________________

Signature ______________________ Expiry Date __________
Name (Mr/Mrs/Miss) ______________________________
Address ______________________________
______________________ Postcode __________
Recipient's name ______________________________
Address ______________________________
____
______________________ Postcode __________
Your message to be included with your order (max 10 words) __________
____
____

(We aim to dispatch your order in 10 days, but please allow 28 days for delivery)

save £10 — WHEN YOU BUY A SET OF ALL THREE 1996 UK JOHANSENS GUIDES	PRICE	QTY	TOTAL
	£35.80		
Boxed presentation set of three 1996 UK Johansens guides with slip case	£39.00		
Johansens Recommended Hotels in Great Britain & Ireland 1996	£21.90		
Johansens Recommended Inns with Restaurants in Great Britain 1996	£11.95		
Johansens Recommended Country Houses and Small Hotels in Great Britain & Ireland 1996	£11.95		
Johansens Recommended Hotels in Europe 1996	£11.95		

ALL PRICES INCLUDE HANDLING AND UK POSTAGE ONLY **15J**

Outside the UK add £3 for each single guide ordered, or £5 for a set or boxed set to cover additional postage. ***PRICES VALID UNTIL 31/12/96***

Post free to:
JOHANSENS, FREEPOST (CB264), HORSHAM, WEST SUSSEX RH13 8ZA

Gift Order Subscription Form

You may use this order form to send a gift subscription to a friend or colleague, or to purchse guides for yourself. Simply indicate which guides you require in the boxes provided. Choose your preferred method of payment and return with the order form (NO STAMP REQUIRED). Remember to include your details and also those of the recipient, if sending a gift subscription.

❏ I enclose a cheque for £______________ payable to Biblios PDS Ltd (Johansens book distributor).
❏ Please debit my credit/charge card account (please tick)
❏ MASTERCARD ❏ VISA ❏ DINERS ❏ AMEX

Card Number ______________________________

Signature ______________________ Expiry Date __________
Name (Mr/Mrs/Miss) ______________________________
Address ______________________________
______________________ Postcode __________
Recipient's name ______________________________
Address ______________________________
____
______________________ Postcode __________
Your message to be included with your order (max 10 words) __________
____
____

(We aim to dispatch your order in 10 days, but please allow 28 days for delivery)

save £10 — WHEN YOU BUY A SET OF ALL THREE 1996 UK JOHANSENS GUIDES	PRICE	QTY	TOTAL
	£35.80		
Boxed presentation set of three 1996 UK Johansens guides with slip case	£39.00		
Johansens Recommended Hotels in Great Britain & Ireland 1996	£21.90		
Johansens Recommended Inns with Restaurants in Great Britain 1996	£11.95		
Johansens Recommended Country Houses and Small Hotels in Great Britain & Ireland 1996	£11.95		
Johansens Recommended Hotels in Europe 1996	£11.95		

ALL PRICES INCLUDE HANDLING AND UK POSTAGE ONLY **15J**

Outside the UK add £3 for each single guide ordered, or £5 for a set or boxed set to cover additional postage. ***PRICES VALID UNTIL 31/12/96***

Post free to:
JOHANSENS, FREEPOST (CB264), HORSHAM, WEST SUSSEX RH13 8ZA

NO STAMP NEEDED

JOHANSENS
FREEPOST (CB264)
HORSHAM
WEST SUSSEX
RH13 8ZA

NO STAMP NEEDED

JOHANSENS
FREEPOST (CB264)
HORSHAM
WEST SUSSEX
RH13 8ZA

NO STAMP NEEDED

JOHANSENS
FREEPOST (CB264)
HORSHAM
WEST SUSSEX
RH13 8ZA